HOOKED ON
CANADIAN BOOKS

HOOKED ON
CANADIAN BOOKS

The Good, the Better,
and the Best Canadian Novels since 1984

T. F. RIGELHOF

Cormorant Books

Canada Council   Conseil des Arts
for the Arts   du Canada

ONTARIO ARTS COUNCIL
CONSEIL DES ARTS DE L'ONTARIO

The publisher gratefully acknowledges the support of the Canada Council for the Arts
and the Ontario Arts Council for its publishing program. We acknowledge the
financial support of the Government of Canada through the Book Publishing Industry Development
Program (BPIDP) for our publishing activities.

Printed and bound in Canada

LIBRARY AND ARCHIVES CANADA CATALOGUING IN PUBLICATION

Rigelhof, T. F.

Hooked on Canadian books : the good, the better, and the best
Canadian novels since 1984–2009 / T.F. Rigelhof.

Includes bibliographical references and index.

ISBN 978-1-897151-75-4

1. Canadian fiction (English)—20th century—Book reviews.
2. Canadian fiction (English)—21st century—Book reviews.
3. Canadian fiction (English)—20th century—Bibliography.
4. Canadian fiction (English)—21st century—Bibliography. 5. Best books—Canada. I. Title.

PS8187.R44 2010   c813'.5409   C2009-906869-9

Cover art and design: Angel Guerra/Archetype
Interior text design: Tannice Goddard/Soul Oasis Networking
Printer: Friesens

 Mixed Sources
Cert no. SW-COC-001271
© 1996 FSC
FSC

The text of this book is printed on 100% post-consumer waste recycled paper.

CORMORANT BOOKS INC.
215 SPADINA AVENUE, STUDIO 230, TORONTO, ON CANADA M5T 2C7
www.cormorantbooks.com

For Judith Mappin, her co-owners,
and the staff of The Double Hook Bookstore;
and in memory of Norah Bryant,
Westmount Public Library's Chief Librarian,
1962–1982.

And, as always, for Ann, my constant companion.

CONTENTS

INTRODUCTION

This book is written from one reader to another — to as many others as possible — in the hope that enough copies will be bought and circulated so that you who read privately and you who participate in reading clubs will find reader-friendly approaches to recent Canadian novels in English that expand the narratives of your own lives — yielding diversion, solace, perspective, comfort, counsel, and insight along your meanders from first paragraphs to last.

Although I've been a college teacher of humanities throughout my working life (specializing in ancient writings from various religious traditions), have reviewed many books of several kinds for a number of newspapers and magazines (notably as a Contributing Reviewer to *The Globe and Mail*'s "Books" over the past decade), and written both fiction and non-fiction with "critical success," I am first, last, and always a reader of contemporary fiction — especially Canadian novels.

In their end-of-the-twentieth-century introduction to *The Modern Library: The 200 Best Novels in English since 1950* (which includes a dozen by Canadians), Carmen Callil and Colm Tóibín assert that the books they chose are "sources of entertainment and enjoyment as satisfying as any Hollywood movie, football match, computer game or rock video." My modest claim is that there isn't a novel singled out for inclusion in my book that I wouldn't buy — full price — to add to the pleasures of days spent occasionally at cinemas or more often in front of the television watching news, hockey, soccer, documentaries, *Masterpiece Theater*, and forever listening to jazz, the classics, opera, the McGarrigles (with and without the Wainwrights), Steve Earle, Tom Waits, and eating generally fresh, generally home-cooked food in a well-loved home. For most contemporary readers much of the time, the reading of fiction includes and encompasses the rest of life's realities but rarely obliterates them for more than a couple of uninterrupted hours at a time — even though reading a book, neurological researchers at the University of Groningen claim, can be as *thrilling* as a real-life event.

Pleasures and thrills are not the only considerations — we read novels to open our eyes to possible experiences beyond our own situations in time and place and judge them, and in judging, judge ourselves and our times. For three centuries, quiet reading of books dominated leisure hours of the literate until inexpensive sheet music and modest pianos, motion pictures, and Edison's phonograph, radio, LP records, network television, and ultimately the contemporary flood of digitalized electronica proved more impulsive and compelling. But, as American novelist and essayist Cynthia Ozick notes in *The Din in the Head* (2006), "the encyclopedic triumphs of communications technology — is an act equal in practicality to a wooden leg; it will support your standing in the world, but there is no blood in it."

There is blood in this book — gusto, passion, zest, good humour, and fellow feeling are the forces driving it. *Hooked on Canadian Books* is a celebration of novels written in English by Canadian writers that made a difference in this reader's life and have the power to do the same for you. These authors are engaged and engaging: they employ whatever abilities at their command to make their works *readable* and they want to be read seriously even when they're at their funniest. Who doesn't? If you think every author writes in the expectation of being bought and read by people serious enough about their lives to pay retail prices for books as readily as they open wallets for fine wines, fresh organic produce, superior restaurant meals, full screen movies, and CDs more sonically alive than MP3 downloads, you're mistaken. Some writers write to be studied rather than read, taught rather than enjoyed, and count success not in sales and readers but in tenure-track points for themselves and friends within academia.

On my desk, there's a yellowing, much-creased Xerox of a column clipped from *Vanity Fair* of February 1986 titled "Tilting at Fame: How to be a well-known unread author" in which James Atlas, Saul Bellow's biographer, lays out the steps necessary to becoming a Famous American Writer everyone has heard of and nobody bothers to read. Stripped of name-dropping, barbed asides, and briefly put, Atlas says that once you've proclaimed yourself to be a writer and chosen your own life — growing up in Brooklyn or the South or on a farm, falling in love, falling out of love, falling in and out of love again and again as you progress through school, college and graduate school, marriage, divorce, remarriage — as your primary subject matter, you must always insist that your writing is metaphorical not autobiographical; you enrol in a creative writing program and write short stories until an editor asks you for the novel and then you write one the size of your life; you collect blurbs from your instructors and from fellow students who got published before you did; you spend a lot of time choosing your picture for the dust jacket and writing the accompanying bio; you use your "best" reviews to get a job teaching creative writing; you assiduously apply for grants, attend writers' colonies, conferences, book launches, and give interviews on any literary topic that has "buzz"; you always insist on how difficult it is to write well and how dedicated you are to doing just that; you become a public character based on your preferred sexual and substance addictions; you form a claque with a half dozen other writers and review one another's books; you travel abroad at other people's expense; you remember to write another book every few years; you become a supporter of imprisoned writers everywhere and a mentor to young writers at home; and then, you're a Famous American Writer. I keep Atlas's satirical shrug on my desk as a warning against taking any writer's academy-approved reputation too seriously. Nobody's reputation (nor sales figures) got their book or books into my book nor kept them out. Nor did my friendships with authors — noted where necessary: this is a book for readers of books not their makers and marketers. I did, however, regretfully omit a wry social commentary masked as a mystery — *Buried on Sunday* (1987) by E. O. Phillips — a current bestseller about a woman who becomes

Montreal's first female doctor — *The Heart Specialist* (2009) by Claire Holden Rothman — and William Weintraub's droll account of coming-of-age in the dying days of the age of burlesque — *Crazy About Lili* (2006) — because their authors have been such near neighbours for so many years that their fictions are too inextricably entwined with who we are when we're not writing for me to be able to strike the balanced viewpoints I hope I've achieved elsewhere. There are winter days when I wake up to such a high, blue sky this neighbourhood feels closer to Saskatchewan than to Peel and Ste-Catherine and Robert Currie of Moose Jaw seems more like the man next door than the man next door. Bob Currie, whose achievements are many, is a distinguished lifetime poet who occasionally writes fictions, including the novel *Teaching Mr. Cutler* (2002): Brad Cutler risks everything to become a teacher and all, really, that this retired teacher has to say about Bob's absolutely authentic account of life in the classroom is that every teacher reading this book really ought to read his novel whenever they start to forget what they're doing and why they're doing it.

In the mid-eighties, the Canadian literary world was headed in the same direction as the American, but we did things somewhat differently than James Atlas "prescribes":

> The standard pattern is easily constructed. A Canadian writer, well-known or not so well-known, is awarded a generous grant to write a particular book; when it is finished, a publisher is provided with a subvention to assist with the costs of printing and distribution — and as often as not the writer in question is then awarded an additional grant for a cross-country tour to help publicize it. And we may add to all this the patent fact that a significant percentage of the eventual readers will be part of the university community, itself largely government-supported.

So wrote W. J. Keith, Professor Emeritus of English at University College, University of Toronto, in his "Polemical Conclusion" to the revised 2006 edition of his *Canadian Literature in English* (originally published in 1985). For Professor Keith, this "basic pattern has changed little" in the ensuing decades. I beg to differ: the first decade of the twenty-first century and final years of the twentieth altered the shape of our fiction in significant ways that weights this book to more frequent astonishments in the last ten years than in the preceding fifteen. I confine my disagreements with W. J. Keith and other commentators to the "Annals of OurLit" that open, close, or interrupt chapters. I strongly recommend Professor Keith's work as a guide to what is worth reading before 1984 and as a guiding spirit to reading for pleasure:

> Despite the trendy popularity of the phrase "the pleasures of the text" a few years ago, "pleasure" is a word that does not occur regularly in contemporary literary discussion.... I read literature unashamedly for pleasure — not the "fun" so distressingly flaunted by bureaucratic committees of adult education, but *pleasure*.

When it comes to Canadian fiction published over the past quarter century, some actually think I've read everything: I haven't — no one could because there are more novels published year after year than ordinary readers can imagine. I've done the *necessary* reading: In order to report with reasonable accuracy on any human phenomena, you have to study a thousand and some "samples" of the "population." The better the sampling technique, the higher the level of probability — that's "the margin of error" pollsters must note as a variable — but the "thousand and some samples" is a constant whether you're investigating vodka consumption in Russia or the musical preferences of anglo listeners to CBC Radio's "New 2" in Montreal (a case where an accurate "sample" would likely exceed the total "population"). And if it's true, as Malcolm Gladwell insists, that you have to put in 10,000 hours of dedicated work to become expert at anything, I've done the time. How I came to read something new in Canadian fiction every week for more than twenty years as an avocation rather than a paying occupation is a story worth telling so the opening chapter has much to do with two remarkable women and the institutions they operated — Judith Mappin and her fiercely independent bookstore, The Double Hook, and Norah Bryant, the Chief Librarian at Westmount Public Library from 1962 until her retirement in 1982. If our literature has any hope of mirroring our rainbow-hued Canadian selves, of keeping us from becoming consumers unattached to the places we live, it can't do it with chain bookstores that are "educentres" and libraries that are "infocentres" modeled on Wal-Mart and Wikipedia.

"The novel can do simply everything," Henry James wrote in his essay "The Future of the Novel" over a hundred years ago: James was stating a fact about the form — "its elasticity is infinite" — and issuing a challenge to would-be novelists to be as "various and vivid" as life itself. Between 1984 and 2009, Canadian novelists attempted many, many things. The failure rate among them is high but that has always been the case wherever novels are widely published. Noting the "contagion" of failed novels in his own time, James placed the blame on the mediocrity of writers, the laxness of readers, and the timidity of editors. He condemned an aversion to risk-taking on all sides and, specifically, the failure of both Anglo-American writers and readers to embrace adult life and examine sexual relations in straightforward ways. He placed much blame on editors and their publishers for fastening on female adolescents as their "ideal" readers. The reshaping of Canadian fiction lies with a surprising number of our novelists successfully addressing "ideal readers" who are adults willing to examine and embrace lives that acknowledge sexual relationships but move beyond physiological encounters into less "romantic" realms of friendship, knowledge, joy, and comfort with variety and vividness and into realms of love and religion more tentatively.

The ways by which the novels recommended within the pages of this book examine, explore, elaborate, and explicate these fundamental aspects of humans becoming more human are loosely catalogued: "Reading by Association" highlights novels of friendship (and enmity); "Reading and Coming to Terms with the Past" underscores knowledge (and ignorance); "Reading Some of 'the Talented Women Who Write Today'" stresses love (and hate), comfort (and discomfort); joy (and sorrow), comfort (and distress) are stressed in "Midnight at the Oasis" but the best of the better novels are without frontiers and their placements are marriages of convenience. My sense of which few of the many matters most is the subject of "Chère Karine: A Letter to a Québécoise Friend in Search of the Canada She Knows She Doesn't Know."

Chronology plays little part in any of this — except occasionally in terms of an individual author's development. Every book, whatever its date of publication, is *new* to those who have not yet read it and — in the cases of the best of them — is an altered, *renewed* experience the second or third or tenth time around. D. H. Lawrence wrote in *Apocalypse* (1931), his final book and one that I'm not tired of rereading — forty-two years after first discovering it:

> Owing to the flood of shallow books which really are exhausted in one reading, the modern mind tends to think every book is the same, finished in one reading. But it is not so.... The real joy of a book lies in reading it over and over again, and always finding it different, coming upon another meaning, another level of meaning ... we are so over-whelmed by the quantities of books, that we hardly realize any more that a book can be valuable, valuable like a jewel, or a lovely picture, into which you can look deeper and deeper.

For me, "reading" a novel means any of at least a half dozen things, three of which are reflected in the phrase "good, better, and the best." Some novels are so familiar in characters, so predictable in plot, so sentimental in spirit, so unwilling to embrace adult life and complex relationships, so innocent of politics, so intellectually blinkered that spending even an hour zipping through them is a waste of forty-five minutes. I have "read" my way through too many such hours but sometimes, the fifteen minutes that yielded pleasure led my eyes back and forth for another hour or two, gathering consciousness of a place and the conditions under which people live that are unfamiliar but ring true: Canada has a lot of geography beyond rocks and trees and lakes and trees and rocks and a diversity of communities beyond hardscrabble farms and down-at-heel villages and one-whore-multiple-idiot towns. Even so, far less cosmopolitanism entered Canadian fiction than entered its music, dance, theatre, or painting until the mid-eighties. Reading, at other times, means testing such rapid dismissals of the seemingly vapid against the opinion of another reader I genuinely respect by going back to a scanned book a second time in the normal way, beginning to end at a more ordinary speed. I'm willing to be proven wrong and can admit to being wrong when I am but, more often than not, my first impression holds and such books are remembered only for quirky settings.

To be "good" reading, a book must insist on being read, beginning to end, in one or two or three gulps. Opening a good novel should be something like picking up a child who needs to tell you — parent, guardian, or sitter — a tale. You hold it firmly and affectionately. You give it undivided attention, accommodate its insistence, and tolerate its inconvenience until you can't keep your eyes open or your stomach from growling or your employer from wondering where you are. As soon as possible, you take it up again until you can finally put it and yourself to rest. A "better" book makes you stop after fifty pages and start afresh immediately — or sometimes days, sometimes weeks later. Better novels impose new rhythms on your reading, alter your expectations of what a story can be, temper your steel, and ultimately win you over to their own complexities — in short, they surprise you. This is the kind of novel that makes you lose yourself in its incidents, has you jumping forward because the suspense is unbearable and flipping back because you want to give yourself another shot of an exchange, an insight, a moment thrumming with life. Sometimes, you catch yourself rereading passages several times and even saying them aloud in empty rooms because the words are so light and nimble. This is the kind of novel that insists on being shared with your journal, if you keep one, and with friends who, you think, *must* read it. The "best" novel is one that can be read over and over again because there is something that lies behind the words and between the words, as complicated an array of tones and shadows and illuminating colours as a Turner landscape or a Mahler symphony that changes and changes and changes again as vision and hearing become heightened as age advances. Or, as D. H. Lawrence writes, such rarities have "power to move us, and move us *differently*; so long as we find it *different* every time we read it ... always finding it different, coming upon another meaning, another level of meaning."

Is this all that aesthetic judgments come down to — the intensities of subjective reaction? No, of course not: reading and writing about novels as a professional reviewer, I've learned much from many editors and more from other reviewers, especially the cold-eyed but capacious humanity of the late Anthony Burgess, an author too closely associated with *A Clockwork Orange* and too little remembered for the Malay trilogy that first brought him to attention, the quartet of Enderby novels, *Nothing Like the Sun*, at least a half dozen more of his many books, and his masterpiece *Earthly Powers*. In his "Introduction" to *99 Novels: The Best in English Since 1939* (1984), lover of wordplay that Burgess is, he notes that "BOOK can be taken as an acronym standing for Box of Organized Knowledge" and that the novel "is a box from which characters and events are waiting to emerge at the raising of a lid." Once opened, he asks, what sort of organized knowledge emerges, what *fictional* truths jump out? First, most certainly, is a sense of gradation in human affairs, a lack of absolutes — even those the author might personally espouse. "Create your characters, give them a time and a place to exist in, and leave the plot to them." Burgess advises fellow novelists:

> imposing of action on them is very difficult, since action must spring out of the temperament with which you have endowed them. At best there will be a compromise between the narrative line you have dreamed up and the course of action preferred by the characters.... [A]ction is there to illustrate character; it is the character that counts.

The novelist who doesn't allow this to happen, who insists on preaching, on being didactic, on seeing himself (and outside the realm of the "romance" and Ayn Rand, it is generally the male of the species who does this) as "a kind of small God of the Calvinists," and is able to predict what is going to happen on his final page is the maker of bad novels, novels that create no surprises, leave nothing new behind. Burgess (who titled his autobiography *Big God and Little Wilson*) continues:

> It is the Godlike task of the novelist to create human beings whom we accept as living creatures filled with complexities and armed with free will.... As novels are about the ways in which human beings behave, they tend to imply a judgement of behaviour, which means that the novel is what the symphony or painting or sculpture is not — namely, a form steeped in morality.... The strength of a novel, however, owes

nothing to its confirmation of what conventional morality has already told us. Rather a novel will question convention and suggest to us that the making of moral judgements is difficult. This can be called the higher morality.

Such *higher* morality is much misunderstood. Does anyone read or even remember John Gardner any longer? Google gives priority to two others of the same name and Wikipedia requests more critical information than it dispenses. But between 1971 and 1979, few American novelists were more popular or prolific. After his third novel, *Grendel*, a retelling of *Beowulf* from the point of view of the monster as foul-mouthed mommy's boy, brought him massive sales and acclaim in 1971, Gardner further enlarged his readership and reputation with *The Sunlight Dialogues* (1972) and *October Light* (1976). There were four other novels in these eight years (including the unjustly neglected *Mickelson's Ghosts*), two books of children's stories, a biography of Chaucer and a book about Chaucer's poetry in 1977, and then a flood of mainstream media attention and a collapse of relations within New York's publishing industry when he published *On Moral Fiction* in 1978. Diagnosed with colon cancer while writing it, he died in a motorcycle accident in 1982 but not before publishing four further novels that disappeared from bookstores much too soon. *On Moral Fiction* argued that fiction should aspire to discover those human values great artists beginning with Homer have always regarded as universally sustaining — *friendship, joy, comfort, knowledge, religion, and love*. Gardner regarded as "moral" (and Burgess agreed) fiction "that attempts to test human values, not for the purpose of preaching or peddling a particular ideology, but in a truly honest and open-minded effort to find out what best promotes human fulfillment; and it does so ... by the kind of analysis of characters and the things they do that bring both writer and reader to understanding, sympathy, and love for human possibility":

The traditional view is that art is moral; it seeks to improve life, not debase it. It seeks to hold off, at least for a while, the twilight of the gods and us. I do not deny that art, like criticism, may legitimately celebrate the trifling. It may joke, or mock, or while away the time. But trivial art has no meaning or value except in the shadow of more serious art, the kind of art that beats back the monsters and, if you will, makes the world safe for triviality. That art which tends toward destruction, the art of nihilists, cynics, and merdistes, is not properly art at all. Art is essentially serious and beneficial, a game played against chaos and death, against entropy. It is a tragic game, for those who have the wit to take it seriously, because our side must lose; a comic game — or so a troll might say — because only a clown with sawdust brains would take our side and eagerly join in.

Gardner felt few of his contemporaries were *moral* in this sense, indulging in "winking, mugging despair" or trendy nihilism in which they did not honestly believe. Gore Vidal famously called Gardner the "late apostle to the lowbrows, a sort of Christian evangelical who saw Heaven as a paradigmatic American university." But he wasn't that — not at all — even if he was rather humourless. His two books on the craft of writing fiction — *The Art of Fiction* and *On Becoming a Novelist* — published posthumously in 1983 — enhance the craft, smooth the rhythms, and develop the continuity of the fictive dream. His books were touched by the redemptive power of art. As are Anthony Burgess's.

For Burgess, as for Gardner, the rules of thumb to a good novel are:

- It never forgets that a novel is about characters — human beings individually, socially, and en masse.
- It operates within temporal and spatial laws of human probability (allowing characters the time it takes for real people to do whatever they're doing and puts them in places in which people can actually do these things and gives them the kinds of bodies that respond to these actions more or less as actual bodies do).
- It doesn't try to get all the details down because there has to be a balance between a journalist's quest for particulars and a philosopher's digging into underlying reality.
- Its speech is lifelike without being transcription.
- It eschews superdeligorgeous verbosity (to be hyperspondulically explicit)

unless such loquacity is necessary to a character.
- It moulds the storyline into a parabola ending in a resolution; some meticulously qualified understanding and assertion.

Because good novels can only be made by artists who subsume themselves to their work, they transcend the intelligence and decency of their makers. That's what makes them "lifes best businesse" as Richard Whitlock noted three and a half centuries ago in *Zootomia, or, Observations on the present Manners of the English: Briefly anatomizing the Living by the Dead*:

> They are for company, the best Friends; in doubts, *Counsellours*; in Damps *Comforters*: Times *Prospective*, the home Travellers *Ship*, or *Horse*, the busie mans best *Recreation*, the *Opiate* of *Idle wearinsesse*, the Mindes best *Ordinary*, Natures Garden, and *Seed-plot of Immortality*.

Whitlock preferred them to doctors, lawyers, and priests. Me too.

Westmount 2010

GETTING HOOKED ON CANADIAN BOOKS

My life as a reader of so many novels by so many Canadian writers needs
some explanation. It became possible only because of a remarkably independent
bookstore — The Double Hook Canadian Books — and Judith Mappin, its
co-founder and principal owner. Throughout most of the four decades I've lived
in Westmount, Quebec, a little city encircled by Montreal, The Double Hook
was a neighbour. When it opened in 1974, it was a five-minute stroll from our
fourth floor walk-up on Clarke — around the corner, over a couple of blocks,
and down another to Ste-Catherine. It soon moved, a minute nearer, to 1235a
Greene Avenue. Eight years later, my wife and I moved fifteen minutes west but,
by then, I was teaching at the original campus of Dawson College, a recycled
pharmaceutical factory in the shadows of the Bonaventure Autoroute. On my
way home, I walked past The Double Hook and dropped in regularly — once,
mostly twice a week. When Judy Mappin, her co-owners, and staff shut up shop
on July 31, 2005, it felt more like the loss of a friendship than the closing of a shop
because The Double Hook was all the things an independent bookstore ought
to be, and it stocked Canadian titles, *exclusively*.

Founded by Judith Mappin, Hélène Holden, and Joan Blake at a time when
the recent loss of important elements of Canada's political sovereignty to the

United States sensitized some of us to the need to battle for cultural sovereignty, The Double Hook gave Canadian books and authors a home of their own in a country that was largely indifferent to them, particularly within a province that was following its own *indépendantiste* agenda. It closed its doors not because the cultural issues were resolved but because unfair and unwise loosening of competition rules generated Chapters megastores, precipitated the debacle and bankruptcy of General Distribution Services, created Indigo's near-monopoly, and killed off a host of independent bookstores.

In its day, The Double Hook stayed open longer hours, stocked more titles by more authors, and sponsored more book launches, author signings, and readings than ever made financial sense. The Double Hook did what it did because Judy and her partners simply wanted it to operate that way. The money the store made at home and abroad (by providing the best special order and mail order services in the country until the advent of Amazon.ca) probably did something to offset the cost of the good wines, fine cheeses, fresh fruits, home baking, and extra hours the owners and staff spent on authors and readers, but it made little economic sense to operate as the kind of cultural venue it was. Even so, it closed only because Judy worked long past normal retirement age and did not want to see it close under somebody else's watch.

Like a lot of other war and postwar babies, I'd started reading unpopular books and listening to unpopular music because there weren't many voices in Regina, my hometown, that were speaking words I wanted to live by. I was looking for a world that was smaller than the know-it-all universalism of the Catholic Church and larger than my family. In Regina, I found the world I wanted at 2439 11th Avenue when a quite different Helene opened the Modern Times Book Store, the sort of place where nobody seemed to want to know anybody's last name — quite unlike The Double Hook, where Judy saw to it that her staff always formally introduced visitors to one another, creating a *Cheers* for people who didn't hang out in bars. Regina's Modern Times was dedicated to "underground" books — including under-the-shelf copies of Henry Miller and D. H. Lawrence — with a sideline in obscure long-playing records on jazz and folk labels. Books were arranged by publisher, not author — there were shelves for New Directions, Evergreen, Modern Library, Penguin, Scribner's,

Doubleday Anchor — and record bins by genre: folk, blues, modern jazz, comedy, poetry, drama. It was on those shelves I found Morley Callaghan, Leonard Cohen, Irving Layton, Jack Ludwig, Mordecai Richler, and started searching out and reading Canadian writers because I was looking for a less myopic Canada — authors who grasped some of its *unknown knowns*:

> Reports that say something hasn't happened are always interesting to me, because as we know, there are known knowns; there are things we know we know. We also know there are known unknowns; that is to say we know there are some things we do not know. But there are also unknown unknowns — the ones we don't know we don't know.

The Plain English Campaign — a British group that lobbies for clear, straightforward public information — gave Donald Rumsfeld its Foot in Mouth Award for saying this and called it the most baffling statement by a public figure in 2004. Academic philosophers immediately countered that Rumsfeld was talking sense and his only fault was to leave out the fourth category of *unknown knowns* — things we know, but don't know that we know — beliefs, suppositions, and practices we pretend not to know about, even though they form the foundation of our public values. To unearth these *unknown knowns* became the *raison d'être* of much of my reading as I sought to become a literary expeditionary into the Canadian psyche.

When The Double Hook first opened in 1974, my habit of reading whichever Canadian writers fell my way from the shelves of independent bookstores in Saskatoon, Ottawa, Hamilton, Toronto, Halifax, and Charlottetown became a more organized compulsion to read all the truth-telling poems, short stories, plays, book-length journalism, song lyrics, essays, social analyses, histories, biographies, memoirs, and novels written locally, provincially, and nationally. As a would-be writer who wasn't at all certain what kind of writer I would become, I was not only satisfying curiosity, I was sussing out the competition, trying to find my own voice and subject matter, not just in books but also in the literary magazines on the wire racks just inside The Double Hook's front door. On October 28, 1981, something special happened: I went into the shop to buy a copy of *From the Fifteenth District* and get it signed by its author, Mavis Gallant. Judy called me to one side and asked me, "Can you stay and talk to her? Hardly anyone has come into the store." One hour turned to two, interrupted by only two or three autograph seekers with little to say, and ended only when the publisher's rep arrived with a car to drive Mrs. Gallant to a radio interview.

Judy introduced me to Mavis, author to author. A month earlier, my first book — half a book, really, since Oberon Press packaged my novella "Hans Denck, Cobbler" together with "The Beautiful Uncut Hair of Graves" by Mike Mason as *A Beast with Two Backs: Two Novels* — was launched from the same table. Mavis Gallant and I talked of many things — the things about her art and her life she has spoken of often in interviews and something she's rarely been asked about: her intricate and intimate knowledge of displaced European peoples and their anti-Stalinist politics (she immediately recognized my rare surname as Volga Deutsch and guessed wrongly, by a narrow margin, that my Canadian roots were in Edmonton rather than a string of smaller places beginning in Altario, Alberta) — but what passed between us was the sure and certain knowledge that no torch was being handed on, writer to writer. What she found most interesting in me was my life as a reader, especially my appetite for her most complex, intense, surprising stories and the refreshing fact that my literary appetites hadn't been limited and gutted by the retrograde literary nationalism that too many smart people confused with cultural independence — that I could read her as she is on the page — an existentialist of the highest order, a comic Camus, a more sardonic Sartre without his overarching sense of self-entitlement — without questioning her Canadian citizenship. She encouraged the nascent reviewer in me. When Russell Banks introduced her in 2006 at the New York City reading series Selected Stories, he said exactly what I think needed to be said twenty-five years earlier:

> She's a post-postmodern writer, a post-postcolonial writer, a post-multicultural writer, one of those artists who refuse the hyphen and reject the claims of national fealty. She belongs to no one but herself and therefore her work belongs to all of us.

I went on to write more fiction and Mavis Gallant read some of it and her polite response spoke volumes: whatever marks I made on paper would be better made expounding on the imaginative works of others than developing my own. She knew before I did that I lacked the single-mindedness "to hold the world of life under a permanent light" as Edmund Husserl, *the* philosopher to a generation of European novelists, put it. I was a taker of notes not a keeper of notebooks.

Now that this book is finished and in your hands, the shelves of books that generated it will have been largely dispersed. *From the Fifteenth District* will stay with me on a couple of shelves of permanent treasures. I'm a reader not a collector. Hundreds and hundreds of Canadian books have passed in and out of my hands and home since I started making notes for this book in 1984 and I never regretted parting with the many I'd given away until The Double Hook closed. The books I presented to others went to people I felt needed to read that particular book just then or were donated to literacy projects. Since 2005, I can no longer easily pick up a copy of whichever Canadian book I want whenever I want, feel it, and scan it before I buy it. How much of a loss is that? Traditional literary writers — upholders of rebellion against the current — are going the way of builders of wooden canoes, decommissioned by fashion celebrities, fitness gurus, juicy teenagers in Juicy couture, drugged and clueless athletes, bloggers, politicians, and historical novelists (the umbrella-menders of literature) as publishers push more and more industry-driven product into trivia-drenched minds. The Double Hook Canadian Books created an "oasis" in Canadian society that was decent, fair, and democratic in ways that no edutainment centre will ever be. Whenever one stopped to ask David, Michael, Francine, Carol, Erika, or any of their predecessors at the cash register, "Have you read …? What do *you* think of the latest …?" If he or she or they (there were some wonderful double acts at the front desk over the years) hadn't read whichever book was being enquired about, the reaction of a customer who had would be relayed and that would prompt a conversation that might draw in bystanders, shoppers looking for specific books, browsers like me, out-of-town authors signing books, or local poets trying to place a few copies of their latest chapbook on consignment.

During its thirty-one years, I didn't read *everything* worthwhile by every Canadian writer worth reading but most of the fiction published in that time — roughly six hundred collections of short stories and a thousand novels (that's an average of one a week) — passed through my hands. Promising ones were scanned and discussed. Many were bought from The Double Hook and more were borrowed from the Westmount Public Library, one of Judy's loyal patrons and the recipient of all the books that remained when her store closed its doors for the last time. Advance copies that came to me for review I tried to write about without fear, envy, or meanness. I didn't always succeed and when I didn't, someone at The Double Hook was always prepared to say so and challenge my taste by arguing in favour of his or her own.

On the evening of October 24, 2005, *The Double Hook: A Celebration* was held in Montreal's Centaur Theatre. There were a dozen platform speakers but the best line of the night came from Aislin — the cartoonist Terry Mosher — who said from the stage, "I'm looking right into Judy Mappin's eyes and I can tell what she's thinking, 'I close my lovely bookstore and all I get is a lousy cartoon.'" The drawing presented (and featured on the *Gazette*'s editorial page the next day) shows two women of a certain age standing inside the famous Greene Avenue window and one is asking the other, "But do you ever wonder if civilization as we know it exists beyond our front door?" This book is the best answer I know how to give.

I would never have been as receptive as I was to what The Double Hook offered me as a reader had it not been for Norah Bryant, the Chief Librarian at Westmount Public Library. Mrs. Bryant (Norah was of a generation that projected formality first, warmth second) had a deep and abiding passion for the Commonwealth as a non-Imperial way of bringing people together and building new communities based on shared language, shared literature, and shared experience. She detested (that seems the *mot juste*) American hegemony, its processes of racial marginalization and bulldozing of local cultures. For eight years, we chatted informally about Canadian and Commonwealth literature weekly and she not only recommended but put into my hands books and articles from the *public* collection she spent her Sundays designing by annotating publishers' catalogues and newspaper sections with her critical eye and exquisite penmanship: if she used a pencil, it was freshly sharpened; when she used her fountain pen, it was filled with Waterman's turquoise ink, a warm and generous colour, softer than her views.

READING BY ASSOCIATION

Kompatibilität and Novels
of Friendship

This is a work of fiction. Any resemblence to people living or dead is intentional and encouraged. Fictional characters and experiences come to life when we compare them with the people and places we know. New experience is always a comparison to the known.

— MICHAEL WINTER

ANNALS OF OURLIT I

SHELVING BOOKS:
ALBERTO MANGUEL'S

The Library at Night (2006)

In *The Library at Night* (2006), an account of designing, constructing, and organizing the library built to house his books in a fifteenth-century barn perched on a small hill south of the Loire, Alberto Manguel tells many odd stories about other libraries and their makers including that of Abraham (Aby) Moritz Warburg (1866–1929), an impulsive and compulsive bookman who exchanged his birthright as eldest son and scion of a prominent Hamburg banking family with his younger brother in return for the promise that the family would buy him all the books he wanted. Warburg's buying and reading from childhood to death was shaped by the notion of *Kompatibilität* — compatibility — experience by association. The underlying question that shaped Warburg's reading was "How are our oldest symbols renewed at different ages, and how do their reincarnations link and reverberate with one another?" Warburg rejected all traditional notions of cataloguing in favour of "the law of the good neighbour." Manguel writes,

> As Warburg imagined it, a library was above all an accumulation of associations, each association breeding a new image or idea to be associated, until the associations returned the reader to the first page.... Warburg dedicated his library ... to the Greek goddess of memory, Mnemosyne, mother of the Muses. For Warburg ... memory is the quality that distinguishes living from dead matter.... Because of its haunting power, Warburg wonderfully described this active memory as "a ghost story for adults."

The law of the good neighbour is a principle more familiarly associated with musicians and visual artists — listen to one or other of CBC Radio-Canada's jazz hosts — Katie Malloch and Dorothée Berryman — and hear amazing sonic ghost stories for adult listeners. Or visit a private art gallery where pictures are hung so that they speak to one another in the language of their owner. *Kompatibilität* — compatibility — with its power of activating memory heightens the adventure of reading any story. But at a cost: Aby Warburg's "project" became unmanageable. As the Great War advanced, he grew anxious, depressed, and began to intuit "bleak concordance between his mental state and the state of the world," and, growing paranoid, perceived hostilities where friendships once prevailed. When the philosopher Ernst Cassirer visited Warburg's library in 1920 — thirty years after it was first constructed — he suffered a panic attack. According to Manguel, he told his guide, "I'll never come back here. If I returned to this labyrinth, I'd end up losing my way." As he explained to another, "Warburg's library isn't simply a collection of books but a catalogue of problems ... the breath of a magician."

What a wonderful phrase — *the breath of a magician*! A novel ought not to impose itself on an adult reader: it should insinuate itself because it speaks (as all good magicians do) to the ghost of a child within each reader:

> Of all the ways we communicate with one another, the story has established itself as the most comfortable, the most versatile — and perhaps also the most dangerous. Stories touch all of us, reaching across cultures and generations.... The story links us to ancestors we can never know, people who lived ten or twenty thousand years ago.... Millions of anonymous raconteurs invented narrative, and simultaneously began the history of civilization, when they discovered how to turn their observations and knowledge into tales they could pass on to others.

Robert Fulford, the dean of Canadian cultural journalism, also reminds us in *The Triumph of Narrative: Storytelling in the Age of Mass Culture* (1999), his Massey Lectures for CBC Radio in the penultimate year of the twentieth century, that assembling facts or incidents into tales is the only form of expression and entertainment that most of us enjoy equally at age three and age seventy-three. Fulford's hyperbole — stories can be traced back six thousand years, not earlier

— is silly but doesn't invalidate his key point that storytelling is the most versatile and dangerous form of communication known to mankind. He demonstrates this by retelling the notorious tale of the cuckolding of Saul Bellow by the Canadian novelist Jack Ludwig that underlies Bellow's *Herzog*. Good stories begin in gossip and are central to "the personal histories people concoct in the course of establishing their identity" and may — ask Ludwig! — have real-life consequences. Jack *Who*? Precisely. Ludwig's *Confusions* (1963), published one year before *Herzog*, merits being as well known and as frequently taught as *The Apprenticeship of Duddy Kravitz*. Yes, it truly does.

Evolutionary psychology has moved the analysis of the impulse underlying storytelling away from inventive anthropology and closer to Darwin's insight that song preceded language by many millennia and gave hominoids the capacity to communicate *friendship, joy, comfort, knowledge, religion, and/or love* — the "six songs" of the title of Daniel Levitin's *The World in Six Songs: How the Musical Brain Created Human Nature* (2008) — and, quintessentially, the double-six packed into The Beatles' *Sgt. Pepper's Lonely Hearts Club Band* (1967), which proves the old point that song cycles (operas in miniature) are to individual songs as stories are to anecdotes: a song can turn Lot's wife into a pillar of salt or Hector into carrion but it takes a libretto to bring ruin to Sodom and Gomorrah or make a man of Achilles.

All that storytelling does and can do to distinguish living from dead *and* animate us in multiple directions simultaneously *and* summon the ghosts of childhood is exemplified by "our Chekhov," Alice Munro. In *The View from Castle Rock* (2006), Munro transports, enthrals, leaves readers oblivious to time, possibly transcends her own intentions, and creates *a novel* of *friendship, joy, comfort, knowledge, religion, and love* to be reckoned among the finest contributions any Canadian has made to world literature. On a shelf in my office — *Kompatibilität* — what Munro summons up so wondrously stands next to her old friend Howard Engel's *Memory Book* (2005), a novel that's all about the inability to remember much of anything. Incongruous? Incompatible? Not to me nor, I suspect, to Alberto Manguel who reads "in a haphazard way, allowing books to associate freely, to suggest links by their mere proximity, to call out to one another across the room."

The books that enter my life as neighbours don't move in Warburgian circles — they travel back and forth, up and down along shelves within the confines of a small workroom. As they call out to one another, they remind me of my first bookcase and my earliest adventures in the act and art of associative reading: *Classics Illustrated*, a series of comic book adaptations of world literature (1941–1962), sought to convey as much of an original book as possible in 48 graphic pages. Ultimately, the series ran to 169 titles but in 1951, at the end of grade one and the beginning of my collection, the series was up to 73 issues, starting from *The Three Musketeers* and running through *Ivanhoe, The Count of Monte Cristo, The Last of the Mohicans, Moby Dick, A Tale of Two Cities, Robin Hood, Arabian Nights, Les Misérables, Robinson Crusoe, Don Quixote*, and many others before reaching *Treasure Island* at #64 and *The Oregon Trail* at #73.

At nine, I could run off the first six dozen titles together with their authors in much the way some of my classmates recited team lineups position by position in the National Hockey League, the Canadian Football League, and *Ring* magazine's top ten boxing contenders — weight class by weight class. By then, whatever law of association Albert Kanter, the creator of *Classics Illustrated*, had been following broke down on my shelves as I grouped Dickens with Dickens, Dumas with Dumas, Fennimore Cooper with Fennimore Cooper, Twain with Twain, Stevenson with Stevenson until every title was configured according to author by alphabet — R. D. Blackmore's *Lorna Doone* to Jonathan Wyss's *Swiss Family Robinson* — as I strove to emulate the conventions of fiction cataloguing in the Connaught branch of the Regina Public Library where I started reading the originals and developed my own taste in reading. Mind and heart sped towards Dickens and Dumas, Cervantes and Stevenson, Fennimore Cooper and Twain, Conan Doyle and Kipling and veered sharply away from Lewis Carroll, Mary Shelley, Jules Verne, H. G. Wells, and Jack London. The child was the father of the man — the world of everyday people and plausible adventures are so richly rewarding that speculative fiction and animal stories then held and now hold minimal appeal.

The late great Kurt Vonnegut (to quote a speculative writer I do admire) begins his novel *Timequake* (1997) about life in a universe that tires momentarily of expanding forever and begins to contract on February 13, 2001, by telling his readers that "I say in speeches that a plausible mission of artists is to make people appreciate being alive a little bit. I am then asked if I know of any artists who pulled that off. I reply, 'The Beatles did.'" In *Timequake* a tired universe stalls, then shrinks back to February 17, 1991, before marching forward once more to 2001 with everybody doing exactly what they did the first time through the decade. "But," as the dust jacket forewarns, "all hell cuts loose when the rerun is over and free will kicks in again. Everybody is so used to being a robot of the past that almost nobody is prepared to think of new things to do and then do them."

My experience of "timequake" is much more modest. In the middle of researching a book that I thought was going to be this one, my life was interrupted on January 27, 2003, by a sudden hemorrhagic stroke that brought a bruising on the left side of my brain and gimpiness in my right leg. I reacted as if little had happened and resumed much of my old life — including working on that earlier version of this book — as quickly as I could. But I was off-balance and out-of-whack in many ways and so was the book I then thought of as a *Literary Atlas of Canada* on good days and as *The Shape of Fiction to Come* when memory gaps fixed my eyes on the future rather than the past. Four years, eleven months less a day later, the same damn thing happened in exactly the same part of my brain but the damage went deeper. So did my reactions. Damned if I was going to relive the preceding five years! Let free will kick in again and all hell cut loose! I resolved to re-read all my favourite post-1983 but pre-2003 Canadian novels and read the most highly recommended of what was published since and write my book in a new way with a deeper understanding of what Vonnegut was saying when he told people that "a plausible mission of artists is to make people appreciate being alive a little bit." That's why Alice Munro's *Castle Rock* stands next Engel's *Memory Book* and ...

Most of us do have issues with friendship, don't we? The younger we are, as adults, the more complications arise. Douglas Coupland titled his debut *Generation X: Tales for an Accelerated Culture* (1991). There and elsewhere in his work, Generation X consists of people born after the Baby Boomers (1946–1957) but before Generation Y (1969–1980) so if you're between forty-two and fifty-two in 2010, you're an X-er. This section of my book begins with four tales of young women written by three former Dawson College students and an erstwhile singer-songwriter who for seven weeks in the summer of 1964 was more popular than The Beatles, then segues to Elizabeth Ruth's story of a young boy befriended by an old doctor and then it's off into the worlds of old people in a retirement home, an old man dying of a stroke, and Michael Ignatieff's gripping account of an elderly mother succumbing to dementia. Readers are invited to dip and dive as they choose but if you're a grandchild or a grandparent, you might find my ordering provides unexpected talking points between generations.

~

ZOE WHITTALL

Bottle Rocket Hearts (2007)

Heather O'Neill, the author of the bestselling *Lullabies for Little Criminals*, describes Eve and her girlish boy and boyish girl roommates in Zoe Whittall's *Bottle Rocket Hearts* as amalgams of "the luminous *joie-de-vivre* of Oscar Wilde and the self-destructive fury of Johnny Rotten." For readers who are less immediately drawn to a tale of a teenage girl from Dorval trying to find a downtown woman who'll want to love her as penetratingly as possible in the demimonde of Montreal's punk rock ethos, tattoo parlour aesthetics, Gay Village nightlife, and Concordia University Women's Centre feminist politics (circa February 1995–December 1996), it should be noted that Zoe Whittall might just possibly be the cockiest, brashest, funniest, toughest, most life-affirming, elegant, scruffiest, no-holds-barred writer to emerge from Montreal since Mordecai Richler staked out the moral terrain that would define and shape his work with *A Choice of Enemies* in 1957.

The robust and beautiful idea that the pursuit of happiness is elastic, immense, cannot be reduced to any fixed system, and fits everyone (no matter how unsympathetic they first appear) took Richler three novels (and some prodding from V. S. Naipaul) to get to. Whittall gets it from the get-go. One novel doesn't make a major writer but *Bottle Rocket Hearts* is a major statement about lessening unhappiness by overcoming the small dishonesties that creep into everyday life:

> [Della] lives in the extreme present. When I am in front of her, I am certain that I am beautiful; I am wanted. When I am tapping my fingers on the cash register at work or standing at school waiting to fill my travel-mug with hot black coffee, thinking of our last kiss, she could be anywhere, kissing anyone, my fingers far from her thoughts. I don't have bad self-esteem, I'm realistic.
>
> This is what we call a Revolutionary Relationship: depending on our own conventions, not falling into traps set by expectations, co-dependency, and unreasonable-romanticism.

No definitions.

The trouble with deciding not to define anything, is that it usually means you have to talk a lot more about what you're not defining than you would if you employed the time-honoured grade nine approach to Going Steady.... When my textbooks are open on my lap, trudging through Foucault or Butler, reading the same sentence over and over again, wondering if I'm secretly mentally retarded and no one has ever bothered to tell me, I pick up a pen and go on and on in the margins about love being a terribly boring preoccupation, a convention, a construct. That's when I know things are not going well.

In order to become overtly responsible for herself rather than merely overly responsive to potential lovers and capable of living with her own choices rather than the rigid systems that ideologues (including polyamorist proponents of the "ultra postmodern Revolutionary Relationship") seek to impose on her, Eve accepts "what it's like to live alone and be lonely" in order that falling in love doesn't happen quite so often nor so disastrously. A "bottle rocket" is a dollar store firecracker that gives maximum bang per buck and is aptly descriptive of both the verbal surface and emotional substance of *Bottle Rocket Hearts*.

~

HEATHER O'NEILL

Lullabies for Little Criminals (2006)

CHRISTINE POUNTNEY

Last Chance Texaco (2000)

Like Zoe Whittall, Heather O'Neill and Christine Pountney both attended Dawson College. Unlike her, they were students of mine — in Humanities courses. I didn't influence their writing but I may have fuelled their ambitions indirectly: if this teacher of theirs could write and get published, why couldn't they? This is less a question of humility than possible projection: it's only after meeting Matt Cohen at McMaster that I made the imaginative jump into thinking myself capable of writing fiction and not just scribbling poetry.

Given that *Lullabies for Little Criminals* won Canada Reads 2007, was shortlisted for the Amazon.ca/*Books in Canada* First Novel Award 2007, the Governor General's Literary Award for Fiction 2007, the Orange Prize for Fiction 2008, and longlisted for the IMPAC Dublin Literary Award 2008, among other honours, it comes highly recommended by others; so too *Last Chance Texaco*, which was longlisted for the Orange Prize in 2000.

Lullabies for Little Criminals (2006)

Nancy Wigston (*Books in Canada*) quotes Leonard Cohen to capture the spirit she finds in this novel of a year in the life of Baby:

> There are heroes in the seaweed
> There are children in the morning
> They are leaning out for love
> And they will lean that way forever.

Baby lives amid the flotsam and jetsam of Montreal's downtown junkieland of decaying hotels, rotten apartments, and dress-up street clothes. She's the child of children: she's motherless, almost twelve, and Jules, her heroin-addict dad, is twenty-six: "Having a young parent meant you had to pack up your stuff and run away," she says. Or be moved into foster homes and, when that doesn't work out, a detention centre. Jules has TB, needs detox, and can't really cope with Baby's pubescence. The sex trade is her only option to doing the hard time the system and Jules's rage and paranoia deal her. And sex is painful, most of the time. School is the focus of her life, literacy the alembic in which her crude experiences are distilled by precocious introspection into intelligence and the capacity to make sound judgments and form healthy friendships that can rescue her.

Much of this is raw but O'Neill isn't a *merdiste*: Baby isn't just plucky and brainy; she may be more bruised than any child should ever be but it doesn't break her spirit or her reader's even when tears are overflowing and the flood-tide is still rising. *There are heroes in the seaweed.*

Last Chance Texaco (2000)

Last Chance Texaco is a road trip and a good one. John Wade, 18, formerly of Bella Coola, BC, sets out from coastal California in a Dodge Omni for New York City. Wade is a bit bland but Hannah, the hitchhiker he picks up along the way, is strong enough to carry a big chunk of the novel (and find herself the centre of its 2005 sequel, *Best Way You Know How*). There aren't nearly enough road novels written and part of the charm of them — from *Don Quixote* down to *On the Road* — is in the impossibility of the task undertaken by the naïf who journeys forth. You don't have to be a car nut to know the Omni won't make it to New York and that John Wade hasn't the stuff to make it there on his own.

What one wants, and what Pountney delivers, is an observant eye and unadorned prose that captures both a vivid sense of multifarious places and our growing suspicion that the protagonist is more out of whack with the realities of every situation encountered than his imagination is capable of grasping. John Wade is blinkered by the new chivalry of political correctness and as full of euphemisms as the Man of La Mancha. It makes him much funnier and fraught with peril than first appears. Pountney is a subtler writer (and a more fully formed comic one) than some reviewers grasped.

∾

MIRIAM TOEWS

A Complicated Kindness (2004)

Has anyone not yet read *A Complicated Kindness*? It won the Governor General's Literary Award for English Fiction, was nominated for the Giller Prize (losing out to Alice Munro's *Runaway*), and engaged so many hearts (including Miss Munro's) that it spent over a year on the Canadian bestseller lists and reappeared on those lists two years later when it won the Canada Reads competition for 2006.

A memoir addressed to a high school teacher by Nomi Nickel, a teenager who longs to escape East Village (a fictionalized version of Toews' hometown of Steinbach, Manitoba) to hang out with Lou Reed in the real East Village in lower Manhattan, *A Complicated Kindness* details the physical and moral collisions between a fresh, engaging voice and a seemingly stale, severe, and severed society of lives less lived than endured. It's a story of Mennonite excommunication told by a writer who knows precisely how to communicate the whole world of her protagonist with a sharp eye, mordant wit, and amazing grace. Here's a taste of Nomi's eye and ear and tongue:

> This town is so severe. And silent. It makes me crazy, the silence. I wonder if a person can die from it. There's an invisible force that exerts a steady pressure on our words like a hand on an open, spurting wound. The town office building has a giant filing cabinet full of death certificates that say choked to death on his own anger or suffocated from unexpressed feelings of unhappiness. *Silentium.* The only thing you hear at night is semis barrelling down the highway carting drugged animals off to be attacked with knives.... People here just can't wait to die, it seems. It's the main event. The only reason we're not all snuffed out at birth is because that would reduce our suffering by a lifetime. My guidance counsellor has suggested to me that I change my attitude about this place and learn to love it. But I do, I told her. Oh that's rich, she said. That's rich.

> We're Mennonites. As far as I know, we are the most embarrassing sub-sect of people to belong to if you're a teenager.... Imagine the least well-adjusted kid in your school starting a breakaway clique of people whose manifesto includes a ban on the media, dancing, smoking, temperate climates, movies, drinking, rock 'n' roll, having sex for fun, swimming, make-up, jewellery, playing pool, going to cities, or staying up past nine o'clock. That was Menno all over. Thanks a lot, Menno.

Nomi smokes. How she smokes!

~

GALE ZOË GARNETT

Visible Amazement (1999)

At 14, Roanne Chappell is sexually developed and curious. When she's seduced by her mother's lover, Roanne heads south from British Columbia to California. Along the way she drops in unannounced on a famous cartoonist — a kind, gay French-Canadian dwarf she considers a mentor. Over the next five months, her encounters become more bizarre — there are born-again country singers, movie stars, rock gods and groupies, a sixteen-year-old alcoholic heiress destined to become her best friend, and relationships with older men.

Roanne, the daughter of a bohemian London artist who has emigrated to Canada, is believably precocious and her journey unfolds through a journal that's frank, perceptive, and sparkling, especially when her sense of the dramatic leads her to riff like a Texas tenorman on the hyper-reality of her orgasms.

Garnett is a child of the sixties — a teenage TV actor who made guest appearances on *77 Sunset Strip* and other shows, a singer-songwriter who scored a Top 10 hit and a Best Folk Recording Grammy with "We'll Sing in the Sunshine," the leader of Gentle Reign, and occasionally a film actress (*My Big Fat Greek Wedding*). She's had early, intimate, and lifelong experience of the improbable and outrageous and has acquired extraordinary linguistic dexterity along the way that supplements and complements her musician's ear for the ways actors and musicians and wannabe's speak to themselves as they talk to one another.

~⌒

TREVOR FERGUSON

Onyx John (1985)

If Wikipedia is your source, then you've read that Trevor Ferguson, the author of nine novels and four plays, has been called Canada's best novelist by unnamed sources, that Dennis Lee called his first novel, *High Water Chants* (1977), "one of the best in the language"; that *Onyx John* "received (arguably) the highest critical acclaim in the history of Canadian literature" inasmuch as "Leon Rooke called it one of the five best novels of the twentieth century." So why haven't you read him? Perhaps you have without knowing it: as John Farrow, he's author of the crime novels *City of Ice* (1999) and *Ice Lake* (2001). How you read him and respond to his work has much to do with how you regard the novels of William Faulkner or, more probably, John Irving.

When interviewed by David Solway for *Books in Canada*, Ferguson's response to a question about "most important literary influences" was that "as a young man I read everything I could get my hands on, and it's that broad, scattered, unstructured absorption that is the principal influence" but

> there was one guy I had to write through, one fellow I had to savage and get rid of as his light flooded such a massive tract of my own internal landscape and bound me to him in a lunar sway, and that was Faulkner. An eagerness to knock down the psychic walls and seek a transcendent language through cadence, to allow cadence to write the book, I owe that to him....

Here's the opening to *Onyx John*:

> The wages of sin aren't bad, everything considered. Old wealth might call this cottage small, and turn up a nose at the crumbling chimney and a kitchen floor, that has heaved awonk; heaven knows the plumbing is cantankerous, and the windows refuse to budge whenever the barometer rises, when it falls no door fits the jamb; yet I bless this house, it's superior to any I've known — and it's mine.... This is an old house. An atmosphere humid with memory and ancestry. Lying awake, I often sense myself being scrutinized, a curiosity here amid creatures from another realm.

Onyx John Cameron is exiled in Camden, Maine, but only needs to phone Montreal to have every whim satisfied by someone who wants to keep him happy and out of the way. He wants a woman? No problem, even if he insists (as he does) that she has to be a Boston girl, between twenty-two and thirty, a Radcliffe grad with honours, slender-waisted, willowy legs, no fat, translucent skin, a yachter who has spent summers on Cape Cod or Martha's Vineyard, so graceful that "men's eyes bug out when she walks past." He's not ordering a whore — he's conjuring a male fantasy, *Sports Illustrated*, the Swimsuit Issue. There's a lot of conjuring that goes on here (Onyx John is the son of an alchemist father and a rodeo mother named Diamond), much of it the backstory the jacket copy describes as "from rodeo life in northern Saskatchewan to small-town Ontario, from the mean streets of Montreal to the underworld of Amsterdam" in "a rollicking one-hand-on-the-wheel ride down the perilous roads of the 50s, 60s, and 70s" to his Camden exile.

Ferguson resolved to become a novelist at sixteen, worked in the north on railway gangs as kitchen flunky, timekeeper, bridgeman, and then west to east hopscotching to Europe and the States and back to his hometown Montreal as a heavy equipment operator, mail sorter, community newspaper editor, printer, bar waiter, taxi driver, and typewriter salesman. Self-education works both ways in his novels: nobody else writes the way he does and the way he writes irritates the hell out of a lot of readers, women in particular — unless they're French. He told Solway,

> I'm probably the only English writer in this country's brief history who owes his survival to the support of French Quebec. Certainly when my novels were being praised, but flushed, in Canada, they were being both praised and read in Quebec, and that gave me the morale boost necessary to keep going.... In Paris I'm referred to as one of the major writers in the English-speaking world, without hesitation or embarrassment (not even on my part!).... France is my inverted universe. Everything's upside down. John Farrow is there and doing well, but he's the little brother to Trevor Ferguson. Good reviews in France mean respectable sales. The same for Quebec. That's just not true in the rest of Canada.

French readers respond to him as they did to Georges Simenon as a dissector of souls and detective of sins. Trevor Ferguson may be Scots and Presbyterian by birth and upbringing (his father was a minister, he has served as a church elder) but he's the most lapsed Irish Catholic novelist this country has produced and *Onyx John* is wondrously of itself, written with more artistic integrity and less regard for commercial success than one senses elsewhere in his work.

But is *Onyx John* "one of the five best novels of the twentieth century"? Leon Rooke is better known for Prophetic Proclamations than Critical Insights, a *provocateur* much given to the subversion of common sense. The "highest critical acclaim" ever dished out in the history of Canadian literature, I'd say, is John Irving's "Robertson Davies was the greatest comic novelist in the English language since Charles Dickens." Rooke and Irving are capable of saying anything and inevitably do. After a decade of artistic and commercial frustration, Ferguson turned himself into the prosperous mystery writer John Farrow.

TERRY GRIGGS

Thought You Were Dead (2009)
(Illustrations by Nick Craine)

The gatekeepers of Havlock House were snarling and yipping behind the dungeonesque front door, hitting the high notes like tiny aggrieved castratos. Although only Bunion qualified for that role, seeing as Hormone was a *grrrrl*. Chellis could hear her nails clicking on the foyer's parquet floor as she danced and yapped, her nails painted some trendy canine colour, like Bitch Black

"Potato I have," he called out. If they were so smart they'd catch the reference. Bunion even resembled a Joyce scholar he knew. Knew of, that is.

That's the opening of the second chapter of *Thought You Were Dead* and it's such a wonderful send-up of *noir* that an unthinking editor would have killed the first chapter and just dumped readers into what one reviewer has termed a "slacker cozy" and left them to figure out for themselves that Bunion and Hormone are "rats with ruffs and canine pretensions" and Chellis Beith is a literary researcher for Athena Havlock, the author of a multiple pseudonymous series of pulp mysteries and the occasional literary novel, who lives in the slumbering southern Ontario town of Farclas near Claymore near the author's actual hometown of Stratford.

Why an *unthinking* editor? Because nothing Griggs ever does is done in the usual way: I can't speak of her children's books — *The Cat's Eye Corner* trilogy (2000, 2004, 2006) — but just like *Thought You Were Dead*, her two previous novels, *The Lusty Man* (1995) and *Rogue's Wedding* (2002), as well as her story collection *Quickenings* (1990), demand an unusual degree of attention. Griggs's stories do have plots and her characters do develop but they're not "givens" — the reader has to discover them by uncovering the layers of linguistic complexity that encase a dominant metaphor. As she says in an interview with John Metcalf,

"In proper metaphor fashion the story becomes in structure, in its very bones, what it is about" and adds, as an aside, "Everything, imagery, symbolism, just piles into the metaphor like kids into a station wagon and the story takes off."

A book reviewer is murdered in nearby Claymore. ("Who would want to kill a lowly book reviewer? ... What would propel a writer to commit an actual murder? Serious plagiarism found out? A vicious rejection ...? The extremes of publicity? Sinister, out-of-control research?") Then Mrs. Havlock disappears. For strength and courage, Chellis Beith draws inspiration from Marcel Lazar, one of his boss's paper-and-ink detectives as he seeks out answers to his life's perplexing problems, which include his inability to act decisively rather than pro-crastinate by comically reacting to everything that might provide genuine solace.

Reading your way into Chellis (and the author behind the author who pulls his strings) is great fun for anyone who enjoys bad puns, good jokes, neat paro-dies, and an excellent set of sometimes-messy allusions to Nabokov, Hitchcock, and others. Wordplay is unrelenting but not without an end — it's Griggs' method of enhancing the role of cultural literacy in a world losing its grip on truth. Chellis (as in Chalice, as in Holy Grail) remarks, "Fiction filtered so surreptitiously into everyday life that you had to keep your eye on it. But not banish it altogether. That would be too too boring. Besides, it was so useful."

A useful clue to what's happening in *Thought You Were Dead* is in the dedica-tion — "For me." There's a quest here and the quest has much to do with exploring the self in ways that have more to do with VN (Vladimir Nabokov) than TM or any other self-help movement going the rounds. The drawings by Nick Craine — who has illustrated Bruce MacDonald's screenplays for *Dance Me Outside* and *Hard Core Logo* and drawn for UTNE Reader as well major news-papers — are a bonus and make *Thought You Were Dead* illuminating viewing as well as reading.

~

ELIZABETH RUTH

Smoke (2005)

Lipstick. Technicolor red. Bette Davis lips. Eyes shoot to the shoes, the god-damnedest do-me-if-you-dare-devil-if-I-care-lady pair of red pumps ever seen on any Canadian author anywhere. It's a meet-and-greet at Bravo studios for finalists and judges in the 2001 Amazon.ca/*Books in Canada* First Novel Award. Elizabeth Ruth is a finalist. I'm a judge. Later in the day, after a banquet that awards the prize to Michael Redhill's *Martin Sloane*, Ruth is taking me across town in her junker, wearing sensible driving shoes, and clutching, braking, accelerating with a zippiness that inspires admiration and trepidation. Still later, her fingers and eyes do what needs to be done with a pool cue to hold her own against Michael Winter in a beer joint on Queen West. At the end of the day, I'm still weighing what to say to her before closing time about her debut novel *Ten Good Seconds of Silence*: it's daring in its insights into single parenthood among women marginalized by psychic states that are all too easily dismissed as psychotic but baffling in its dependence on Timothy Findley's overwrought sentencing.

Ten Good Seconds of Silence has been adopted by several university courses and its German translation is creating a buzz similar to the one that made Barbara Gowdy more widely read and discussed in Europe than in Canada in the early stages of her career. Ruth is as equally direct and disturbing as Gowdy when it comes to human bodies and the transfigurations in flesh that love impels and has as much to say about the spiritual crises of our time and the ways tolerance gets tested in everyday life. Both writers speak directly to the urbane and cosmopolitan even when their settings are as provincial as *The White Bone*'s herd of elephants or the tobacco harvesting crew in *Smoke*.

Smoke seems the kind of CanLit novel that upmarket downtown hipsters sneer at. Set in 1958 in Ontario's tobacco country, it tells the tale of a sensitive farm boy on the verge of becoming a man and what he learns by listening to the stories told by the town's elderly doctor. But this isn't Jake and the Kid revisited: Elizabeth Ruth is closer to Pedro Almodovar, Todd Haynes, and other leading members of the New Queer Cinema than to W. O. Mitchell. Like Haynes in *Far From Heaven*, Ruth recreates the fifties with affection, understanding, and uncanny accuracy in a virtuoso performance that subverts the past by challenging us to rethink what is normal and what is not without mocking anybody.

Fifteen-year-old Brian "Buster" McFiddie falls asleep with a cigarette in his hand and wakes up with his bed on fire. While burns are cleaned and fresh dressings applied to Buster's face, Doc Gray tries to distract Buster by recounting true crime stories of The Purple Gang — the Prohibition era mobsters who smuggled liquor from Windsor to Detroit. When the bandages come off and Buster has to face the world outside his bedroom, a gangster's fedora and a couple of other gifts from the Doc teach him how to move forward even as the physician continues his descent into the past. There's not a lot more that can be said about the plot of *Smoke* without, as cricketers say, queering the pitch. It addresses the timeless gap between how we see the maimed and deformed and how they see us — think about *The Hunchback of Notre Dame*, Cyclops in *The Odyssey*, Episode 12 in Joyce's *Ulysses*.

Elizabeth Ruth is an innovative storyteller, full of quirky surprises, who has the courage to confront basic preconceptions about self-identity and is much more herself and less Findley acolyte the second time round. *Smoke* is an unconventional probing of the anxieties of outsiders in a decade infamous for conformity — a notable achievement for any writer and utterly remarkable for a self-confessed "city girl" born at the end of the sixties. The child of a single mother who moved around a lot, Ruth has worked on the midnight shift at a Chrysler minivan plant and as a counsellor in women's shelters and mental health centres. The result is a keen sense of the everyday things ordinary people do with considerable grace under the pressure of earning a living and making homes for themselves and their families in sexually inhospitable circumstances such as those she's anthologized in *Bent on Writing: Contemporary Queer Tales* (Women's Press, 2002).

JOAN BARFOOT

Exit Lines (2008), *Luck* (2005), *Critical Injuries* (2001)

Exit Lines (2008)

Joan Barfoot is the most frequently overlooked and underrated major Canadian novelist — at least in her own country: overseas and in the USA, she's ranked alongside Anne Tyler, Carol Shields, Margaret Drabble, and Margaret Atwood. At home, she's won the *Books in Canada* First Novel Award (*Abra*, 1978) and been nominated precisely once for the Giller (*Luck*, 2005). *Critical Injuries* (2002) was longlisted for the Booker and shortlisted for the Trillium. Go to her website and you'll see that she's a minimalist when it comes to self-promotion: her eleven novels take pride of place.

In a 2006 interview, Barfoot mentions that she never called herself "a writer" (even though she'd published several novels) until she stopped working as a journalist. Then, she adds, "I still don't have a business card. What would it say? 'Joan Barfoot: Thinks, feels, types; re-thinks, re-feels, re-types.'" Writing is "strangely hard work, even broken into just one word after another. But it's entertaining and often enough I amuse myself." Her amusement isn't self-indulgent — *thinks, feels, types; re-thinks, re-feels, re-types*. She's a self-described "fierce reader" and, as a reader who writes, knows what Jane Austen knew — that her novels are hers alone only until they go into the world "at which point readers (and occasionally reviewers) take over creating 50 percent of its content and meaning out of their own experiences and perceptions." When asked "Do you have a favourite story to tell about being interviewed about your book?" Barfoot replies:

> ... an interviewer spoke of her own writing, and her desire to be published, but the hurdles she was facing because publishers kept turning her down and editors kept suggesting she might do this or that to improve her manuscript. But what right, she wondered, did anyone have to recommend changes to her perfect intentions? So we had a little chat about *the beyond-measure value of a good editor*, although I

failed to convince her. I think I also failed to dislodge *her firm belief that writers should not be readers, lest their pristine personal styles be contaminated by the influences of others.* Mind you, that discussion turned out to be not about my book at all. But it was certainly entertaining, in a depressing sort of way. [my italics]

Asked, "If you could have written one book in history, what book would that be?" she answers:

It would have been fun to discover/think up/stumble onto the novel form, and to have written the very first one. Maybe the second one, too, just to develop and play around with the form. Imagine the world without novels, and then the world suddenly with them — what an explosion of knowledge, possibilities, big questions, and willed, deliberate empathy. A brilliant invention.

Exit Lines is a brilliant invention that's reminiscent of The Beatles — not because one of its central quartet is George, but because of the harmonic interplay of four voices as they reflect different melodic interpretations of friendship, loyalty, and love. This tale of a four-way friendship begins on a "blessedly balmy day in mid-April" when move-in time comes to the Idyll Inn, the latest link in a small chain of retirement homes run by a management group on behalf of investors, mostly doctors and dentists. As new residents begin to settle into unfamiliar surroundings on the banks of a small river city in Ontario, the foursome of Sylvia, Ruth, Greta, and George band together in pleasurable rebellion, fuelled by a private supply of decent wines. Their spouses are dead or beyond recall. Their children are distant — physically or emotionally — and their pasts are more or less loosely interconnected: George ran the best shoe store in town; Greta was the immigrant single mother who clerked in his shop; Ruth was the city's child welfare officer; Sylvia was a lawyer's wife and civic-minded volunteer. But Greta is also George's former lover and glimpses into their steamy past and abstinent present are a powerful reminder that the distance between knock-kneed passion and knackered passivity can be frighteningly short.

"I'm intending to die, and I'd like your assistance."

Greta's scarf loses two stitches. Sylvia is gape-mouthed, blindsided, when she'd have sworn she was by and large beyond shock. While George remains unruffled, assuming he's heard wrong, as sometimes he gathers he does.

Ruth cannot be serious. Except if she's not serious, she's making a far worse and more unlikely joke than anybody among them has yet managed to crack. "You're kidding, right?" Sylvia asks, but Ruth shakes her head. Who would kid?

Then who does she think they are?

Perhaps she considers them cruel people, or arrogant, or compassionate or righteous or vulnerable or guilty.

Or she thinks they're her friends. And so they are, in a haven't-known-each-other-very-long way. Only friendship is supposed to be companionship, compatibility, trust, empathy, challenge, warmth, goodwill, consolation and sustenance. Not this. What she's asking has to be — or is it not? — beyond all possible bounds.

Exit Lines is subtitled *A Darkly Comic Novel about Everything that Matters, from Sex to Death* and encompasses companionship, compatibility, trust, empathy, challenge, warmth, goodwill, consolation, and sustenance. This tale of growing old disgracefully, as Julie Wheelwright noted in *The Independent* (just one of the many enthusiastic reviews that appeared in the United Kingdom), is "powerful stuff ... [with] plenty of bite ... a poignant read that unsettles, haunts and disturbs with the best literary sensibility." Barfoot's dry, distinctly black humour is empathetic and uncondescending, sardonic, sly, and so subversive that it's no surprise that she's widely read in Britain where she's admired as a writer of depth, originality, and unembarrassed honesty. In the interview quoted above, she remarks, "It interests me (although no longer very much) that people tend to stick to the surface of novels that are located within households.... I could wish, in short, for more ... that paid more attention to the mind, and focused on ideas rather than only personalities and feelings."

Barfoot gives open-minded readers much to think about and it's limiting to think of *Exit Lines* as a book of interest only to those who are middle-aged with aging parents. It should be on senior high school curricula across the country. Why? *Exit Lines* explores the world of disempowered people whose independence is studiously ignored or bureaucratically circumvented. Residents of the Idyll Inn have to keep too much of themselves carefully concealed, locked up because they're all-too-easily robbed of dignity, autonomy, and erotic vibrancy. Patronized and pushed around, these people whose lives are so difficult in so many ways are constantly faced with the question of what makes life worth living.

Luck (2005)

Like Margaret Laurence (a major influence), Barfoot's world includes Africa. Barfoot didn't live formative years there as Laurence did but she has "travelled through Niger and Mali in times (fairly perpetual) of drought and hunger" and knows just how *lucky* she, her friends, and her readers are to be unoppressed, comfortable, free, and safe no matter what hardships we might face, including 9/11 . Those terrorist attacks led her to ask what accounts for most people living in perpetual viciousness, violence, poverty, hardship at best, and we're exempt. *Luck* offers a crapshooter's answer: no gods, no fates, no system of virtue and sin, reward and punishment, including karma, accounts for how lives unfold. This is what Alice Munro thinks of it:

> *Luck* took me right out of myself. I read it in one gulp, and it never let me down. Sharp and surprising but always responsible, no tricks for tricks' sake, so satisfying, with its shifting and puzzles. So much fiction turns out to be diversion, in spite of fancy claims, and doesn't really look at anything. Well — this does.

Nora Lawrence wakes up to discover her second husband dead in bed beside her. Phillip, a furniture maker, has died quietly in his sleep but leaves an unconventional household to mourn him — Nora is an artist with a live-in model,

Beth, and a housekeeper, Sophie. Their relationships with one another and with Phillip unfold over three days. Some reviewers didn't know what to make of *Luck* because its humour is so mordant and its philosophic stance so radical in its amorality. Reviewing it for *Books in Canada*, Ann Diamond did nail its most interesting features:

> The principal colour in every scene is a dull grey-green — the colour of money, disappointment, cynicism, thwarted affection. The scenes themselves take place in sedate, recognizable places: a bedroom, a kitchen, a living room, a funeral home, a roadside, a fashionable art gallery. The homes are well furnished and tasteful, endowed with lovely gardens. The principal emotions are, in order of frequency and novelistic significance: envy, doubt, resentment, financial dread, and vindictiveness. (Maybe financial dread is not precisely an emotion, but it might as well be in this world.)

But even Diamond had difficulty knowing what to make of a narrative "which at times mimics the convoluted blankness of the characters' souls":

> I was never sure what to make of all the repetition, the attention to appearance and surfaces. I think that it's most likely a form of ironic social commentary. Barfoot definitely has an ear for inflated, pompous dialogue. Over coffee after the embalming, Hendrik, the funeral direc-tor, earnestly bares his beliefs to the grief-stricken Sophie: "I like the idea that sometimes I can make sorrow easier to bear. You can't take grief away from anyone, but sometimes you can lift it a bit. Make it easier or more comprehensible, whatever seems required. And I like being able to acknowledge the people and the lives that I know and the ends of their stories. Respecting all the family and community and how it unfolds, in the end." This is quite a mouthful for an undertaker, even if he is, in a way, the novel's real hero.

Luck was shortlisted for the 2005 Giller Prize won by David Bergen's *The Time In Between*, a book whose narrative voice was well described as "tightly controlled monotony." *Luck* is wickedly amusing social satire of the kind that Russell Smith is forever saying he'd more willingly write if only there was a readership for it. Careerists seek to inherit existing audiences — enduring writers build readerships by *thinking, feeling, typing; re-thinking, re-feeing, re-typing* book by book by book. As the eminent painter Betty Goodwin never tired of saying, "you push and push and push, and there is a moment when the work begins to pull you."

Critical Injuries (2001)

Critical Injuries pushes off from a random encounter between strangers — Isla, a middle-aged mom, happy in her second marriage and Roddy, a truly stupid seventeen-year-old who accidently shoots her and paralyzes her in the midst of holding up an ice cream parlour. Told in alternating chapters, their backstories show us who they were before the shooting; the foreground is what they both need to do to come to terms with the present and figure out the future. Like *Luck*, this is all about how life can be as unpredictable and potentially topsy-turvy as a playground where what you gain on the swings, you can lose on the roundabouts. Comic relief and a way of interlocking the stories is provided by Isla's spacey daughter Alix a.k.a. Starglow, a member of a religious cult called Serenity Corps who thinks — if thinking is the word for it — that her mother's involuntary "stillness" is a chance to achieve inner peace.

MICHAEL IGNATIEFF

Scar Tissue (1993)

"Novelist" isn't the first word that comes to mind when Michael Ignatieff gets discussed these days. In 1991, he wrote *Asya* — a well-told, unpretentious tale of the life and loves of Asya Galitzine, who loses everything during the Russian Civil War, goes to Paris, pregnant and alone, and joins other Russian émigrés before being forced into exile in London where she loves and loses a Canadian officer. In 2003, *Charlie Johnson in the Flames* was published, the story of a veteran war correspondent in Kosovo in 1998 who loses objectivity and much else in the face of one particularly grotesque brutality. *Charlie Johnson* is hurried, formulaic, thin, and lacks the intellectual rigour and emotional intensity of *Scar Tissue*, which was shortlisted for both the Whitbread Novel Award and the Booker Prize for Fiction (along with Carol Shields's *The Stone Diaries*) won by Roddy Doyle's *Paddy Clarke Ha Ha Ha*.

Scar Tissue, narrated by a philosophy professor, the younger brother of a neurologist, is about the losses that accumulate over a lifetime within a generally fortunate family. As his mother nears her sixtieth birthday, the philosopher begins to observe her decline into *dementia* with clinical precision: Alzheimer's is in her genes and not entirely unexpected. She has always been a high-spirited woman, a portrait painter Bohemian enough to prefer bare feet to shoes, uninhibited enough to belt out Broadway show tunes in her house and in her studio. Now, more suddenly than ever anticipated, she stops painting and starts fumbling words and jumbling ideas and memories. As his mother declines at home and then in a nursing home and his father dies, the narrator's distressed relationships with his wife and children stretch, snap, break. Guilt-ridden, his struggles to find meaning to life in the face of death gradually brings him closer to his brother and the light neuroscience can shed on disease, not as metaphor but as pre-condition for life.

The title comes from "the dark starbursts of scar tissue" that indicate a brain being destroyed. This is tough but necessary reading as the narrator recounts in embarrassing and excruciating detail his mother's decline and death. But it's only through such attentiveness that he (and his readers) begin to grasp a self-examined-life's hardest truth — "We have just enough knowledge to know our fate but not enough to do anything to avert it." What makes this book more than bearable — almost pleasurable inasmuch as such dark things can ever be so — is Ignatieff's artistry in capturing and celebrating moments in life when all we really need to do is exclaim (in the words of Kurt Vonnegut's uncle) "If this isn't nice, what is!"

~~

HUGH HOOD

Near Water (2000)

Near Water is the twelfth and concluding volume of *The New Age/Le nouveau siècle* (1975–2000), Hugh Hood's novel-series that attempts to capture the texture of Canadian life in a Proustian way. Any reader wanting to understand the depth and comprehensiveness of his achievement and why it deserves serious consideration as a masterpiece of world literature will find W. J. Keith's *Canadian Odyssey* (2002), a most accessible and insightful companion.

The final text of *Near Water* was prepared for posthumous publication by Professor Keith, and take his word for it that "*Near Water* ... though it frequently refers back to people from the earlier books, resembles none of its predecessors" and is *initially* so bewildering that "an essential prerequisite for coming to terms with the book is to banish from one's mind all previously held assumptions about traditional novels." The things that make it unique include no human conversation and very little action in its voyage through one man's consciousness in the last hours of his life. Matt Goderich, the central figure in the series, is either alone or surrounded by angels — not New Age guardians and guides but the choirs of spiritual entities from the world of Dante's *Purgatorio* and *Paradiso*. There are nine chapters and each takes its title from the Angels, Archangels, Powers, Virtues, Principalities, Dominations, Thrones, Cherubim, and Seraphim that, in ascending order, form the hierarchy of beings that stand between man and the Holy Trinity in the "great chain of being" constructed by the Church Fathers from biblical references, early Jewish apocalyptic writings, and Christian traditions.

Near Water begins, almost conventionally, with Matt (he's in his eighties) driving to his lakeside cottage in southern Ontario. Anticipating a reunion with Edie, a woman with whom he's had a long and tangled relationship and from whom he's been estranged for thirty years, he free-associates as he drives — beginning with the word "periplum."

> Around 1950 some admirers of Ezra Pound, and many others of a small literary elite, made a great fuss over their discovery, as they considered it, that the *Odyssey* had the form of a periplum, a literary work having the overt and public form of, say, an account of an epic journey, as well as a private, concealed form and purpose. This secondary, covert design was not usually put to a malign purpose but existed more for the fun of the thing than anything else. The work was an essay in the making of double meanings as an artistic exercise, periplum.

Matt gets to the lake, suffers a stroke while lying on a recliner some distance from his cottage, is paralyzed, and will survive only if he can somehow work his way back up to the house. As he does what he does, we witness ourselves becoming his friends and he ours with a level of involvement that reminds us just how powerful a companion a book can be when the author is as much in love with *home* as Homer and Dante wanted us always to be.

Hugh Hood's own sense of fun was utterly *audacious*. As a young man, he was a connoisseur of drunkenness and mastered the art of savouring its every phase, including oblivion. Promising himself a massive drinking bout only after he'd completed *The New Age/Le nouveau siècle*, he went cold turkey and fuelled his writing with conversation. Talking to him (listening, actually) was intoxicating. Among all the authors I've reviewed, Hood was the only one who phoned me every time I reviewed one of his books on the very day the review appeared. Those conversations are memorable for their pattern, a pattern that recurs throughout his work. In the thirty or forty-five minutes between opening and closing, we'd romp through his periplums, his texts within texts within the texts within the text he'd written. Had I caught the doublings and treblings he'd intended, his literary three-in-ones? Had I seen, had I really seen how a moral sense lurked behind the literal, how an allegorical sense made war upon the symbolical, how each of these was at the service of the anagogical? "The Blessed Trinity," he'd say, "is everywhere in everything." He'd chuckle as he said this and then he'd invite me to lunch to discuss the book he insisted only I could write about periplums in the novels of David Adams Richards! I'd decline and hangup with one hell of a hangover, his chuckles reverberating like bent-out-of-shape notes from Jimi Hendrix's guitar. How I miss him!

~

HOWARD ENGEL

Memory Book (2005)

Howard Engel suffered a critical injury in 2001: a stroke left him with a very rare condition, *alexia sine agraphia* — he can write but he cannot read in a normal way. (Oliver Sacks provides the details in an afterword and Engel elaborates on them in detail in his 2007 memoir, *The Man Who Forgot How to Read*). Until this happened, Engel was better known for his work as a producer of literary programs for the CBC, the once-upon-a-time husband of the novelist Marian Engel, a co-founder of the Crime Writers Association of Canada, and the creator of the first truly Canadian private eye, Benny Cooperman, who is more Woody Allen than Sam Spade.

Memory Book is the eleventh and the best of the Cooperman series. What makes it a good novel are the ways in which it transcends its own genre. Benny is a different character when he wakes up in a Toronto hospital with a traumatic brain injury: he's been in a coma for eight weeks and he shares his creator's neurological condition. Hit on the back of the head, he's found in a dumpster beside the body of a dead woman — that's the generic mystery. But the real mystery is what happens inside Benny as he attempts to re-establish his own identity. Engel succeeds at creating a character that transcends the demands of the plot. Cooperman in hospital is ruled less by the laws governing murder mysteries than by his own free will operating within a straitjacketed brain. *Memory Book* is a living, breathing radiant novel because Cooperman struggles for knowledge (and self-knowledge) and what he learns about Benny-in-a-state-of-traumatic-brain-injury is more gripping and less easily discerned than the solution of the murder. Benny's vivacity lifts the book to heights Engel never attempted before his stroke.

~

BRAD SMITH

Big Man Coming Down the Road (2007), *One-Eyed Jacks* (2000)

Big Man Coming Down the Road (2007)

People who complain that they can't find a good Canadian novel with a strong storyline need pointing to Brad Smith. A carpenter by trade (he's also been a farmer, railway signalman, insulator, truck driver, bartender, school teacher in Alberta, British Columbia, Texas, and South Africa) who builds things near the north shore of Lake Erie when not writing, Smith gets details right when he describes how people do many things — handle tools, horses, machines, and make music, love, and fools of themselves. In less than a decade, Smith has developed an enthusiastic following by writing intelligent novels that are perfect for summer reading. As Dennis Lehane of *Mystic River* fame says, "Brad Smith has got the goods — he's funny, poignant, evocative, and he tells a blistering tale." Smith's ability to create down-to-earth characters as authentic as Lehane's has attracted the interest of filmmakers who have bought rights to all of his novels: *One-Eyed Jacks* (2000), *All Hat* (2003), *Busted Flush* (2005), and *Big Man Coming Down the Road* (2007).

What makes Brad Smith different and sets him apart from just about every Canadian writer east of Douglas Coupland is his use of Elmore Leonard's device of establishing character through honest-to-the-ear dialogue, James Ellroy's criss-crossing storylines to broaden social contexts, and Walter Mosley's race and gender consciousness to get at some overlooked truths about the rest of our lives without becoming captive to crime genre conventions. Everett Eastman, the ruthless dynamo who electrifies and magnetizes the plotlines of *Big Man Coming Down the Road*, is old, ill, and estranged from his children. Daughter Kathleen is a documentary filmmaker who has maxed out her credit cards filming the effects of natural gas exploration on cattle ranching. Ethan, the younger of his two sons, is a bipolar stoner musician who isn't interested in taking his meds and hasn't managed to interest anybody in his songwriting. Ben, the eldest and heir apparent, has allowed the family's major source of wealth — an auto parts manufacturing plant — to run on its own momentum as he ignores his wife, fondles his implant-assisted mistress, and daydreams of what he'll do when he gets his hands on daddy's millions. When the old man dies and the will is read, his children discover that he has paid more attention to them in death than in life. In a final effort to make them stand up for themselves, Eastman leaves each of them a less-than-thriving company in the Waterloo region but the bequests come with a rat's nest of codicils and his only remaining friend, Will Montgomery, as executor. Will is a former NHL fourth-line winger who knows when to take off the gloves and when to take a hit and keep moving.

Smith's characters are quirky, colloquial, and never quite as bright or alert as circumstances warrant. Kathleen is given a publisher of audiobooks on condition that she makes a comeback album with a country singer as principled as Johnny Cash, as cantankerous about paying taxes as Willy Nelson, as hard-living handsome as Kris Kristofferson, and full of misgivings about getting involved with any and all record producers. Ethan gets a distillery. Ben, who is more interested in wresting both companies from his siblings, keeps the auto parts company only if it can fulfil a major contract with Toyota. Is that enough plot for you?

Big Man Coming Down the Road documents with sly good humour the not-so-graceful ways in which conflicting views on the environment, global capitalism, and female–male relationships get played out at ground level in the Ontario heartland over a couple of double-doubles at the Tim Hortons in the mall or a couple of Coors at a backyard barbecue. It's a world view that's been under-represented in mainstream Canadian fiction since the death of Matt Cohen and Smith presents it with both the geniality and bite it deserves. As an added bonus to Bob Dylan fans, Ethan says and does little but when he speaks or acts, it's with fragments of Dylan's lyrics on his lips.

One-Eyed Jacks (2000)

It's 1959 and Tommy Cochrane at 35 is still ranked number 9 among the top 10 contenders for Floyd Patterson's heavyweight boxing championship. That's his only asset and it's useless because he's got an aneurysm and can't fight. When Tommy comes riding into Toronto the Good on a freight car with his sparring partner, T-Bone, he's broke and homeless and hoping he has enough friends to raise the few thousand he needs to buy back his grandfather's farm and start scratching out some kind of subsistence. Tommy and T-Bone encounter a city of gamblers looking for luck at all the wrong tables. The small lives and narrow minds of a provincial city long gone are vividly recreated by an author who was a mere four years old in the year his story is set. Smith is guilty of a couple of howlers — could any sexualized male not have known who Marilyn Monroe was in 1959? — but the story he gets right is that nobody, no matter how strong, ever gets to be the hero of his own life. We all get rescued by those who love us. *One-Eyed Jacks* has good sex, bad beatings, stupid thefts, and senseless killings but it's also a novel about friendship that gets closer to the spirit of Charles Dickens than stuff that's taken more seriously. Brad Smith uses T-Bone as a lightning rod to attract all the racist impulses of Toronto. It's risky, but Smith finesses it without reducing T-Bone to stereotype and caricature.

M. T. KELLY

Save Me, Joe Louis (1998), A Dream Like Mine (1987)

Save Me, Joe Louis (1998)

M. T. Kelly is overwhelmingly intense — in person and on the page. He was born with one layer of skin less than the rest of us. Or had it stripped away in boyhood.

Save Me, Joe Louis is about Robbie Blackstone, a sixteen-year-old boxer about to turn pro, and his relationships with his mother Lucy, her boyfriend Shiner, his trainers Stu and Jimmy, and Rocco, an ex-world championship contender. They're all less mature, far more confused than he is. Kelly's characters are characters.

The setting is Toronto in the 1960s when most of downtown wasn't fashionable and never expected to become so; a *noir* city of diners, taverns, boxing clubs, pool halls inhabited by men nursing grudges and women nursing broken hearts.

Kelly's been in the ring. He knows the ropes. His sentences are compact, strong. Robbie learns to bob and jab and punch hard. There's no butterfly bullshit here, just the stinging truth when and where the author sees it. The late Carole Corbeil, a writer as strong as they came, wrote:

> There is a kind of alchemy in the very best writing that allows it to disappear so that its peoples and themes — in this case the desperate expectations adults place on children — become a part of the reader's heart long after the book is put down. *Save Me, Joe Louis* is that kind of book.

When Robbie begins asserting his independence, you get more than a plot twist — you get raw emotion that makes you remember that while you may be getting older, you ain't old yet if you can feel his heartbeat in your chest.

∾

A Dream Like Mine (1987)

In 1987, M. T. Kelly was awarded the Governor General's Literary Award for Fiction for *A Dream Like Mine*, a novel set in the real-life situation of land claims disputes and environmental pollution in and around the community of Grassy Narrows. Kelly weaves his tale around a First Nations activist, a sympathetic reporter, and a kidnapped lumber company executive. When the story was tranferred to the screen as *Clearcut* in 1991, the journalist became a lawyer and mercury pollution replaced logging but the central conflict was left intact. The movie is well worth watching for its mesmerizing performance by Graham Greene and the book is essential reading for Kelly's ability to realize his intentions. In his Governor General's acceptance speech, he said:

> Because of the themes of *A Dream Like Mine* I cannot conclude without speaking of the land claims of the Lubicon Lake Indians.... I am not one of those for whom literature or poetry — in W. H. Auden's words — "makes nothing happen," flowing "on south / from ranches of isolation." I believe that to change people's minds — and governments are people — we must not rely solely on economic or other arguments, but must create a sense of imagination. The Lubicon Lake Indians — all Native peoples and their cultures — are not simply artifacts to be displayed in museums or societies that are part of our multiculturalism and are interesting from an ethnological point of view. They are people and cultures from whom we can learn another way of looking at the world. This is not misplaced pantheism or aesthetic luxury; it is essential if we ... are going to leave our children anything that is wild, anything that is beautiful. Listen to these Indian voices, harken; they seem to me the very breath of the Americas.

Kelly makes something fine and true out of anguish and ugliness and does it in a way that opened publishers' doors and readers' hearts to unheard voices. *A Dream Like Mine* predates Joseph Boyden's *Three Day Road* by eighteen years but it feels more like a lifetime.

JOHN HARRIS
Small Rain (1989)

In the world of *Small Rain*'s narrator, people fall into two camps: *Voters* and *Indians*. *Voters*:

> are not fractions, but they are able to live like them. They are "nice." They own .25 of a house, drive .5 of a car, have 1.3 kids and are relatively happy. They dream of wholeness at 65 years of age. They are the backbone of civilization. They belong to parties, support charities, watch the news and suffer angst. Given a bar of soap and told to line up for a shower, they are convinced by the time they reach the head of the line that they need a shower and are going to get one. Most of the time they are right.

Indians:

> don't believe in fractions and can't learn to live like them. They don't vote. They refuse to believe that Germans stink, young people can't think or write, civil servants are lazy, and communists evil. They have the ability to walk away from houses, cars, etc.... They fall in love and stay there, write poetry or paint pictures. They are over the edge. Given a bar of soap and told to take a shower, they know that something is wrong. Usually they are right.

The narrator is a middle-aged English instructor in a community college in a town a lot like Prince George, BC. He's a recently separated father of two adolescents, a funny self-deprecating man who finds himself becoming transformed from Voter to Indian as the pressures of his new life with a new lover unleash roiling undercurrents of sarcasm, flippancy, and idealism from living too long at the back of a standstill line.

My ex-wife has a plumpish body and Brenda has a thin, nervous one. My ex-wife has very nice breasts and Brenda has hardly any. My ex-wife is a psychiatric nurse and Brenda writes surrealistic stories in the Laundromat. These are the factors that change the universe.

What a spillway of passionately comedic words bursting out of him as he observes and analyzes the collisions between his old world and his new one!

There are some people (possibly the author himself) who'll argue that *Small Rain* is a suite of 15 connected short stories but it's actually a novel of character and locale in 15 episodes because a fragmented life is shaped into a semblance of quotidian unity by book's end as this teacher (who daydreams of becoming a university lecturer in Toronto) realizes that at York U, he would have

students who would not write "the chainsaw is busted." They would believe in freedom of thought and would know how to get ahead by saying yes.... They have never gone outside the walls after dark, never been yelled at, shit-kicked, and pissed on. At the college, this is an everyday event.

When Diane Schoemperlen reviewed *Small Rain* for *Books in Canada*, she declared it "wonderful," wrote that it deserved "serious attention," could not believe that a writer this good had previously gone unnoticed, and mused that Harris was "a pseudonym for another well-known Canadian writer who chose to remain anonymous." Her off-the-record guess was Brian Fawcett and that made a lot of sense (both in terms of the eye for nonsense and the ear for local sensibilities) except that John Harris did and does exist: over the past two decades, he's published a less robust sequel, *Other Art* (1997), and *Tungsten John: The South Nahani River by Foot and Bicycle* (2000), co-written with his partner, the travel writer Vivien Lougheed. After *Small Rain* and *Other Art*, Harris has devoted much of his energy to mastering the art of the occasional essay, two dozen of which are posted at dooneyscafe.com, the webzine hosted by Brian Fawcett.

∾

PAUL QUARRINGTON

Galveston (2004)

Long before launching his band Porkbelly Futures, Paul Quarrington started writing fiction in idle moments while playing bass for Joe Hall and the Continental Drift. From 1978 to 1990, he created half a dozen novels (including *Home Game*, *King Leary*, and *Whale Music*) that are hysterical and historical in the way pubescent boys are.

All follow a plot line that's deeply meaningful to any man still bright-eyed enough to revel in tales of emotionally crippled, socially withdrawn, and inept wet fish getting hooked, netted, landed, and transformed by some minor divinity (a young woman, ghosts, whatever) into a more sensible and less-thin-skinned version of himself. The process is always wildly comic and the setting larded with arcane knowledge and precise period detail — as perfect a reading for a summer's night with beer in Canada as P. G. Wodehouse is for an afternoon with tea in England.

In the summer of 1988, *King Leary* (the best of them) felt like reading the work of a thirteen-year-old literary prodigy, a rink rat who hangs out at his grandpa's nursing home and takes in every detail of every story the old guys tell about the days when hockey was really hockey. For the next decade, Quarrington's writing went off in directions I wasn't interested in following; then, he hooked me again with *Galveston* (2004).

Galveston is ideal fare for that inevitable low in every summer holiday when black clouds gather, the sky turns to thunder, plans fall apart, and a paper world is preferable to the real one. It'll keep you engrossed until the daylight fades, the power goes out, and the beer turns warm. At the end, you'll be swept away imagining Quarrington's cast of castaways doing what the last sentence says they do as they "rode these rafts upon the waves until they came to the shore of a small island where the natives, naked and smiling, greeted them with gifts."

They're on a different island at the beginning: Dampier Cay is a "narrow strip of land, a few miles long" that lies to the "southwest of Jamaica, making a triangle with that land and the Caymans." Once the haunt of pirates, there's not

much to Dampier: private estates owned by white Americans with golden para-
chutes, a tiny hamlet populated by the native black population, a big hotel at
the south end, and a ramshackle resort at the northern end called the Water's
Edge.

Two accidental tourists and three obsessively deliberate ones occupy the
Edge, together with the owner, her lover, and the handyman, as Hurricane
Clare eyes them up. The obsessives are "weather weenies," storm chasers who
travel in order to encounter the sort of extreme conditions most of us do what
we can to avoid. When the storm advances, these characters bend and blend
seamlessly into a story that sticks so fast to the mind that you can leave the book
behind and drop it into the life of whomever occupies your comfy chair or bed
after you, a special gift to entrance people buffeted by things worse than the
weather. I've read it twice since 2004, while recuperating after each of my
strokes.

Gail and Sorvig, a pair of New York cable TV girls looking for the kind of
long drinks of trouble in surfing shorts that itsy-bitsy thong bikinis are likely to
attract, are on Dampier Cay by mishap and provide the kind of genial, comic
relief that a Quarrington novel includes. The three other visitors are Jimmy
Newton, a.k.a. "Mr. Weather," an American videographer with an insatiable
need to photograph things that no one else has ever caught, and two Canadians
— a lottery winner named Caldwell, and Beverly, a woman with no luck at all,
both looking for psychosexual panaceas, sea changes in their fates.

Galveston is one of those books where everything depends on the power of
description and little hangs on unexpected turns in the plot: Newton gets the
shots he most wants and readers get a really bad storm with lovemaking in
the middle that's more graphic than is usual in mainstream Canadian writing.
Like *Saturday Evening Post* storytellers of the mid-twentieth century whom he
emulates (and they include Hemingway), Quarrington knows his way around
such a variety of everyday things — fishing rods, hammers, CB radios, boats,
cameras, nipples — and how each responds to gentle and rough handling that
there's a minimum of disbelief to suspend. What's more, he knows precisely
which words need to be lined up in what order to show how people can manip-
ulate their bodies to gain advantage of whatever they find at hand: "Herbert

struck the pole with sufficient force that both halves flew out of the boat ... and then the sky cracked open. The lightning hit the rod at the apex of its flight, and the rod carried the power into the water and the water carried it away, and that was why they were all still alive."

~~~

WAYNE TEFS

Red Rock (1998)

When Larry McMurtry (*The Last Picture Show, Lonesome Dove,* and so many more, including *Walter Benjamin at the Dairy Queen,* a meditation on a heart beating to the love of books and what open heart surgery did to it) was profiled in *The New Yorker,* he wore a black T-shirt emblazoned "Minor Regional Novelist" for the occasion. It was ironic not iconic but more than a few New Yorkers didn't get the joke. Once tagged a regionalist, the epithet lives a life of its own, overshadowing all broader achievements of its casualty. This has been the fate of Wayne Tefs, a novelist often described over the past two decades as "that guy in Winnipeg" or, more academically, in *The Encyclopedia of Literature in Canada* (2002) as a writer whose encounters with

> Robert Kroetsch, Dennis Cooley, and David Arnason, and his experience with Turnstone Press in Winnipeg helped solidify his commitment to writing a kind of fiction that shaped the landscape of the Prairies rather than one moulded by it.

The one broader note in a couple of inches of clanging text is that his 1985 novel, *The Cartier Street Contract,* "shows his awareness of and response to the Quiet Revolution and Quebec Nationalism." While Tefs surely derives satisfaction from mentoring and editing more acclaimed Winnipeg writers such as Miriam Toews and David Bergen, and bittersweet pleasure from the substantial readership he's acquired as the author of *Rollercoaster: A Cancer Journey* (2002) (an absolute *must-read* for those suffering from cancer, and for their loved ones and care-givers), the indifference of Toronto publishers must leave him confused. Asked to nominate a book for Canada Reads, *Red Rock* would be among my first five choices.

Born in St. Boniface, Tefs grew up in a mining town that was "a place of young transients who were paid the highest hourly wage on the continent in the fifties, where cash flowed freely and so did impulses and urges," he told me. In the decade lived in "Red Rock," there were several brutal murders motivated by sexual jealousy or marital infidelity. With the death penalty still in effect, the murderer's life hung in the balance and "every detail of the trials was followed in the community with breathless absorption."

The thing that makes Tefs difficult to "regionalize" is that each of his novels addresses a different literary problem. In *Red Rock*, he gives away in the opening lines what is usually withheld until the closing pages of a murder mystery — the identity of the murderer. The rest of the novel, he explained to me,

> undoes that revelation, undermining it, so that by the final pages, where conventionally this issue is clear, in *Red Rock* it became as murky as is usually the case ... in the opening pages. Multiple points of view were of great use in reaching for this objective. I wanted to suggest how complicated a thing such as a murder can be. I wanted, too, to explore the complexities of social relations as well as the darker sides of the human heart, and in so doing pose the question, What are the failures in a community that make murder a solution to its social, sexual, and interpersonal issues?

Everything is examined retrospectively. The boy next door, the pharmacist, the wife's best friend, the Chief of Police, the babysitter, and the out-of-town reporter who arrives years later to investigate the old story — offer differing explanations and different judgments. Through the voices of townspeople who think they know every secret but reveal their own prejudices at every turn, we learn about unions, bosses, family myths, the class struggle, the cult of violent hockey in a place where strikes loom, tempers flare, old jobs are casually lost and new ones rarely found. What have to figure out for ourselves — the mystery that makes this "mystery novel" so soul-wrenching — is what makes young women in such places so prone to wanton self-destruction.

CAROL SHIELDS

Swann (1987)

Count me among those readers who have never understood the *literary* celebrity Carol Shields acquired in the 1990s — starting with the 1993 Governor General's Award and the 1995 Pulitzer Prize for *The Stone Diaries*, the Giller nomination for *Thirteen Hands* in 1997, and the culmination of the National Book Critics Circle Award and The Orange Prize in 1998 for *Larry's Party*. The only one of her novels that requires attentive, nuanced reading, start to finish, is *Swann*, which won the Arthur Ellis First Mystery Novel Award in 1988.

Swann was Shield's fourth novel and eighth book (there were a couple of volumes of poetry, a critical study of Susanna Moodie's writings, and a book of short stories). The gentlest thing one can say of the three earlier novels is that they lack credibility in plot or dialogue or character or all three. *Swann* is like them (and all her subsequent work) only in preoccupation with the conjunctions/disjunctions between domestic and artistic impulses, in pleasant and accurate domestic observations, and in a search for consolation and celebration at the intersection of the everyday and the unusual. What sets it fully on its own is the jealousy that enrages Angus, Mary Swann's farmer husband. He's impatient with her secret life as a reader of books borrowed from the library in Nadeau, Ontario, and the time she steals from domestic duties to write poems. When he starts to think she thinks she's better than he is, impatience turns to cruelty and cruelty to rage. What happens between them, and how it unfolds in the telling, makes *Swann* compulsive reading and fascinating, a worthy shelf mate to Wayne Tefs' *Red Rock*.

Though her *literary* celebrity may seem incomprehensible, Carol Shields has a nurturing appeal for multitudes of women readers who peer into her writings and find words they wish they could use as gallantly and genially to plumb their own unsatisfactory domestic arrangements with as highly developed a descriptive power, and this makes her a valuable force in the continual struggle for equal rights and equal opportunities.

~

GEORGE ELLIOTT CLARKE

George & Rue (2005)

A white devil moon haunts the black 1949 brand-new four-door Ford sedan when a black hammer slip out a pocket and smuck the taxi driver's head, from the side. Not just a knock-out blow, the hammer was a landslide of iron. It crashed down unnervingly.

Note the "white devil" and doubled "black" in the opening sentence of George Elliott Clarke's *George & Rue*, a novel that telegraphs its intentions early and often: this is a dark tale of race relations told with cinematic touches of *noir* and bloody daubs of *sang-froid*. Clarke's story is "based on several actual persons and one actual crime" that "employs facts not found in mere trial transcripts" and is actually a retelling and retailing at more commercial length of the crime and punishment that won its author the Governor General's Literary Award in Poetry in 2001 for *Execution Poem*, a slim and handsome book that gave readers the same kinds of pleasures found in Michael Ondaatje's *The Collected Works of Billy the Kid*.

George and Rufus Hamilton "always lived outside boundaries (including knowledge, including history, including archives)" and "fell like dominoes" from a double gallows constructed under the direction of Arthur Ellis, the Dominion Executioner, on July 27, 1949, for the blows Rufus hammered into the skull of Nacre Pearly Burgundy, a white Fredericton taxi driver. The Hamilton brothers were Africadians (descendents of slaves who had intermarried with Mi'kmaq) and the author's matrilineal first cousins, once removed, who were born where Clarke himself was born in Three Mile Plains, Nova Scotia, a few miles southeast of Windsor. Unlike another cousin, the contralto Portia White, or himself, who are both celebrated at home as well as abroad, the Hamilton brothers had their names blotted from the registers where they were christened and Clarke grew up "innocent of their existence — and their destruction — until May 1994" when his mother generated those poems, this book, and a screenplay-in-progress by commenting "abruptly and briefly, on their homicide and their hangings."

In English that "ain't broken" but is deliberately "blackened" into a visceral dialect, Clarke reveals the ways in which poverty enrages the Hamilton brothers in pages as evocative as James Baldwin's. The "stunted-hearted" George and Rufus are rough, impoverished country boys badly damaged and deranged by alcoholism and physical abuse at home ("The belt touched them so much it was like their best suit of clothes") and beaten up by life in the world at large where their impulsive thievery and menace ("They wanted to incubate *Fear* for miles around") are as ill-suited to the Canadian army which expels George as they are to the Halifax underworld ("a goldmine of prostitution") which rejects Rufus. George Elliott Clarke is an ebullient writer and his lush and luxurious language captures the bodies of both men with all their appetites. George is a man of enormous muscles who could "hack up rampikes into logs and logs into kindling like none of your business." His hands "were bad-assed carpenters, ingenious mechanics." His first love is food and "life was a meal" of bread "as intoxicating as molasses-distilled home brew." His older brother Rufus — "Rue" or "Rudy" — is more complicated, less willing to work and settle into family life: "Rue ached to be spiffy, a nappy Napoleon, with maybe a flower in one lapel. He'd become an expert in the way to wear a tie that's shiny, the way to make sure the suit drops right, just right, around the frame, the way to wear shoes that are natty, snazzy, and jet-spanking black. He knew how to hold a cigarette, how to wear a hat — with gangster poise." What he didn't know was how to play piano that inspired "dancing, drinking, coupling, tippling, or any of the merrymaking that should accompany moneymaking."

When George's hard work for white farmers doesn't pay enough for him to heat his shack or feed himself and his young son or pay the doctor's bill that will release his wife and newborn daughter from the hospital, the brothers decide to "snitch and snatch." The victim is an ex-veteran like George and known to him. Afterwards, they clumsily dispose of his corpse and spend his money so freely that they are readily caught and convicted. It is a brutal, gruesome crime in which the victim's last breaths make "a noise like hardwood cracking" and it's as well described as these things can be.

ANNALS OF OURLIT II

MATT COHEN AND AFTER

I knew Matt first as a creature of contradictions. He was a lone wolf with a marvellous gift for friendship. He was also a city guy who came into his own when he connected with the land. A spiky intellectual in love with the physical world; a brain with a killer jump shot. And a workaholic who just hung out. For the first ten years I knew Matt, I tried to find a key that would resolve the contradictions. And for the next twenty, I realized I'd been missing the point. There was nothing to resolve: Matt simply was a denizen of opposites, and it was that multiplicity that made him himself.

Dennis Lee said this in his eulogy at Hart House on December 5, 1999. Matt died of cancer three days earlier — four weeks short of his 57th birthday. For thirty years, he'd lived *wholly* as a writer. This was the life Cohen wanted. As Graeme Gibson and Wayne Grady note in the Preface to *Uncommon Ground* (2000) a volume of essays, photographs, and author interviews celebrating a writing life that "covers almost every genre except the theatre ... he wrote short stories, novels, poetry and kids' books, reviews and magazine journalism ... edited anthologies, translated writers from Quebec and ghosted memoirs for passing celebrities" — twenty-three adult books, another eleven children's books (most of them under the pseudonym "Teddy Jam"), excluding the translations, the "ghosts" and three added posthumously — a story collection, another children's book, and a memoir *Typing: A Life in 26 Keys*. Among them, there are, Dennis Lee asserts, "three or four of the classics of our literature."

Uncommon Ground's contributors include Daniel Poliquin, Cohen's translator, who examines Matt's ability to live and love the French within their own language; Monique Proulx, who Cohen translated, writes of "how completely he sabotaged the prejudices" of Quebec writers; Margaret Atwood suggests that if "Matt Cohen had himself been a character in a fable, he would have been Rumpelstiltskin — the artist as odd little outsider and grumbling isolate ... engaged in an improbable activity that transmutes base matter into precious essence.... In his own eyes he could sometimes spin straw into gold, although on other occasions he suspected he was only spinning straw into straw." Recollecting their mutual involvement with House of Anansi Press in 1971, she writes,

> In *Typing*, however, I find myself making a cameo appearance: "Atwood was slim and elfin, with a mop of frizzy hair, piercing eyes, a sharp tongue and a manner that was both brusque and friendly." The elfishness, the slightness, the mop of curly hair, the sharp tongue and the rest of it — this sounds like the Matt Cohen of those days looking in the mirror.

Atwood is one of many friends intrigued but disconcerted by the fierce and unexpected voice that informs *Typing: A Life in 26 Keys*. Written in his final months, the memoir is a sketch of the writing life in Canada by a leader in the movement to decolonize Canadian literature.

Matt was the first contemporary I met who wanted to write novels and intended to live entirely from what he wrote. I was an acquaintance at McMaster in 1969 when he threw away a promising academic career to do just this; afterwards, I regularly read and occasionally reviewed his books and we spoke sporadically at writers' meetings. That sums up our relationship until the final months of his life when we exchanged letters, in one of which I wrote about the books of his that mattered most to me. On September 20, 1999, he responded:

> I tend to like whatever I'm working on the best — or at least to believe it has that potential — and if there are moments I doubt it can be brought to that level (and there always are many!) I wonder why I'm doing it. But the above aside, *Emotional Arithmetic* has been, until

Elizabeth, the book of which I was most certain. Also some of the stories in *Café Le Dog* and *Living on Water*, and now my new book....
All in all, however, I wish everything I've written would disappear and I could start over. I still have an endless supply of books I'd like to write and figure I could do much better with them than I did in the past. Oh well.

Faced with that devastating "Oh well" and the loss of life it portended, I should have written back and told him how much I admire the stories gathered together as *Lives of the Mind Slaves: Selected Stories* (1994). It accomplishes more in fewer pages and stands up better to repeated readings than any of his novels. Those stories teach how we ought to read the rest of his fiction.

In the story that gives the collection its name, Norman says to his friend Elisabeth, "I have looked into the mirror of the oasis, woman, and I have seen what I am not to be. I am not to be a mind slave, an intellectual, a member of the employed class." Cohen considered those who work in English departments in Canadian universities to be colonial officers in outposts of a twinned British and American empire. In an interview, he said:

> Here we are, we're Canadians, we all converse in English, naturally, and *English* isn't our invention. Say we were lumberjacks ... we'd be right in the heart of the empire of lumberjacking. We wouldn't say, "well, let's do it the way they do it in England" ... what a joke that would be! We'd do it the way we do it. So, the interesting thing, and the strange thing about English departments, is that they are ... a double outpost ... talking in translation about a series of traditions that really were invented for another country.

In "Why I Write," George Orwell asserted that "the opinion that art should have nothing to do with politics is itself a political attitude." Commenting on Orwell in "Forethoughts" to the essay collection, *Quarrel & Quandary* (Knopf, 2000), Cynthia Ozick writes:

The central question, perhaps, is this: is politics a distraction from art, or is it how we pay attention to the life that gives rise to art? And might not the answer be: both, depending on the issues and the times?

The life Matt Cohen lived as a politicized writer in this country — thirty-seven books in thirty years — can no longer be lived except by a writer — such as Douglas Coupland — who manages to surf the leading edge of the age in ways that fully command the attention of his own generation and the next one. There's just too much competition: Matt writes in "Trotsky's First Confessions,"

We live in an era when — despite all the new big words — ideas are less important than biography.

On August 22, 2006, Douglas Coupland blogged in *The New York Times*, "What is CanLit?"

"CanLit" is a contraction for Canadian Literature, and I'm often asked by writers from other lands, "Doug, what, exactly, is CanLit? ... Basically, but not always, CanLit is when the Canadian government pays you money to write about life in small towns and/or the immigration experience. If the book is written in French, urban life is permitted, but only from a non-bourgeois viewpoint.... One could say that CanLit is the literary equivalent of representational landscape painting, with small forays into waterfowl depiction and still lifes. It is not a modern art form, nor does it want to be.... CanLit is not a place for writers to experiment, and doesn't claim to be that kind of place. CanLit is about representing a certain kind of allowed world in a specific kind of way, and most writers in Canada are O.K. with that — or are at least relieved to know the rules of the game from the outset and not have to waste time fostering illusions.

Coupland gets to say his piece not because of its validity but because he's Douglas Coupland, a prolific typist who until recently showed little evidence of carefully reading anything written in this country, least of all his own books. Happily, his arrogant disregard of editorial advice seems to have waned: In *JPod* (see below), he writes with a watercolourist's delicacy about many things, including the kitchen and basement of his narrator's parental house.

~

MATT COHEN'S

Elizabeth and After (1999)

In Matt Cohen's most fully realized novel, *Elizabeth and After* (1999), Elizabeth McKelvey was "51 years old, a white female 66 inches tall and weighing 128 pounds, the possessor of chestnut hair and 27 teeth" when she takes "an unplanned trip through a suddenly stationary windshield attached to a car that had accordioned into a large oak tree." Ten years elapse in the turn of a page and her much older husband, William, has broken out of the local old folks' home and is sitting in a spanking new stolen Pontiac. There's the scrunch of car wheels on a gravel road and something wildly destructive and very funny happens that hastens the return of Elizabeth and William's son Carl. Many things come together in the weeks after Carl's homecoming that link up with the three decades Elizabeth spent in that town.

West Gull, population 684, is on a small lake not far outside Kingston. Once upon a time, it was part of a prosperous and useful timber, farming, and cheese-making economy: now it's home to weekend country hideaways for people from cities and McJobs for the locals — Carl manages a video shop and does odd jobs for the real estate agent who is selling off the town's heritage lot by lot. These same roads, woods, and waterways appear much earlier in Cohen's career as "Salem" in several novels between 1974 and 1981 but are never before so well drawn nor deeply understood. The villages are agonized, melancholic, smouldering juxtapositions of criminality and commerce, learning and ignorance, academic elitism and agrarian democracy, gentrified pretentiousness and drunken squalor.

Carl is a good old bad boy trying to put booze and brawling behind him and stretch into being responsible for Lizzie, his seven-year-old daughter. He's likeable because he's ruefully aware of his shortcomings. Scanning the personals in the local newspaper, he mockingly writes his own:

> *White trash male, late twenties. Seeks understanding woman to do all the work. Nursing experience not required but would be helpful. Don't be afraid to apply if you're rich, beautiful and lonely. If ex-wife, must be willing to offer bond to guarantee good behaviour.*

Cohen plays plot, setting, style, and characters off one another in ways that delight even as they disturb. Cohen's penetrating intelligence is distinct but he's like the Australian director Fred Schepisi (*Fierce Creatures, IQ, Six Degrees of Separation, The Russia House*) in his ability to keep imperfect pasts alive in a tense present and to glide ominously back and forth without turning the tale into a disaster epic. If that isn't reason enough read this book, buy a copy for any literate accountant you might know: Elizabeth's accountant is some kind of hero and there aren't many of his kind in our literature.

$\sim$

DOUGLAS COUPLAND

Duet: *Microserfs* (1995) & *JPod* (2006)

Love or loathe his writing (and I often do one then the other moving from chapter to chapter within the same book), Douglas Coupland is a cultural force of extraordinary magnitude within the global literary world. He's now so physically rooted (garden and squirrels are reportedly making serious inroads into his Ron Thon-designed house) in the West Vancouver neighbourhood where he grew up that it's worth looking at some of the forces that shaped him and his aesthetics.

Coupland was born on the Royal Canadian Air Force base in Baden-Söllingen, West Germany, while his father was serving as a military doctor. After studying physics at McGill, Coupland trained as a sculptor at the Emily Carr Institute back in Vancouver and furthered his training as an artist and designer in Sapporo and Milan before spending two years (and graduating with honours) at the Japan-America Institute of Management Sciences in Tokyo and Honolulu. He worked for lifestyle and business magazines in Vancouver and Toronto before turning to fiction and sculpture full time.

Boomers may take a little longer than X-ers to get what Coupland is doing because much deliberately goes against the conventions we're most familiar with in fiction, unless our primary literary influences are the same pre-Boomers as his — Truman Capote, Kurt Vonnegut, Joan Didion, and Andy Warhol (as author). What comes first for him (and them) is the culture we inhabit rather than character as it develops. The unexpected shifts created by new technologies trump plot twists. Whatever else they are, Coupland's fictions aren't as aimless, artless, and arbitrary as they first appear; it's a mistake to write him off as a literary Faith Popcorn — a sociologist without her corporate client base.

Microserfs is narrated in the form of Powerbook entries by Daniel, a computer programmer for Microsoft, who observes the misadventures of six code-crunchers ("microserfs") spending sixteen-hour days writing software, eating "flat" foods (such as Kraft slices that can pass beneath closed doors), and obsessing over the company's internal emails to see what the great Gates might be thinking. Seizing an opportunity to form their own start-up company and live communally (and claustrophobically) in "Our House of Wayward Mobility," the microserfs attempt to find unprogrammable loves and non-default lives amid a pre-Windows 95 industry. Much of the book's layout is grounded in Andy Warhol's Pop Art and Jenny Holzer's Text Art, which prefigures blog formatting by a decade. Coupland also accurately predicts the actual bursting of the dot.com bubble a couple of years beforehand.

Eleven years later, *JPod* arrived as "a sequel in spirit" to *Microserfs* as Coupland takes Pop Art and Text Art further and with greater accomplishment. It's the work of a fully formed literary intelligence with a set of skills to match ambitiousness and a seriously funny book, a rolling thunder of sustained comedy first page to last, as it skewers the shamelessness and amorality that defined the past decade. With as sharp a scalpel as Richler employs in *Cocksure* to dissect corporate boneheads, greed-driven marketers, and sexual wastrels in the conglomerate-fuelled, celebrity-driven publishing and movie-making worlds of the Swinging Sixties, Coupland targets the vacuous and vicious who control and market the computer games that redefined the face and formula of mass entertainment in the first decade of the new millennium. Coupland's timing is once again impeccable — the right book at the right time; early warning of what lies beyond the bend of the dead man's economic curve we rode into the fine mess we're now in.

JPod is Ethan Jarlewski and his five co-workers (whose first or last names all begin with the letter J) — a team of software geeks working on a game for a Vancouver video design company. When the new head of marketing insists that Ethan and his crew retroactively insert a charismatic cuddly turtle character into the skateboard game one-third of the way through its production cycle, a classic situation develops. The rules of Marketing must be obeyed in defiance of logic and consumer taste because the new guy "took Toblerone chocolate and turned it around inside of two years." Can Ethan's ill-assorted pack of undermutts find focus and bite the hand that feeds them by turning that turtle into something far more dangerously reptilian? (This turtle and much else of interest can be viewed online at www.jpod.info.)

The author has described his protagonist as "non-Doug" and Ethan is distinctly different from any of Coupland's previous narrators. Ethan is smart, a lot of fun, and convincing in his capacity to see himself as behaving normally while everyone around him is "going random." He says, "I look at most people like recently lit Roman candles, unsure if they're about to go off, or if they're merely duds." Away from work, Ethan's life is fused to his Boomer parents "in the gloomy evergreen cocoon of the British Properties" and confused by a mom who runs a marijuana grow-op with a built-in death trap in her basement and a dad who has given up marine engineering to get into "acting, mostly TV ... copping ... tiny crappy, non-speaking parts in TV commercials where he always seems to be left on the cutting-room floor, as well as gigs as an extra in crowd scenes" because it gives Dad the opportunity to philander with young and restless stagehands. Brother Greg is a realtor in "West Van's bizarre Canterbury neighbourhood, a rainforest bull-dozed to make way for jumbo houses that resembled microwave ovens covered with cedar shake roofing" inhabited by "mostly sports stars and abandoned Asian housewives sitting out their three-year sentences required for citizenship." Kam Fong, a client of Greg's, becomes criminally involved in everybody's businesses and pleasures.

As plot and subplots twist and turn around Vancouver and over to China and back, Coupland writes in a non-doctrinaire, anti-ideological way about a lot of big issues — globalization, multiculturalism, fast food, genetic modification, drugs, people-smuggling, intellectual piracy, slave wages, Chinese factories — and smaller ones such as spam, lesbian jargon, secret ingredients in soft drinks, and, first and foremost, computer games. He also writes himself into the story as a character named Douglas Coupland, a "fatuous prick" and "asshole," who grasps what everyone else in *JPod* fails to see, namely that "The only money remaining is in hardware, and only hardware made offshore at that, preferably in some unregulated, uninvestigated Asian backwater where you can get a day's labour and a hand job for the cost of a bag of Skittles."

When *Cocksure* was published in 1968, the Canadian literary establishment, as represented by such reviewers as Marian Engel and George Woodcock, was pissy and prissy toward it: Engel admitted freely that she wasn't quite sure what

Richler was satirizing but did know that it was "smart-alecky stuff" that didn't "cut any deeper than the Sunday-paper set it's aimed at." Woodcock wrote it off as the "sexual fantasy and bawdy jokes that beguile adolescent boys." Although Richler went on to win the Governor General's Literary Award in Fiction that year, it took much longer for him to achieve literary respectability in this country than people nowadays generally acknowledge — the fate of any Canadian writer who has highly receptive cultural antennae and are brazen enough to exploit them. A more legitimate reason for Coupland's outsider status is the reckless extravagance that has fuelled his prodigious output. As a writer, he's doesn't always give his readers enough breathing space to get to know his characters on their own terms and learn to love them as he does but he's getting better at establishing sufficient distance between himself and his creations. That said, Ethan is very much like Coupland in his deep and abiding fascination with mass culture for its abundance of images and simply revels in its powers of replication. Among a host of other delights in a visually astonishing book, *JPod* contains printouts (with intentional errors embedded) of *pi* to a hundred-thousand digits, the 8,363 prime numbers between 10,000 and 100,000, and the 972 three-letter words permitted in Scrabble.

~o

RUSSELL SMITH

The Princess and the Whiskheads (2002)
(A Fable with illustrations by Wesley W. Bates)

If you stumbled across a defaced copy of the erotic fable, *The Princess and the Whiskheads*, from which the author's name and the place and date of publication had been torn out, you might think that you'd found something written more than half a century ago, say, about the time George Orwell published *1984*. Princess Juliana and her land of Liralove seemingly could have been imagined amidst bombed-out Coventry or Oxford by a young man inflamed by the writings of Oscar Wilde and whose private parts were engorged exclusively by beautiful, wealthy, and socially prominent young women who would shamelessly end his sexual uncertainties, elevate his social status, support his artistic endeavours, house and dress him gloriously, and free him completely from the necessity of earning a humdrum living by taking hold of him firmly and boldly.

The Princess and the Whiskheads is a charming, naive but not innocent, fantastic invention that might helpfully assist inexperienced seducers of sexually seasoned but romantically unversed young women — if, that is, there are aesthetic seducers and idealistic temptresses left in this era of "hooking up" among the decorously urban. But this little book isn't anonymous and isn't the product of the post-WW II revival of English Romanticism that collapsed under the weight of the Suez Crisis. The author is Russell Smith (or Mr. Smith, as he's now known to readers of his advice column in *The Globe and Mail* and www. dailyyz.com), the unabashedly self-as-fine-art-object culture columnist and radio commentator who is less read than he insists he ought to be for his satires of the lives of green, fidgety, never-quite-hip-enough Torontonians in the novels *How Insensitive* (1994), *Noise* (1998), *Muriella Pent* (2004), and the story collection *Young Men* (1999). Because *Princess* was published in 2002 and Smith is now identified with the kind of masculine attire he espouses in *Men's Style: The Thinking Man's Guide to Dress* (2005), the fact that his fable (when it was actually written isn't clear) is a throwback to the New Romanticism of the early 1980s is worth a moment's notice.

Manufactured in London nightclubs such as Billy's and The Blitz, the New Romantic movement was associated with ABC, Human League, Duran Duran, Visage, Culture Club, Adam and the Ants, Spandau Ballet, Brian Eno, and Roxy Music. The bands and their followers favoured flamboyance and androgyny: eyeliner, frills, quaffs, lots of black and white or black and red contrasts. In his London period, Russell Smith did his über-utmost to flit past the doormen and fit in. Out of this experience emerges his allegory of the conflict between art and industry.

Art in the form of whimsical towers and industry in the form of sewer construction clash (much like New Romantics and Punks) as the state of Liralove moves to the brink of revolution but the fundamental polarity is one between beauty and necessity and how a powerful woman must shape her sexual desires to both.

Smith's tale is forthright in its atheism: not even Orwell entirely escaped Christian underpinnings and trappings of allegory to the degree that Smith does and consequently no one has ever written so erotically in this manner. It's casually said (especially by the out-of-shape) that the brain is the primary sex organ but Smith writes his Princess and his Whiskheads into being with absolute conviction that art that is unsexed is worse than trivial. His tale is worth reading as carefully as the epic of Gilgamesh, which also deals with a ruler whose subjects are dissatisfied with their monarch's sexual practices. And reading it is a pleasure — at least to socialists and anarchists who don't think any great harm befalls children of the ruling class who are deflected from the paths of industry and progress by artists who know how to turn a screw or a screw-up into works of art.

In his other fictions (notably *Muriella Pent*, which André Alexis insists was the best novel published in Canada in 2004), Smith tries too hard to capture an audience that no longer exists (most of Kingsley Amis is out of print) rather than create his own. Wittily drawn characters do memorably silly stuff but novelistic intentions are undone by an underlying desperation to play readers like Noel Coward played Las Vegas audiences. Smith's talent to amuse is at its best when he works as a miniaturist. Note his response in "Ask Mr. Smith" of March 31, 2008:

Dear Mr. Smith,

This guy who I have been casually dating recently asked me to "ask him out some time." Who's in charge here?

I love it when I get to address sexual and linguistic questions at the same time. Here is a classic example of a euphemism, and it's so fascinating which of these the young are currently using to describe fornication. "Casually dating" is what the kids are calling it, I see. Okay. What I'm guessing here is that you have had sex with this guy on a few occasions, but with enough time between each encounter that neither of you feels justified in having "The Talk."

I wonder if the guy in question refers to you as someone he is casually dating or as someone he banged a few times, but no matter. "Dating" it is.... Don't ask him out, though, of course — just call him at midnight when you want to, uh, "date." Which is exactly what you're already doing, am I right?

Russell Smith

The full answer runs 368 words and attains standards of clarity, brevity, and focus that nine out of ten writers never achieve.

~

C. S. RICHARDSON

The End of the Alphabet (2007)

C. S. Richardson's *The End of the Alphabet* delivers a gem of a book for anyone romantic enough to think a few thousand words artfully arranged and hand-somely printed are worth every bit as much as the price of a couple of bottles of *vin de pays* and of greater emotional depth than a greeting card on Valentine's Day. Like a bouquet of roses, beauty in this elegant and witty tale is barbed.

When Ambrose Zephyr has his annual medical around the time of his fiftieth birthday, his doctor diagnoses a fatal condition that will "kill him within a month. Give or take a day." The doctor bluntly tells him his "faculties may dull a bit. Blurred eyesight, ringing ears, numbed fingertips. That sort of thing" and advises him "to make arrangements." The air turns "thick as custard, sauna hot" for his wife, Zipporah (Zipper) Ashkenazi, sitting beside him. "None of this is happening to us," she thinks. "Ambrose is not unravelling into the sweating, pasty stranger sitting next to me." But, of course, it is:

"Fatal?"

"Yes, quite. Very sure."

Zephyr has worked throughout adulthood "as the creative wallah" for a London advertising agency and is considered by co-workers "to possess an inventive if journeyman approach to the creative process: on time, on budget, realistic, reasonable." In the face of imminent death, he seeks refuge in the deepest pleasures of his otherwise average childhood — planning trips to foreign places and constructing alphabet books that imaginatively populate a map of the world pinned to his bedroom wall: "*D* is for a Beach in the Dutch Antilles, *E* is for the Windy Coast of Elba, *F* is for Palm Trees in Florida." As he'd explained to his parents, "things didn't always have to be the way you'd expect."

Fleeing present pain for past pleasures, Ambrose lays out a new A to Z of "Places ... Things" to fill out twenty-six of the twenty-nine or twenty-eight days of the month, give or take, remaining to him, an expedition to spend some precious hours walking in places he has loved or viewing others that he has longed to see, starting in Amsterdam at the Rijksmuseum in front of Rembrandt's *The Night Watch*. In the face of such manic intensity, Zipper's mind spins, "There was no mention of putting affairs in order, no alternative remedies.... This was not her Ambrose, she thought at first. But then, apparently, it was." Zipporah is "the literary editor for the country's third most-read fashion magazine." As is her habit, she edits everything, including pencilling "a stroke through Valparaiso" and "in the margin" adding "Venice" to Ambrose's Grand Tour.

As they travel by trains, taxis, and planes from Amsterdam to Berlin, Chartres, Deauville, the Eiffel Tower, Florence, Giza, and miss a connection to Haifa on their way to Istanbul, where their journey takes an unplanned turn, Ambrose and Zipper remember the chance encounter that brought them together, falling in love, wedding and honeymoon, previous trips to Paris and Venice, and a multitude of small events that tie them together as an affectionate and humorous childless couple living an ordinary life of good fortune and casual contentment in a row house in Kensington. Unnerved and disturbed, alone and together, they consider and re-consider unsettled questions about what their love has really meant to each other and what the burden of being on your own at the end of life truly is.

The End of the Alphabet is more elongated short story than conventional first novel. Although characters, locales, and comic touches will put many readers in mind of Mavis Gallant's European stories, C. S. Richardson's style is as minimalist as Norman Levine's. This is a very difficult book to put down even when the final page is turned. Richardson writes with such visual and emotional density that the end of one reading readily becomes the start of another. As Scott Richardson, he's a multiple recipient of the Alcuin Award for excellence in Canadian book design and has exhibited his work internationally. The design of *The End of the Alphabet* is the work of his protégé Kelly Hill and it's more than a tribute to a master, it's a masterpiece in its own right.

~

TIMOTHY TAYLOR

Stanley Park (2001)

Douglas Coupland is impossible to imitate but that hasn't stopped other writers of his generation from attempting to emulate his success by replicating carefully chosen aspects of his sensibility. Timothy Taylor's debut novel *Stanley Park* succeeded in getting shortlisted for the Scotiabank Giller Prize, an honour Coupland has yet to achieve.

The Couplandesque idea behind *Stanley Park* is that global corporate culture threatens local connections with ruinous personal and professional consequences. Jeremy Papier, locally born but French-trained chef-owner of The Monkey's Paw Bistro, creates cuisine for foodies from mostly local ingredients but he's at least five years ahead of the culinary curve and going broke. When he tries to cut losses by forming an alliance with Dante Beale, old friend and owner of a national chain of coffee shops, Jeremy discovers that the cost of doing business with a maggot transmutes his restaurant and his cuisine into transnational crap. In his misery, he seeks out his father, an anthropologist studying the homeless in Stanley Park by participating directly in their lives. The "low probability event" so beloved by Coupland upon which the plot turns is a decades old mystery involving two children killed in the park.

Taylor has a much stronger sense of Vancouver as a leading character in the lives of his characters and of food as an obsession around which urban life increasingly revolves than attracts Coupland. And Taylor writes with greater attention to craft and passion for detailed description — there are food preparation scenes (both in the kitchen and by campfires in Stanley Park) as carefully constructed as anything you'll read elsewhere or see, say, in *Babette's Feast*. To cap it off, the novel ends with a wonderful prank.

~

MICHAEL HELM

The Projectionist (1997)

Born in Eston, Saskatchewan, Helm uses a small prairie town — Mayford — as internalized landscape in *The Projectionist*. He's said, "The land is important because it's part of the consciousness of anyone living in a prairie town. Your life comes from it, your work, and the book is trying to establish a consciousness, and that consciousness is one that's always aware of the land and the weather and the physical space of the place."

The Projectionist asks how much of the past has to be recovered in the present to move on into the future? There are echoes and re-echoes of T. S. Eliot's meditations on time in *Four Quartets* in Wesley "Toss" Raymond's sense of what he does as a high school history teacher and what he is — a cuckolded husband whose parents and brother haven't provided him with much sense or sensibility in domestic matters and matters of the heart.

It's the summer of 1988 and Raymond is finishing off the school year as the board builds a case for his dismissal. Toss is more concerned with pursuing Karen, a Mayford single mother who has come back from Vancouver to care for an ailing mother, and with Dewey Beyer, the projectionist of the title, who runs the local movie house and relentlessly battles the Mayford community over its small-mindedness.

Plot and characters are less complex than Raymond's awareness and self-awareness (his voice speaks throughout): Raymond is clever, not bright. As a "thinker," he inclines towards the moody and ironic, the pose of a loner who fancies himself an insightful renegade but doesn't "get" the fact that he's his own best joke/worst enemy. That's how I read him: another reviewer labelled it "a poignant story about home: losing it, returning to it, making it your own ... deliver[ed with] sustained moments of absolute clarity and grace." Take your pick. The Michael Helm I've met in Toronto seems very comfortable with bright lights and big cities and throwing poses that "poseurs" don't quite get either.

~

MICHAEL WINTER

Duet: *This All Happened* (2000) & *The Big Why* (2004); *The Architects Are Here* (2007)

This All Happened (2000) & *The Big Why* (2004)

In twelve chapters and 365 entries, Michael Winter's *This All Happened* presents a year in the life of Gabriel English with this disclaimer:

> Caveat: This is a work of fiction. Any resemblance to people living or dead is intentional and encouraged. Fictional characters and experiences come to life when we compare them with the people and places we know. New experience is always a comparison to the known.

Gabe wants to write a novel and has the potentially lucrative idea of writing one about the American painter Rockwell Kent who abandoned New York's art world in 1914 in favour of roughing it for a year in Brigus where he met up with Newfoundland's fabled arctic explorer Bob Bartlett. Gabe's creating a master-piece but is distracted by jealousy — is his partner Lydia sleeping around? — and a mystery — who's breaking into their homes, stealing food, and doing laundry?

Winter's writing has been called "literary pointillism" and is painterly in the way Norman Levine's is (the oddities in punctuation are similar and deliberate):

> There is no colour in the hills now. Whatever quality affords colour in colour film is no longer in those hills. Below the hills in dry dock is the trawler *Wilfred Templeman*. It looks like a part of the sentinel fishery.... The roofs are white. But the roads have melted to black. All the windows are black or a very dark green. Windows allow light but offer darkness.

The novel that Gabe is writing morphs into Winter's own *The Big Why* (2004) and creates a more complex double helix than Coupland's *Microserfs–JPod* duet. Set in 1914–1915, it feels as contemporary as *This All Happened*. *The Big Why* isn't a historical novel because people and places persist differently offshore: Rockwell Kent's house might be ramshackle but it still stands where it ought to be when Gabe goes looking for it and a neighbour takes him inside and shows him things that correct the "historical" record of its construction. And Kent himself is remembered by those who know him only from the tales of fathers and uncles — a New York boho who was radical in politics, carefree in lovemaking, perverse, grandiose, a self-described "asshole" who encouraged rumours that he was a German spy by painting "Bomb Shop" on his door. Winter's portrait of him in *The Big Why* is compulsive reading in the way a Rockwell Kent painting is compulsive viewing — intensely bright.

The Architects Are Here (2007)

The Architects Are Here IS a tangled love story in which triangular relationships intersect at sharp and odd angles. Winter is four years younger than Douglas Coupland and, at first glance, his main characters could blend seamlessly into any Couplandish pre-apocalyptic scenario about Generation X college friends whose fortunes diverge sharply. Now living in Toronto, Gabriel English has become a luckless slacker, seemingly content to photograph used cars for *Auto Trader* while David Twombly is a high-flying "techie" breezing his way through penthouse parties from Harbourfront to Yorkville. But Winter is faster getting past consumer-junkie surfaces and inside the skins of people driven by darker forces than Coupland's.

Gabriel narrates the tale after David's death but it's not a eulogy. There's too much intensity, too much immediacy, too much need for truth for Gabe to gloss anything about the roguish David who was fond of quoting the code words used to signal Julius Caesar's assassins — "The architects are here." With these buddies, bad times are only a motion away.

Friendship begins in boyhood when they're building igloos and have a close call with a snowplow, a scrape and escape that sets the tone for the relationship they develop as college roommates and continue to turning forty. That relationship also involves a third person — Nell Tarkington — who enters their lives as the teenage lover of David's father and stays as David's business associate and Gabriel's enigmatic girlfriend. Nell changes them both, Gabe says, "in complex and idiosyncratic ways." Until Nell, their strongest tie is that they are both outsiders — David's parents are American and Gabriel's are English — in the Newfoundland milltown of Corner Brook.

Winter has a knack for capturing points where the natural world intersects with the industrialized, the raw with the half-baked. His previous novels were praised in *The New York Times* for portraying Newfoundland and Newfoundlanders with sharp, simple strokes. Some readers may regret that *The Architects Are Here* leaves Newfoundland for Toronto before returning to Corner Brook via a road trip so filled with confrontations (including encounters with both the Prince of Wales and President Bush), revelations, and denouements that no summary can do it justice. But "the Rock" and "Away" and all that comes between them are essential to capturing a generation in crisis:

> As he drove ... I thought of David's phrase from university: the architects are here. I think of it because we all wonder if we're at the end of the good times. Our generation will be the last, we think. And if not the last generation, then the last of the old generations.... These were the last days before ... we strapped on sensory devices and experienced other places without leaving our bedrooms, before the West sent robots

to war instead of real American soldiers. It was a complicated time ... that made many of us skip having children because we couldn't muster the hope needed to pass the new world off onto youngsters. The architects are here, we said.

Because Gabriel remains a man of genuine and genuinely surprising hope despite all the physical and psychic damage done, one can say of Michael Winter precisely what V. S. Pritchett wrote in his review of the final volume of Henry James's *Letters*: "In serious matters, in sorrows, in the sad concerns of his family, especially, he is deeply tender, wise, and concerned. He is a great praiser and healer, the care showing as much in his sentences as in his feelings." This puts him in the front rank of writers worth reading and Henry James is worth remembering while reading *The Architects Are Here* because Winter's flamboyance is so wide-angled and crowded with dramatic incident that it stretches even a generous reader's literate mind and loving heart beyond normal limits as he attempts more of everything with fewer words than James used on anything. In the seven years since *This All Happened*, Winter has embraced adult life and now examines sexual relations in just the sort of straightforward way that James insisted novelists must do to enlarge rather than diminish our sense of human possibility. He gets outside bed and bedroom and into the daylight side of life even when the weather is most unpromising.

∿

LISA MOORE

Alligator (2005)

According to her publisher, "Lisa Moore's *Alligator* gives dramatic birth to a new kind of fiction: North Atlantic Gothic." According to Moore herself, "*Alligator* is about greed and survival and the line between those things" and it has more to say about the way money excites the reptilian core of human consciousness than generally suits mainland sensibilities. Lisa Moore is a lifelong resident of cold-blooded and chronically mismanaged St. John's and has more in common stylistically with, say, Nancy Huston or francophone writers in Montreal than she does with most of the women or men writing in Toronto or Vancouver today.

Colleen Clark is "seventeen ... forthright and blankly innocent" except "she has been recently caught trying to destroy several thousand dollars' worth of privately owned forestry equipment." While she pays for an environmental protest with community service and keeps out of the way of Beverly, her chronically weepy mother, Colleen hangs out at her Aunt Madeleine's as Madeleine produces a feature film about two young men who "stole a priest's collar and went up the Southern Shore hearing confessions" in the 1830s. Madeleine casts Isobel in the lead role and the film has drawn the Toronto actress back to her birthplace and into a love affair with Valentin, a violent Russian criminal and erstwhile seaman who jumped ship in Newfoundland. Valentin turns extortionist when he realizes just how much money Frank, a kid with a hot dog cart, is making from the best location in St. John's. Frank, to close the circle, falls in lustful love with Colleen when he spots her in a bar "dancing with her arms over her head, biting her bottom lip.... Her hips swing and he sees she has a rhinestone in her navel the size of a dime.... The rhinestone winks lewdly at him."

Moore's tale — which also includes Mr. Duffy, the owner of the damaged forestry equipment, and a homeless mall rat named John Harvey — unfolds in brief scenes that shift perspective from character to character. As with a Robert Altman film, it's difficult to determine at the beginning who are the key characters and what will emerge as the dominant storyline as relationships criss-cross various anxieties, arts, cultures and sub-cultures, economic conditions, families, genders, generation gaps, legal systems, moral positions, phobias, politics, and icebergs of regret. Moore uses her enormous skills to deepen and enhance both the emotional intensity and intellectual profundity of her portrait of the existential crises that underlie contemporary St. John's. And she's sensual in ways few others of her generation are willing to be in print. Her writing, bluntly, is a terrific turn-on for all sexes and all ages. You don't have to be male or young to get a jolt from:

She has a rhinestone in her belly button. She's slender, her arms are golden, her neck is golden, and there's an elastic riding over her hip, a part of her red thong and it makes him crazy to think about sliding a finger under that elastic. He'd like to take that elastic in his teeth. Her arms are raised over her head, and her face is turned down and to the side and she's biting her lower lip to keep from smiling to herself because she's so sexy.... He is very close to just walking up to her. She lifts her arms and gathers her hair and twists it and piles it on the top of her head and he sees her bare neck and he should ask her right now and she drops her hair and gives it a shake and it falls in a straight curtain down her back.

Moore started out as a visual artist and she's not only bold, vivid, imagistic, resonant in her depiction of young and middle-aged and old, rich and middling and poor, innocent and corrupt, but her joy at being alive and living among her people and getting them down as honestly as she can is irrepressible.

~

TREVOR COLE

Norman Bray in the Performance of His Life (2004)

Almost all the really interesting fictions written about Canadians at home and abroad are being created by writers born after 1960. There's no great surprise in this: as Ronald Wright notes in his splendid *A Short History of Progress*, "few people past fifty can keep up with their culture — whether in idiom, attitudes, taste, or technology — even if they try." What is surprising is how very good the current crop of younger novelists is at absolutely nailing the idioms, attitudes, tastes, and technophobias of their parents' generation. Trevor Cole's great achievement in *Norman Bray in the Performance of His Life* is "to write seductively and sympathetically about someone as narcissistic and bullying as is actor Norman Bray, leaving the reader in a wonderfully uneasy state of delight and horror." Those are the words of the adventurous 2004 Governor General's English-language jury that shortlisted Cole's first novel *and* first books from Colin McAdam as well as David Bezmozgis to go alongside the two slam dunks of the literary year — Alice Munro's *Runaway* and Miriam Toews' *A Complicated Kindness*, the ultimate winner.

Everybody knows at least one Baby Boomer who is very much like Norman Bray. He's ubiquitous. No, he's not Everyman. *Au contraire*, the Norman Brays of our world are anything but *common*. As they are the first to tell you, they are precious, very precious. Why? Because to their way of thinking (and their way of thinking is the only one that really matters), they have superior talent, finer sensitivity, and more refinement in clothes, drink, music than the rest of the world. They are artists who never compromise and we are not. To most of us, of course, most of the time, they are something else entirely: lazy, lecherous monsters of self-absorption, petty moochers, and annoying time-wasters, addled and raddled misfits who never quite connect with our everyday world of earning a living, paying bills, establishing and maintaining reciprocal relationships. We'd ignore them if we could but they won't let us. They insist on making their larger-than-life presence felt in the smallest of circumstances. Besides, they do have a talent to amuse and charm in small and endearing ways even if we only ever get their full attention by putting their name in front of whatever we have to say to them.

Norman Bray is an aptly named jackass. He's a fifty-something musical theatre actor who likes to think that his very best role is Don Quixote in *Man of La Mancha*, which he last played at a dinner theatre in Beverly, Ontario, an hour north of Toronto. Despite being given "The Mirror Award" because he "saved it from disaster" as the solitary professional in an amateur production, the only work he's had since the curtain dropped on his knight errant three years earlier is as the voice of Tiny in *Tiny Taxi*, a cheaply animated toddler show on a cable channel. At the novel's hilarious opening, Bray is lunching at The Skelton Arms prior to taping new episodes at a Jarvis Street studio. As he fails to interest his pub waitress in finding him his favourite brandy or noting his gastronomic preferences in shepherd's pie or succumbing to his "potent charms," Norman decides, she is obviously a girl who doesn't know what she wants, doesn't know what sort of man he is, has no idea of his range of knowledge or experience. So, with some effort, he manages to feel sorrier for her than for himself. He will be satisfied with the shepherd's pie, even if it is slightly less meaty than he prefers. He will make a point of it.... It will require a unique strength of will but, in his life and work, Norman has found it necessary to overcome discomfort, and so he has mastered the skill, a fact he would be happy to share with the waitress, if only she were less grumpy.

Feeling chronically underappreciated, Bray never connects the grumpiness of the women in his life with his obliviousness to his failings as a lover, friend, surrogate parent, brother, and "leading man." When Amy, the daughter of his deceased long-time companion, nervously reconsiders the appropriateness of the outfit she's chosen for dinner with him, she stops in mid-thought, "Norman would hardly notice if she came wearing a clown's baggy pants and big-foot shoes."

When the bank sends a foreclosure notice (Norman has ignored making a year's worth of payments on the mortgaged house in Parkdale that he inherited from Amy's mother), Bray finds that to keep his home on not-yet-gentrified Sorauren Avenue he has to take on windmills truly worth tilting against — a Latin American boarder who is more willing to suffer indignities on behalf of her art than even he is and a bank-appointed job counsellor who takes his job as seriously as the actor takes himself. It's at this point that Norman Bray discovers he has more in common with Cervantes' protagonist than ever imagined. When Henninger, the man from the bank, talks to him about the "basic necessities," Bray asks if "joy" and "the pursuit of inspiration" are included.

Trevor Cole is reminiscent of England's Nick Hornby (*High Fidelity*, *About a Boy*): they have similar eyes for the physical and emotional minutiae that obsessive-compulsives feed upon but Cole has digested Cervantes: *Norman Bray in the Performance of His Life* is a subtle work of art that transforms the story of a mundane actor into something older and less fathomable than a trendy tale of self-redemption among the self-absorbed. By having others (the surrogate daughter Amy in particular) demand answers from him that he's ill-prepared to give, Bray increasingly senses the limits of his own awareness and asks questions "he can't remember ever asking before." As the actor grudgingly wins a little admiration and affection from us through his resiliency, we "confront a reflecting mirror that awes us even while we yield to delight" as Harold Bloom says of Cervantes. This is a remarkable achievement, a book to be cherished both for the depths of its ironies and the breadth of its responsiveness.

∼

RAY ROBERTSON

Moody Food (2002), *Gently Down the Stream* (2005)

Moody Food (2002)

Now that Richler is gone from the scene, there's plenty of room up in the front line for writers willing to take a chance on being urban and ironical. Ray Robertson made that move with his third novel. *Moody Food*, now a cult classic among certain kinds of undergraduates, is a debunking of a cultural myth and the *poseurs* who created it. It's Yorkville in the sixties and hippie country-rockers are the heart of uptown Saturday nights in a twisting of F. Scott Fitzgerald's tale of Jay Gatsby with amphetamines and cocaine as the tonics of choice.

As in *The Great Gatsby*, *Moody Food* begins as a confession: Bill Hansen looks back three decades and sees

> Thomas Graham in a bank.... In white cowboy boots and a red silk shirt with a little silver cross peeking out underneath, all topped off with a white jacket covered with a green sequined pot plant, a couple of sparkling acid cubes, and a pair of women's breasts. The jacket glowed, I swear, and I'd had nothing stronger that morning than a cup of coffee. He was also the only other guy in the bank in blue jeans and with hair hanging down past his collar.

Thomas Graham is from Mississippi, an evasive draft-age American who claims to be many things he is not. The son of a good-old-boy southern businessman, he's a mid-twentieth century remittance man with a large annuity at his personal disposal as long as he stays away from the family's antebellum mansion. In Toronto, he passes himself off as a folkie following Bob Dylan's lead away from acoustic protest music into electrified rock with a Southern country twang. His grandiose vision as a musical trailblazer becomes enmeshed in various lunacies and tomfoolery as he puts together the Duckhead Secret Society, a band with Hansen as the drummer, and takes it on a unruly and harebrained run of gigs from a Cabbagetown tavern to the Whisky A Go Go in Los Angeles and into studio recording sessions in Hollywood and Toronto.

Interstellar North American Music ("a heaven-sent musical hybrid fusing together all honest forms of sound into one great big soulful stew. Just music, understand, just one kind of music — good music") is Graham's mistress and it's young and beautiful but less innocent and more restless than any Daisy Buchanan: its devils dance faster and a neo-Gatsby as guitar-slinger falls faster and further into idiotic pursuit of sensation, incredible stupidity, triviality, and swinishness. It's just the sort of high carnival that Fitzgerald revelled in depicting.

Robertson is a sharp social historian and accurately captures the looks, sounds, tastes, and smells of a Toronto he's too young to remember first hand. Better than that, he gets the feel of the place dead-on. The occasional anachronism that does pop up highlights the unreliability of a narrator who is no brighter than a cipher needs to be. Robertson playfully includes a lot of winking references to the fabled career of Gram Parsons for those who care about such things. What's really important here, what raises *Moody Food* higher than the generality of rock and roll novels, is the way the stylist challenges the social observer. Having studied philosophy before creative writing, Robertson is wise about the possibilities of seeing through, understanding, and helping readers experience the rattle and hum, the hullabaloo and shakiness, the follies and vices of everyday life by using English with great gusto, ingenuity, exactness, and delight. In the end, what Lionel Trilling wrote of *The Great Gatsby* fits *Moody Food*:

The book has no real scale: it does not rest on any commanding vision, nor is it in any sense a major tragedy. But it is a great flooding moment, a moment's intimation and penetration ... [that] strikes like a chime through the mind.

Gently Down the Stream (2005)

If you (or anyone you care deeply about) is thirty-ish, urban, basically monogamous, more dog lover than cat fancier, and not so hip as to be offended by oldies radio, *Gently Down the Stream* is just what you need to read if you've got the blahs or the blues. With a geniality that is more readily associated with midwesterners than west-end Torontonians, Robertson asks his readers to consider this question: Can an overeducated and underachieving thirty-something male find the answers to life's persistent problems of how to stay sane, solvent, sober, and satisfactorily coupled amid the gentrification of his neighbourhood with no more powerful weapons than Sudafed-laced coffee, a karaoke microphone, a tin of spray paint, a pair of wire cutters, and the love of a woman and a dog?

Hank Roberts, the man on this mission is something like the slacker his creator might have become but didn't: Robertson has said that if he hadn't become a writer, he'd be "a well-read but bitter security guard with a profound drinking problem who doesn't understand why he's so damn bitter." What redeems Hank, what makes the questions asked of him comic in the posing and sober in the answering is that he is just bright enough to understand his bitterness and find his way to a sweeter life. While his wife Mary pays more than her fair share of the bills by working as a graphic artist four days a week and has begun to establish herself as an artist with the paintings she creates evenings and weekends, Hank has pissed away the first decade of their marriage devoting himself to the same pursuits he followed when he was a university student — drinking beer, shooting pool, reading poetry, and endlessly discussing rock and roll music with a shrinking number of like-minded pals. When Mary finds both the will and the money for them to move out of semi-basement apartment and buy a little house of their own in a better part of Parkdale, Hank scratches his way out of resignation and into a more mature understanding of who he is and what he can do to make his small part of the world a better place.

Robertson holds back on the verbal pyrotechnics and structural devices he employed to such wonderful ecstatic effects in three earlier novels in order to dissect Hank's emotions with surgical precision. Hank is heroic in terms that would have endeared him to Mordecai Richler by working out his own code of honour and system of beliefs in a time and place where there is no real agreement on values.

BRUCE MacDONALD

Coureurs De Bois (2007)

Unlike Heather O'Neill or Rawi Hage, Bruce MacDonald didn't get a break from any prize jury when his first novel was released. That's a shame because *Coureurs De Bois* deserves to be as well known and widely read. Like those two writers, he has perfect pitch for capturing the voices of the half-crazed and a cinematic eye for the urban surroundings where they drink too much red wine and acquire too little self-knowledge.

William Tobe is taking a timeout from his family and the rest of his life by living in a rooming house near the Gladstone Hotel in Toronto's Parkdale. He's white, young, and a trained economist who connects with Randall "Cobb" Seymour, a recently released ex-con of Ojibwa and Mohawk descent. Like the seventeenth-century "runners of the woods" of the fur trade in New France who broke from the government monopoly, Cobb and Will live outside the official system, selling untaxed cigarettes, weed, and kinky sexual services and investing the profits offshore.

MacDonald's exceptional extra-literary strength is his ability to understand economic systems well enough to explore the operations and question the ethics of black markets with the indignation and insight that John LeCarre brings to larger scale but no less reptilian business deals and dealers. Like LeCarre, MacDonald senses precisely how far he can go in mismatching his characters without engendering disbelief. Tobe and Cobb are prophets guided by antithetical visions, spirit versus flesh in a carnal part of town:

> Cobb knew the white man was no longer a thing that could be seen.... The white man was an idea, like money, a commodity.... The white man could appear in a 30-year-old Guatemalan bank teller. She didn't even know she was a white man. Most people who are possessed never know.

Amid the smoke, pills, and perversity ingested, digested, and spirits drunk, characters just this side of those who inhabit graphic novels explore how and why we spend time with those we do and raise all the relevant questions we should be asking ourselves about the nature of justice, law, religion, spirituality, the ethics of shock therapy as a treatment for mental illness, and what a social contract really means — all wrapped in a package that contains a voodooesque scene, a chicken, and a dungeon mistress that's worth the price of the book. MacDonald's literary strengths begin with flamboyance, include impudence, "a deadpan ironic tilt to his prose" that echoes Vonnegut (as Jim Bartley pointed out in *The Globe and Mail*), and culminate in a degree of risk-taking that is exhilarating and seductive.

∼

IAN McGILLIS

A Tourist's Guide to Glengarry (2002)

Ian McGillis is the hardest working book reviewer in the country and one of the best. He's from Edmonton but lives in Montreal when he's not travelling elsewhere. In 2002, Ian asked me for a letter of recommendation for a grant. Having read the still-unpublished chapters he showed me, I asked if he had anything else on hand and he hesitantly handed over the manuscript of *A Tourist's Guide to Glengarry*. After reading it in a single gulp, I phoned John Metcalf the next day and asked him to read it over the weekend. He did and offered Ian a contract within a week. Published with minor edits, it is one of the bestselling Canadian literary press novels of the decade, much loved in Alberta and all-too-rarely read elsewhere. This is what Yann Martel thinks of it:

If J. D. Salinger or Mark Twain had lived in Edmonton, they might have written *A Tourist's Guide to Glengarry*. Prepare to slip into the mind of a nine-year-old. Prepare for a trip like Huckleberry Finn's, except here it is not a river that is travelled but a single day in the life of little Neil McDonald. Prepare for a story that is simple, deep, psychologically dead-on, minutely observed yet worldly — and very funny.

This is how his publisher describes it:

Nine-year-old Neil McDonald has always wanted to write a book. Every time he tries, though, it comes out "like the Hardy Boys or something." But when a maverick substitute teacher challenges him to record all the events and thoughts of a single day, the doors of creativity swing open. It helps that the day in question is, in Neil's words, "pretty weird." The time is the fall of 1971; the setting is "North America's northernmost Metropolis." The cast includes Neil, his best friend Keith and his gnome-like baba, a budding Black Power advocate, the heavy-smoking son of anti-war activists, and a very small boy wielding a very large axe in a public park. Neil thinks his day will climax with the broadcast of the first night game in World Series history, but what he's in for is something much deeper, a surprise that will teach him much about the world and his place in it. In the end, Neil has his book. And it's nothing at all like the Hardy Boys.

This is a seriously funny book, more Mark Twain than Salinger. I feel very privileged to have played a small role in bringing it into print.

～

ANNALS OF OURLIT III

STEPHEN MARCHE

"CanLit hates youth, says young author"

In *Shut Up, He Explained* (2007), John Metcalf writes,

> It has been borne in on me during the last forty years that it is unusual
> to find Canadian writers who even read other Canadian writers.... It is
> not at all unusual to find aspiring writers who have never read Leon
> Rooke, Clark Blaise, Norman Levine, Keath Fraser, Mavis Gallant....
> Similarly, older writers remain resolutely ignorant of Caroline
> Adderson, Michael Winter, K. D. Miller, Sharon English ... while all
> of them seem to be cognizant of, say, W. G. Sebald.
>
> If the country's writers do not read each other — an aesthetic and
> competitive necessity, one would have thought — why should we
> expect an audience to read us? If writers do not care, why should
> anyone else? ... Is it that Canadian writers hold Canadian achievement
> in contempt?

Ignorance doesn't prevent writers complaining over who gets grants, who goes
to which literary festivals, who makes the long- and shortlists for prizes and,
especially, who wins or doesn't win each autumn when mainstream media exhibit
otherwise dormant interest in our literature. Stephen Marche, Robert Fulford's
son-in-law, drew considerable attention with "Raging against the tyranny of
CanLit" in the *Toronto Star* on October 20, 2007. Here are some of the more
notorious things he had to say after moving from Brooklyn to Toronto the
previous month:

- In the middle of prize season and the authors' festival, the differences
  between the two literary capitals couldn't be starker to me. Brooklyn is so,

so young and Toronto is so, so old: It felt like moving from a frenetic day care to an old folks' home.

- It's not just that young people write in Brooklyn; writing itself is considered a youthful activity. It's the kind of thing that 32-year-old men who go to work by skateboard do. Literature in Toronto is something your smartest aunt does once she's cozied up in her favourite sweater.

- Setting is everything in Canadian fiction. Plots don't matter much. There are only a few plots anyway: recovering from historical or familial trauma through the healing power of whatever (most common); uncovering historical or family secrets and thereby achieving redemption (close second); coming of age (distant third place).

- The characters are mostly the same: The only thing that changes is the location of the massacred grandmother, what kind of booze the alcoholic father drinks himself into fits with, what particular creed is being revealed, in deft and daring ways, as both beautifully transcendent and oppressive.

- Innovation, whether in language or form, is a dirty word.... Brooklyn's books are like toys, meant to excite and give pleasure and challenge a little bit. In Canada, we are the oatmeal of world literature. We are on the cutting edge of blandness.

- The danger is that the Giller, like the CBC, will become just another institution for boomer self-congratulation. Theirs is the greatest generation in the history of the country at inventing awards to give one other.

- The problem may be the sheer gravity and intensity of boomer self-regard. In literary terms, they are represented, as they always have been, by Margaret Atwood. Her career, much like CanLit itself, has entered a Shavian twilight, where every book she produces takes away from her legacy.

- The old generation of writers is dead or dying; the men are mostly dead — Mordecai Richler, Irving Layton, Robertson Davies, Timothy Findley. The question is really whether CanLit as a phenomenon is more than one generation long.

- There are young writers in Canada, lots of them, but they tend to be Brooklynish. They, too, write about kids: Heather O'Neill in *Lullabies for*

Little Criminals, David Bezmozgis in *Natasha*, Sheila Heti in *The Middle Stories*, Yann Martel in *Life of Pi*. These are the exciting books that have come out of Canada in the last little while. All of them were written by young people. All of them found their success outside of Canada: Heti at *McSweeneys*, Bezmozgis at *The New Yorker*, O'Neill through a friend at *The New York Times Magazine*, Martel through the Booker. None of them was nominated for the Giller. The message for young Canadian writers could not be clearer: If you want success, you're going to have to find it elsewhere. Wasn't the whole point of Canadian literary nationalism, begun so long ago, to avoid exactly this situation?

You'd never guess from Marche's comments that the previous year's Giller had gone to Vincent Lam for *Bloodletting & Miraculous Cures* or that Rawi Hage's *DeNiro's Game* had made the 2006 shortlist as did Pascale Quiviger for *The Perfect Circle* or that the 2007 shortlist contained Alissa York's *Effigy* or that in 2005 the shortlist contained David Bergen's *The Time in Between*, Camilla Gibb's *Sweetness in the Belly*, Lisa Moore's *Alligator*. It may be true that none of these writers are quite so young as Marche would like them to be or as in the money: Toronto's publishing mavens have always been slower to get on top of bright young things than Manhattan (at least since the collapse of the Sordsmen's Club — Marche can ask his father-in-law for the story on that one! Everybody else can read about it in the recent biography of Pierre Berton by Brian Mckillop). Are these writers (and Eden Robinson, George Elliott Clarke, Elizabeth Ruth, Douglas Coupland, Timothy Taylor, Michael Winter, Trevor Cole, Ray Robertson) ponderous, plotless, sanctimonious, or lacking in innovation? And that's just a starter kit to post-Boomer writers in English Canada these days.

While it's the duty of every novelist who believes that novels "that do not discover a hitherto unknown segment of existence" are worse than useless (Milan Kundera, *The Art of the Novel*, revised edition, 2000), to weigh up existing talent and create a readership for himself (yes, it's alpha males who rush to these judgments), what's insulting in Marche's self-serving are his off-hand colour-blindness and anglophilia (among the old men of the first generation, Austin

Clarke is alive and well and flourishing as is Josef Škvorecký), and lack of rudimentary historical perspective. Hasn't he read at least enough of Coupland (whose views on CanLit 14 months earlier in the *New York Times* blog — cited above — are paraphrased closely enough to imply some causal relationship) to know that Atwood (and Leon Rooke, Clark Blaise, Keath Fraser) as well as the other writers he does name are pre-Boomers who have largely given way to an established generation of actual Baby Boom writers (born between 1946 and 1957) that is doing some of its best work under pressure from Coupland's own excellent-at-innovation Generation X (born between 1958 and 1968) as well as Marche's Generation Y (born between 1969 and 1980)? Has he read enough Atwood of the early, middle, and later periods to judge her as he does? Her talent remains robust; Michael Ondaatje is the only established author whose career has entered not a "Shavian twilight," but the Klieg day-out-of-night of Planet Hollywood where every new novel sadly reduces his legacy. But Marche takes the cheap shot, the one he knows he can fire off without burning up his own career: Atwood has better things to do than piss on his natterings but Ondaatje's friends at *Brick* and elsewhere might just help his career along in some way that's sweller in his imagination than in reality.

Yes, there are bad Canadian novels. There have always been bad novels everywhere they're written. And yes, some of them have too much setting and too little plot but this isn't peculiarly Canadian any more than the limiting of plots to "recovering from historical or familial trauma through the healing power of whatever (most common)" which, for example, might define Twain and Tolstoy; "uncovering historical or family secrets and thereby achieving redemption (close second)" which, for example, might define Dickens and Dostoevsky; "coming of age (distant third place)" which, for example, might define Conrad and Goethe. More than a century ago in "The Future of the Novel," Henry James complained about the *gross quantity* of bad American and British novels — stories and characters that lacked both variety and vividness — but blamed *the mediocrity of writers, the laxness of readers and the timidity of editors for their proliferation.* James bemoaned the aversion to risk-taking on all sides and, specifically, the failure of both Anglo-American writers and readers to embrace adult life and examine sexual relations in straightforward ways. He placed the greatest blame on *the timidity of editors who invariably seem to fasten on female adolescents as their "ideal" reader*. Female adolescents or the adolescent that remains firmly botoxed in women uncertain of maturity remain the favourite targets of Manhattan's editors. Such readers are no longer sanctimonious — those who find their way past the Young Adult vampire fantasy sections of Big Boxes of Books and don't stop at the shopaholic pyramids — devour the less-than-adult sexual relations that Heather O'Neill delivers in *Lullabies* and Marche attempts to service in his own debut, *Raymond and Hannah* (2005).

As a critic of our literature, Marche is a *pissenlit* (dandelion): as a novelist, does he have anything to offer? *Raymond and Hannah* has a plotless sex scene in an empty apartment that moves a hook-up to a somewhat committed relationship over a cottage weekend setting that are both worth reading: they are fine, compact, lucid short stories shoehorned between a novella about Hannah's attempt to discover Jewishness by moving to Israel and studying at a yeshiva with a rabbi who once was a fisherman in Maine that involves a lot of typing of the kind Nino Ricci does (whenever he forgets he's a mature married man and not a morose grad student). While Raymond works at a doctoral dissertation in Toronto on — *quelle surprise!* — Robert Burton's *The Anatomy of Melancholy*, Hannah comes of age as Raymond doesn't. None of this prevented Nicholas Dinka from exclaiming in *Quill & Quire*:

> Stephen Marche's debut novel, bearing all the hallmarks of Leonard Cohen's influence — poetic language, urban hipsterism, explicit sexuality, Jewish philosophy — is a rare creature, then. And judging by the book's many strengths, it's perhaps a loss to our literature that more young writers haven't followed in Mr. Cohen's footsteps.... Marche's writing is both muscularly clear and infused with powerful poetic rhythms....

More young writers ought to have read Cohen's *The Favourite Game* and might have done so if our country's high school and college teachers had the wit and cunning to teach it rather than J. D. Salinger's *Catcher in the Rye*.

READING AND COMING TO TERMS WITH THE PAST

Vergangenheitsbewältigung and
Novels of Knowledge

It is bad taste to be wise all the time, like being at a perpetual funeral.

D. H. LAWRENCE

The man who doesn't read good books has no advantage over the man who can't read them.

MARK TWAIN

Novels contain more than settings, plots, and characters: they yield knowledge that may be factual or fantastical but which, in either case, gets behind, underneath, in front of or on top of imagined realities in search of something else:

> Thomas Gradgrind, sir. A man of realities. A man of fact and calculations. A man who proceeds upon the principle that two and two are four, and nothing over, and who is not to be talked into allowing for anything over. Thomas Gradgrind, sir — peremptorily Thomas — Thomas Gradgrind. With a rule and a pair of scales, and the multiplication table always in his pocket, sir, ready to weigh and measure any parcel of human nature, and tell you exactly what it comes to. It is a mere question of figures, a case simple arithmetic. You might hope to get some other nonsensical belief into the head of George Gradgrind, or Augustus Gradgrind or John Gradgrind, or Joseph Gradgrind (all suppositions, no existent persons), but into the head of Thomas Gradgrind — no sir!
>
> In such terms Mr. Gradgrind always mentally introduced himself, whether to his private circle of acquaintance, or to the public in general. In such terms, no doubt, substituting the words "boys and girls", for "sir", Thomas Gradgrind now presented Thomas Gradgrind to the little pitchers before him, who were to be filled so full of facts.
>
> Indeed, as he eagerly sparkled at them from the cellarage before mentioned, he seemed a kind of cannon loaded to the muzzle with facts, and prepared to blow them clean out of the regions of childhood

at one discharge. He seemed a galvanizing apparatus, too, charged with a grim mechanical substitute for the tender young imaginations that were to be stormed away.

So begins *Murdering the Innocents*, Chapter 2 of Charles Dickens's *Hard Times* (1854), his state-of-the-nation novel set in Coketown (Manchester) not London. It's been called everything from "sullen socialism" (Thomas Macaulay) to "passionate revolt against the whole industrial order of the modern world" (George Bernard Shaw) to an "unsurpassed critique of industrial society" (Walter Allen) to "a moral fable." *Moral fable* sounds right to this late modernist ear: the heart, soul, braininess, spirituality of the novel reside with Sissy Jupe, in particular, who does not thrive in Gradgrind's school. Sissy's father rides and tends horses for a travelling circus that moves from one small fun fair — what the French term *la kermesse* — to another. If Gradgrind is "Fact," she's "Fancy."

In her Penguin Lives *Charles Dickens* (2002), Jane Smiley writes that

Dickens appeals to that part of the reader that recognizes that much is left undiscussed by reasonable discourse, that people and institutions often do populate our inner lives not as who they are but as what they mean to us, and that we often do not see them whole and complex, but simple and strange. This view, of course, has an affinity with childhood, as Dickens had an affinity with childhood, but it also has an affinity with many states of consciousness throughout life, including madness or obsession and exalted states of love or spiritual transcendence.

The following novels shout out to one another about the state of our nation from one end of the twentieth century to the other with madness, obsession, love, and transcendence while leaving regions of our Sissy Jupes intact.

～

ANNALS OF OURLIT IV

LA KERMESSE:
DANIEL POLIQUIN'S

A Secret Between Us (2007)

If there wasn't some basis to Stephen Marche's complaint that in Canadian fiction the characters are "mostly the same: The only thing that changes is the location of the massacred grandmother, what kind of booze the alcoholic father drinks himself into fits with, what particular creed is being revealed, in deft and daring ways, as both beautifully transcendent and oppressive," Daniel Poliquin's *A Secret Between Us* would not be what it is: "Achingly moving and darkly funny, *A Secret Between Us* (translated by Donald Winkler) earns comparison to the best of Günter Grass's novels. A masterwork."

Michael Redhill's blurb on the back cover says precisely what a patient and perceptive reader will find between the covers of a novel that is defiantly a Grass-inspired *Vergangenheitsbewältigung* — a coming to terms with dualities in Canada's past. Like Grass's Danzig Trilogy of *The Tin Drum*, *Cat and Mouse*, and *The Dog Years*, Poliquin's *A Secret Between Us* deals with the way a war and its aftermath are experienced in a unique cultural setting where ethnicities intermingle against a complex historical background, rendered in prose that blends hyperrealism with kinetic lyricism.

A Secret Between Us was originally published in French as *La Kermesse* (a small-town fun fair) and Ottawa on the Rideau, our fledgling nation's capital, to which antiheroic protagonist-narrator Lusignan returns from the trenches of the Great War, is a working-class town in which the inhabitants of the working-class Flats are mightily amused by the false-fronted pretentiousness of the uppity folks who live in thrall to Parliament Hill. Lusignan is a full time drunk and liar, a radical but disgraced novelist, a run-of-the-gin-mill journalist, an incompetent translator to the Senate and a less-than-illustrious veteran of Princess Patricia's Light Infantry who wobbles his way through the postwar world careening and carousing between social and sexual indiscretions, guided and misguided by his tragicomic Catholic childhood and infatuation with an aristocratic fellow officer, Essiambre d'Argenteuil.

D'Argenteuil has all the charm, manners and nobility Lusignan might have acquired if his mother had married the local notary rather than her village's carpenter and had stayed out of the district madhouse. Seduced spiritually and physically (the "secret" of the English title), Lusignan returns from the trenches with a cunning plan to reconnect with the love that dared not speak its name by bedding Amalia Driscoll, d'Argenteuil's prewar lover with whom he has been corresponding under the other man's name. While trying to fight his way free of the drunken ghost that drags him from blind pig to blind pig in Hull and leaves him utterly loose-limbed and disordered on the streets of Temperance-bound Ottawa, Lusignan fumbles his way towards Amalia with help from Concorde, a sexually voracious housemaid who has also been to bed with d'Argenteuil. Assistance of another kind comes from Father Mathrun, a Capuchin monk with a martyr complex.

Poliquin has absorbed Rabelais and incorporates grotesqueries and bawdiness into his comedy but his sense of satire owes more to Grass's (and Thomas Mann's) Germanic love of parody and subversion than to the French (Voltaire and his descendents) penchant for farce and fantasy. Poliquin, like Mann, is almost too good a mimic: the letters from Amalia to d'Argenteuil that interrupt Lusignan's reveries seem so true to the straightened circumstances of a gentle-woman of the era that it's easy to fall victim to the trickery and lose track of the larger sense of this novel. *A Secret Between Us* is a remarkable send-up of the earnestness, the self-importance, the whining, the pretentiousness that passes for artistic seriousness and social responsibility among the generality of those who write historical novels in either of our official languages. It's very funny if you enjoy seeing un-ironic *merdeists* and careerists get the drubbing they deserve but if you don't, *A Secret Between Us* might seem nothing more than what it is for *Quill & Quire*'s reviewer, Michel Basilières, "just one damn thing after another, with the characters weaving in and out of each other's lives over the years, everyone's dreams unrealized and their lives inconsequential."

What accounts for such obtuseness? Patience is a virtue and there's a marvel-lous sense of accomplishment that emerges from reading this book through to the end at tempos that allow each of the voices to speak in distinctive time signatures. As Redhill asserts, there is much more to *A Secret Between Us* than a finely turned literary joke. It has the power to move readers "achingly" because it opens eyes wide shut to the darker realities of the past by exploring reversals of fortune in the lives of the gentlewoman and the housemaid, Amalia and Concorde.

Daniel Poliquin is better placed and better prepared to lead us to come to terms with Canada's collective and doubly colonized past than other writers of his generation. Raised in Ottawa, highly educated, and deeply immersed in both French and German literature, he's a writer for whom the personal has always been political. That's not surprising since he makes his living as a parliamentary translator, as a literary translator (Jack Kerouac, Matt Cohen, Mordecai Richler) and, most recently, as the man who turned Jean Chretien's *My Years as Prime Minister* (ghost written in English by Ron Graham) back into French as *Passion politique*. He's a superb mimic. The Giller nomination ought not to have surprised: *A Secret Between Us* is world class in its deflation of the earnestness, self-importance, whining, pretentiousness, and self-entitlement that persuades all too many writers that serious and responsible artistry can casually co-exist with careerism in the successful and *ressentiment* among the failures.

JOSEPH BOYDEN

Three Day Road (2005)

Among foreign readers (it's available in American, British, Dutch, French, Italian, Spanish, and German editions) Joseph Boyden's *Three Day Road* has supplanted Timothy Findley's *The Wars* as the great Canadian novel about the First World War. For the best of reasons — it's gripping, wrenching, eye opening, illuminating, stirring, moral (not moralistic) fiction rooted in closely observed fact.

What's utterly novel about the treatment of the Great War (and specifically the contributions of Canada's fighting men) in *Three Day Road* is its point of view. Xavier Bird is a young Oji-Cree whose experiences alongside his childhood friend and hunting companion, Elijah Weesageechak, parallel those of the non-fictional Francis Pegahmagabow: "Peggy" was one of only thirty-nine men in the entire Canadian Expeditionary Force to receive the Military Medal with two bars and was the most highly decorated Aboriginal soldier in the conflict. Corporal Pegahmagabow, the subject of Adrian Hayes' *Legendary Warrior, Forgotten Hero* (2003), was an Ojibway from the Parry Island Band who worked as a sniper and is reputed to have killed as many as 378 German soldiers, one shot at a time. Pegahmagabow was a loner who worked without a spotter and won his medals for his work as a scout, runner, and guide at Mount Sorrel and Passchendaele. The fictional Xavier provides Elijah with the second set of eyes Pegahmagabow never had. As both witness to his friends "kills" and author of his own, Xavier gives voice to the conflicts felt by "savages" in the slaughterhouse of "civilized" France and Belgium.

Xavier, a runaway from residential schooling, has been raised mostly in the bush beyond Moose Factory in northern Ontario. His aunt Niska, who has been mother and father to him, is one of the last of those who refused to enter the reserves and took to the woods where she has lived as a shaman and executioner of *Windigos* — those who consume human flesh. Xavier barely speaks English when he arrives in France and takes in everything according to the traditional beliefs and customs in which he was reared. Elijah, by contrast, is a product of a Roman Catholic residential school. Elijah speaks English as impeccably as the nuns who taught him how to live in the non-Native world. Able to mimic the accents of the officers and dialects of the men he serves among, Elijah uses jokes, tricks, and stories to keep himself and Xavier out of as much trouble as can be avoided in an army that is both ruthless and racist. Elijah has heard of Pegahmagabow's exploits and competes to exceed them. A man of twists and turns, a cunning Odysseus to Xavier's reluctant Achilles, Elijah seeks opportunities to risk both their lives in a theatre of war that is both tragic and comic in ways Homer's ancient warriors never imagined.

The story of what seriously wounds Xavier and ultimately destroys Elijah is told in flashbacks as Niska returns her nephew to his birthplace at the end of the war. On a three-day canoe trip back into the woods, Niska's voice complements and counterpoints Xavier's. She provides the larger context of European and Native relations in Canada against which the experiences of the young soldiers are weighed by an author who is as morally complex as Tomson Highway.

Joseph Boyden grew up in Willowdale, the son of Dr. Raymond Wilfrid Boyden, Canada's most highly decorated medical officer of the Second World War. Part Métis, part Mi'kmaq, part Scots, part Irish, Boyden is also the grandson and great-nephew of veterans of the First World War. This merely suggests but doesn't fully explain the familiarity and intimacy with which he handles military and Native materials. Well-informed but non-specialist readers won't find themselves feeling distracted by the obviousness of underlying research or shaking their head over improbable coincidences. Although the voices of both narrators seem at first unconvincing, *Three Day Road* quickly takes on the texture of lived experience and feels uncannily as if its author has known these people and traversed the Canadian wilderness and the killing fields of the Western Front with them.

Like the young Homer of *The Iliad*, Boyden is precise and unflinching in his descriptions of the ways in which soldiers fall in battle. Men die in agony: they drop screaming, writhing, bleeding, spewing, gasping, clawing the ground, reaching out to beloved companions; they die bellowing, weeping, whimpering, roaring. They are barraged, gassed, machine-gunned, knifed, bludgeoned, blown apart by mortars and grenades, left to bloat and stink in the wastes of no-man's lands or to feed trench rats and wild dogs. And death is their end: there is no comforting vision of life beyond the grave, no blessedness, no great promises fulfilled. Darkness engulfs them and their bloodied, scarcely recognizable remains haunt the survivors.

The noisy, brutal deaths of *Three Day Road* are not only historically indispensable, they are required as contrast to the quieter, long range, technically precise, caught in the telescopic crosshairs, one shot at a time, bullet to the head, clean kills that are Elijah's and Xavier's specialty as snipers. As Elijah becomes more and more both lover and victim of the will to violence and Xavier is compelled to do what he has never imagined, readers are led to a renewed and deeper understanding of Robert E. Lee's words as he watched Hooker's men fall into his trap at Fredericksburg: "It is well that it is so terrible or we should grow too fond of it."

~

JANE URQUHART

The Stone Carvers (2001)

The Stone Carvers was published at the height of Urquhart's critical and commercial success: *Away* (1993), shortlisted for the the International IMPAC Dublin Literary Award, remained on the national bestseller list for a record 132 weeks; *The Underpainter* (1997) won the Governor General's Literary Award in Fiction. Reviewing her interweaving of a tale of the impact of the Great War on siblings from a farming community in southern Ontario for *The Globe and Mail* left me feeling giddy: I sensed this wasn't just another bestseller but the best book Urquhart had in her.

The stone carvers of the title are craftsmen who turn Walter Allward's technical drawings and plaster models into the shaped, polished, and inscribed Yugoslavian marble of the Vimy Memorial in the 1930s on the few hectares near Arras ceded to Canada by France. All are Italians except for three Canadians and two-thirds of the novel provides the backstories that bring the trio to this project in middle age. The rest deals with how their lives are altered by the experience of building a public monument to their countrymen. The Canadians come from pioneering attempts to graft Western European culture on to places that cling to the *wild* in *wilderness* — the Italian community in Hamilton and the dominantly Bavarian town of Shoneval, in southwestern Ontario. Juxtaposing remnants of Europe in Canada with a part of Canada memorialized in Europe provides an opportunity for Urquhart to tackle something more ambitious and riskier than she's done before or since.

Germans in Canada don't attract the voracious readership that the Irish draw and readers of *Away* were disappointed that Eamon O'Sullivan, the only significant Irishman in Shoneval, doesn't get more attention than he does. The heart of the book belongs to Klara Becker, a seamstress and spinster, whose affair with Eamon is interrupted by the declaration of war in Europe. Klara is the granddaughter of one of the Bavarians who turned Ontario trees into lumber for European manufacturers but Joseph Becker wasn't a simple hewer of wood: he's a skilled carver who passes his techniques and his chisels on to his grandchildren — Klara and her brother Tilman — after devoting all the free time in his long lifetime to sculpting altarpieces and statuary for an elaborate stone church financed by that great builder of architectural follies, King Ludwig of Bavaria.

Klara lives within sight of the church and of a brewery that's the town's second most important edifice. She aspires to no greater use of her gift than adding a carving of her own to those of her grandfather's in the church until Tilman draws her to Vimy. Following Homer, the progenitor of tales of soldiers returning from war, Urquhart interlinks historical events, legends, folk tales, visions, anecdotes, longings, and journeys into a complicated but unified exploration of history, perception, memory, and transformation. Unlike Homer, whose intentions are dominantly ethical, she focuses on the power of chisels chipping stone to impress on the world "light and strength and consolation."

Read once, *The Stone Carvers* delights and refreshes the imagination. Read a second time, it's more engaged with the public realm than you'd first imagined as Urquhart makes a case for public art as the necessary expression of populist experience, insisting that art is the interface between our private and public selves and essential for a whole life. The changes a book make in a reader's inner life are difficult to predict but this book is guaranteed to change the way you look at a war monument the next time you pass one.

~◡

WAYNE JOHNSTON

Duet: *The Colony of Unrequited Dreams* (1998) & *The Custodian of Paradise* (2006); *The Navigator of New York* (2002)

The Colony of Unrequited Dreams (1998) &
The Custodian of Paradise (2006)

The Colony of Unrequited Dreams centres on Joey Smallwood, the final Father of Confederation who brought Newfoundland into Canada and became the tenth province's first premier. *The New York Times* said of it, "this prodigious, eventful, character-rich book is a noteworthy achievement: a biting, entertaining and inventive saga ... a brilliant and bravura literary performance." Exactly so: the book captures Premier Joey's sense of his place in Newfoundland and Newfoundland's place in the world even as it satirizes both.

Smallwood wants to rise "not from rags to riches, but from obscurity to world renown." Driven by earnestness to self-importance, he confuses self-serving with public service as he transforms himself from a socialist journalist in New York to union organizer walking the railbed across the British colony (signing up members all along the route) to political schemer *nonpareil*. While championing the poor and Newfoundland's place within Canada (rather than post-colonial political independence), Smallwood's story is entwined with that of Johnston's fictitious Sheilagh Fielding, a hard-drinking newspaperwoman of irreverence, wit, and go-straight-for-the-jugular satirical instincts. Her columns, journals, and work-in-progress, a *Condensed History of Newfoundland*, add saltiness as they pepper the Smallwood narrative.

In *The Custodian of Paradise*, Johnston takes up Fielding's own story and haunts readers of the earlier book by creating what Kate Pullinger brilliantly describes in her *The Globe and Mail* review as "not really a new novel at all, but a ghost novel, a shadow novel ... a Gothic double ... books [that] stand in almost complete opposition to each other; if *Colony* is Dorian Gray, then *Custodian* is the portrait in the attic." Pullinger nails the contrast:

> *Colony's* narrative is large and all-embracing, vast and universal, while at the same time highly culturally specific. *Custodian's* story takes place almost entirely inside Fielding's own head; psychological, internal, repeatedly returning to pick over old wounds. *The Colony of Unrequited Dreams* is large (though Smallwood himself was small) and male, self-aggrandizing, firmly placed on the world stage, while *The Custodian of Paradise* is small (though Fielding, of course, was very tall) and female, self-lacerating and completely domestic.

Pullinger finds *Custodian* the lesser of the two works ("At times reading the novel feels like being trapped on a train with a teenager — a Goth, probably — who feels compelled to recite all the clever comments he has ever made") and ends her piece expressing the hope that Johnston will turn his duet into a trilogy. Take the work as it stands — novel and ghost — because it's a duet that dances its way through North America's postwar politics with Shakespearean scope and Dickensian intensity.

Wayne Johnston does not write historical novels. He's made that absolutely clear in numerous interviews by direct reference to Shakespeare's history plays — seeing himself as chronologically close to Smallwood as Shakespeare was to the Tudor ascendancy and claims an Elizabethan liberty to invent outsized characters in small scenes to capture substantial truths. Speaking of *Colony*, he's said the title is meant to evoke

> the nostalgia Newfoundlanders have felt for the possibilities of the island, and that they still have for the future. Joe is always searching

for something commensurate with the greatness of the land itself, but he can't find it, and it's driving him mad.... Newfoundland is that kind of place. It makes you want to live up to the landscape, but on the other hand it offers you no resources to do so.,.. I couldn't think of a bigger character whose life touched on more themes, involved the whole of Newfoundland more completely than Smallwood did. He was so prone to making mistakes and so fallible, and he combines so many contradictions in his personality. His quest, like that of many great literary figures of the past century, is to overcome these divisions.

Johnston invents Fielding as a spokesman for himself and for comedy lived in the midst of tragedy: in this, he comes as close to Shakespeare and Dickens as David Adams Richards does to the Bible and Tolstoy but he's more at home with modernist techniques than Richards: *Custodian* opens (and the opening scene is one of the great moments in Canadian literature) with Fielding in self-exile at Loreburn, an abandoned island off the south coast of Newfoundland. Half-Caliban, half-Prospero, Fielding sometimes reads from journals or letters but just as often soliloquizes or invents dialogues of extraordinary complexity and range.

In 1984, Dilshad Engineer (who had acquired and edited my first novel for Oberon Press and seen it through to publication the previous year), remarked a little tactlessly over the phone that she had just acquired the most brilliant novel ever to fall or ever likely to fall into her hands: *The Story of Bobby O'Malley* by a twenty-six-year-old Newfoundland journalist, Wayne Johnston. For too many years, Johnston had far too few readers enthusiastic for storytelling that's as brilliant, bravura, beautiful, mesmerizing, spellbinding, magical, splendid, entertaining, evocative, cavernous, capacious, operatic, hypnotic, and impassioned as American reviewers, in particular, say it to be while being so very funny that its intended targets, Canadians in particular, didn't get the point of what he was doing in *The Time of Their Lives* (1987), *The Divine Ryans* (1990), or *Human Amusements* (1994) until he found in Joey Smallwood and Sheilagh Fielding characters capable of the erudition to carry the weight of the very strange thing that is Shakespeare's comedy.

The Navigator of New York (2002)

Set at the close of the nineteenth century and the beginning of the twentieth, *Navigator* moves from near-rustic St. John's to the pandemonium of Manhattan and Brooklyn as Gotham becomes a city with cathedrals to commerce, mansions, and streets darkened by elevated trains for its immigrant population. From a New York where nothing is today as it was yesterday, *Navigator* transits to the windswept emptiness of Arctic ice packs. Read this book simply for the force, beauty, and accuracy of its images and you'll feel your time has been well spent. But this is a novel of love between characters as oddly and variously shaped as the places they inhabit.

Devlin Stead grows up in St. John's in the house of his aunt and uncle. Unusually solitary, he enters into correspondence with the explorer Dr. Frederick A. Cook. Cook's letters take Devlin to Brooklyn, Alaska, and the Arctic and teach him what it is to love and remain loyal to a man full of twists and turns in a story as old as Telemachus and as current as Tom Hanks' *Road to Perdition* as a pure-hearted boy tries to connect to an irresolute, guilt-ridden, unreliable man. Stead is Johnston's invention but Dr. Frederick Cook was leader of the North Polar Expedition of 1908–1909, the man who went to his grave in 1940 insisting that it was he and not Commander Robert E. Peary who first discovered the North Pole.

Johnston has become a cagey witness to the dishonesty and betrayals of our time. His works are all about the ways in which tricks, dodges, ruses, impostures, subterfuges, and deceptions don't just betray those who love the liar but alter the social fabric. Cook was sent to prison for fraud in the promotion of Texas oil shares. Anyone twerpish enough to think that the story of the New Yorkers who destroyed him in order to protect Commander Peary, who was one of their own, isn't intimately connected to Canadians, here and now, can't have much stake in any pension plan or any interest in the centrifugal forces that draw the rest of the Northern hemisphere to New York. *The Navigator of New York* contributes to the vindication of Dr. Cook, "the American Dreyfus of the North," in startling ways.

DAVID ADAMS RICHARDS

The Friends of Meager Fortune (2006),
River of the Brokenhearted (2003); Trilogy: *Nights Below Station
Street* (1988), *Evening Snow Will Bring Such Peace* (1990), &
For Those Who Hunt the Wounded Down (1993)

The Friends of Meager Fortune (2006)

> One cannot, somehow, think of him as a revolutionary, in the sense
> that James Joyce and D. H. Lawrence are revolutionaries, yet his
> contribution to literature is as original as theirs. He has given us a new
> formula. He is of the generation and yet not of it. His novels are only
> possible because he has cut himself off from twentieth-century civiliza-
> tion, and yet could not have been written in no other century than this.
> He owes little or nothing to contemporary literature; all his debts are
> to the past.... But it is probable that future generations will regard him
> as standing of the same relation to this generation as Blake did to his.

So wrote William Hunter of T. F. Powys (1875–1953). Much the same is true of
David Adams Richards whose thirteenth novel, *The Friends of Meager Fortune*,
is one of the greatest Canadian novels. It has the power, immensity, and melancholy of which Nobel Prize winners are sometimes made (Solzhenitsyn comes
to mind). So why did it fail to even be shortlisted for prizes Richards has won
in the past — the Governor General's Literary Award in Fiction (for *Nights
Below Station Street*), the Giller (for *Mercy Among the Children*)? Is it that Richards
doesn't employ irony (he's very humorous but his comedy is rooted in an absur-
dist's delight in the illogicality of thinking processes raddled by alcohol and
drugs or addled by greed and vengeance)? Or is it that his books burst with joys
that emerge from tragedy not in spite of it? Or is it that he's just too scathing
about middle class people who sacrifice simple decency on the altar of social
acceptability? It's certainly not through any lack of plot, character, or clarity in
his storytelling. Richards' novels have beginnings, middles, and ends in exactly
that order. As a storyteller, he has a better ear for speech patterns, a better eye

for details of dress and manners, and a more realistic feeling for the effects of physical and emotional deprivation than any contemporary not named Joan Barfoot (who is even less appreciated by literary powers-that-be). At this late date in both their careers, can it be tastemakers are as clueless about Richards' visionary poetics as they are about Barfoot's uncondescending, sardonic, sly, subversive, unembarrassed honesty?

There's such strong thematic, stylistic, and religious continuity between Powys and Richards that one suspects direct influence except that T. F. Powys is so little read beyond a circle of devotees (tinier than the one that regards older brother, John Cowper Powys, as the most-underestimated writer of the twentieth century). Powys and Richards are originals who share sources of inspiration in the Bible, Bunyan's *Pilgrim's Progress*, and Blake's *Songs of Innocence and Experience*. Other lines of influence are unimportant. Both novelists invent small, essentially rural worlds that are large enough to contain every quality ever imagined in mud and God. Such worlds are elastic enough that love and death, good and evil can be present in characters that are honourable or despicable while serving larger purposes as symbols and allegories of an unorthodox Christianity that intertwines strands of pantheism, quietism, and mysticism.

The Friends of Meager Fortune is a tale set against the backdrop of the lumber trade in 1946. Owen Jameson, a heroic officer who fought with the Canadian First Army "on the left flank of Monty for ten months" until wounded in France and was awarded the Victoria Cross, returns from the war to take over the company founded by his father and elevated in the world by his older brother, "the great Will Jameson" who died prematurely. Owen's "family was in lumber, or was Lumber" and it's his intention — despite his bookishness, sensitivity, and injury — to restore its primacy in the New Brunswick woods by directing the most ambitious cut ever undertaken "further up the river, past where anyone had gone before ... on Good Friday Mountain."

This is the end of the age of handsaws and axes, teams of men and teams of horses, "and how a good man lived then would try the best men now." Trees the diameter of two or three men are felled and scraped and sledged to the banks of tributaries of the Miramichi River through winter until spring run-off drives the log booms to the mills. To get the logs off Good Friday, teamsters run "the devil's back" — "a drop that seemed to plummet into the void." As the men, trees, and mountain resound to countless physical blows, the milltown downstream is flooded by rumours about Owen Jameson's relationship with Camellia Glidden and the role it may have played in the mysterious disappearance of her husband, his loyal friend Reggie.

That's the barest description of a novel that begins with a prophecy passed on through drink and a deck of cards from a Mi'kmaq woman to Owen's mother "that her first-born would be a powerful man and have much respect — but that his brother would be even greater, yet destroy he legacy by rashness," then proceeds through folly, drunkenness, and betrayals to a sensational trial and its aftermath to culminate in a meditation on fate and destiny in all their misery and glory.

David Adams Richards' mature novels achieve more than the sum of their parts because his overriding vision is not only poetic and religious but religious in a very special way: he cites Hardy, Conrad, and Tolstoy, Shakespeare and the Bible as essential influences but his brand of Catholicism and that of his characters is unthinkable without the *Pensées* (1670) of Blaise Pascal. Pascal's notion that life is a gamble that you'll always lose if you wager against God's inscrutable existence makes Richards potent because it's the just kind of thinking that threatened to turn every man into a King and the Sun King to nothingness seventy-five years before the French Revolution. Richards' storytelling is as anguished as Pascal's aphorisms — "we never live but we hope to live," "faith is God perceived by the heart not by reason," "the heart has its reasons which reason knows nothing of," and "we shall die alone."

After winning the Giller in 2000, David Adams Richards told an interviewer that he thought he only had two novels left in him. There's a valedictory feel to *Meager Fortune* as traces of earlier characters and storylines weave in and out. Then the tale's narrator (whose presence is barely felt except as the source of a nagging sense of narrative unreliability) announces his own birth and brings the consequences of the logging of Good Friday Mountain in 1946–1947 seamlessly into the present. He looks out his upstairs bedroom window and sees,

> the new generation traveling on their skateboards off those old pipes at
> the side of the mill Will Jameson once owned. They teeter and move

like princes in the wind, their shirts behind them, and manouever across the cold railings in this desolate broken lot, thirty feet above the ground. They are the out-of-work children of out-of-work fathers whose grandfathers worked in the long ago. They are as tough as stone and as kind as a day is long.... And they move like their forefathers before them, as if in their primitive years a fortune was at stake.

Watching them and thinking of their forefathers, hewers of wood seem now lesser than that. But to think merely this, you have to read without vision, without poetry. Richards' allegory is a subtler plombing of innocence and experience. Read slowly, intensely, it leaps into tongues of flame and vanquishes our deepest fears.

River of the Brokenhearted (2003)

My father Miles King once told me that some are damned by blood, by treason, by chance or circumstance, some even by the stars themselves, or as Shakespeare, denying that, said, by ourselves. This in a way is a journey back in time to see how I was damned.

The speaker is Wendell ("Wendy," his father calls him) King, the narrator of River of the Brokenhearted. Like his father, Wendell is a man who needs few excuses to raise many a glass to anything. But he drinks most heartily to the nobility of his father's sufferings. Blood feuds, traitorous acts, reversals of fortune, cosmic forces, and self-consciousness have plagued Miles King's life and turned him alcoholic and eccentric, a seeker among "old tracts, deeds, family history" after secrets that might make his own life comprehensible. It's quite the task. When his wife exclaims, "All you Kings are idiots!" His reply is, "Well, I know — but why?"

Miles is his father's son ("a howling failure ... must be the English side of you") rather than his mother's. Mother is Janie McCleary, a fiddle-playing Irish Catholic teenager of the Miramichi, who marries war-ravaged, recently-arrived-in-Canada from Liverpool, English Protestant, piano-playing George King against family's wishes and scandalizes Newcastle. Together, they open the Regent, the first movie theatre in northeastern New Brunswick, and incur the wrath of Joey Elias, another immigrant who dreams of making his own fortune by showing silent films to families of fishermen and woodsmen. Because Elias knows how to cater to the tastes of the less moral and exploit their weaknesses, he enlists the Drukens who have been feuding with the McClearys ("because both their families ... lost boys to a British hangman in 1791") in an attempt to ruin the Kings and take over their theatre. When George dies, Janie not only escapes the machinations of Elias but also prospers by seizing exclusive rights to "talkies" with help from Lord Beaverbrook. The price Janie's children and grandchildren pay for her early feminism and sizeable end-of-life fortune forms the crux of *River*, a novel of greater historical sweep than Richards had written since *Lives of Short Duration* (1981), an early tale ripe for rediscovery.

In scope and ambition *River* resembles the kind of book that Robertson Davies was forever attempting to write (a visiting circus even plays a key role in Richards' plot) but Richards merits the comparison to Dickens that Davies never earned. Janie McCleary is based on incidents in the life of the author's grandmother and her film palace. As a bonus, Richards contributes his own ardent moviegoer's sense of how a generation was altered by the experience of Hollywood movies in its Golden Age.

These are not the only two novels Richards has had in him since 2000 — there's been a third, *The Lost Highway* (2007), a novel some claim is superior to the other two.

Trilogy: *Nights Below Station Street* (1988), *Evening Snow Will Bring Such Peace* (1990), & *For Those Who Hunt the Wounded Down* (1993)

Richards won two great battles with this trilogy: one against internal demons and the other with the reading public. Put plainly, he taught himself how to write wholeheartedly and his audience how to read his characters as people of character troubled by bearing true witness in communities ruled by gossip, rumour, innuendo, mythmaking, demonization, and idolatry. He draws on everything he learned in the movie houses run by his family, storyboarding his narratives in such a way that he became a notable scriptwriter in the process (the first and third were made into films worth viewing). All three begin with simple premises that lead to much mischief. Start reading and you won't stop — they get better and better with as each chapter unfolds. *Nights Below Station Street* explores the day-to-day lives of folks from the wrong side of town, especially Adele, a strong-headed fifteen-year-old rushing into womanhood. *Evening Snow Will Bring Such Peace* takes up a quarrel over money between Cindi and Ivan Basterache who are in the second year of their marriage. *For Those Who Hunt the Wounded Down* centres on Jerry Bines, a violent man, feared by his town, who is trying to get back on the good side of the law and stay there.

Marina Endicott has said this about David Adams Richards as an influence on her writing: "It's not so much that I think about him when I'm writing, but I think about him while I'm living, as I move through neighbourhoods and classes, and that percolates into the writing." And then, she adds, "I can't think of anyone I know who hasn't been touched by David's influence. Call me crazy, but what about Joseph Boyden, in a way? Michael Helm, Michael Crummey. Some ... might not have been directly influenced by DAR, but have been able to write the books they write because of his opening up the provincial town underbelly genre: there's where I see Lynn Coady, but also Lisa Moore in some of the short stories ('Grace,' for example, seems to me to owe a hereditary debt to *Nights Below Station Street*), Susan Juby, and especially Dianne Warren." Endicott, a scintillating voice of sanity, isn't "crazy" in any of her judgments. But speaking of DAR's influence, what about Donna Morrissey?

~◞

TERRENCE HEATH

Casualties (2005)

The Globe and Mail assigned *Casualties* to Margaret Cannon for review in her "Crime Books" column, an understandable mistake that didn't help a tragic novel of the Dirty Thirties find the mainstream readership it deserves: as Cannon admitted, "This intriguing novel doesn't really fit any category."

There's mystery, crime, and detection but they aren't genre-driven — quickly read, digested, and discarded. *Casualties* is the work of a superb social historian wrestling with moral complexities endemic to our time. In present-day Toronto, Clara Stemichuk finds a confession of murder, signed by a man whose name she's never heard, in the pocket of her dead husband's dress suit shortly after his funeral. The extent to which she really knew her husband Peter (nick-named "Chuck") is called into question when she receives a phone call from a man who claims to have fought in the Spanish Civil War alongside him. Unsettled, she sets out to discover the meaning of the note and why her husband never spoke of his involvement in Spain. Clara unravels Chuck's story as she travels to Vancouver, Regina, and the west of England.

Central to her quest are Chuck Stemichuk, Thomas Pennan, and Margaret Long, young people of the Canadian Dust Bowl who survive the Regina Riots and join the Republican side in Spain. *Casualties* zings when their lives take centre stage in the RCMP-fuelled mayhem in Regina and in the hills of Spain as they follow their passions for social justice and economic reform. It is "terrific," as Cannon says, "in the battle of Teruel, when Spain is falling and everyone's dreams are dying." The "casualties" of the title are not just truth, the first victim of all wars, but also love, friendship, hope, and trust.

Terrence Heath is no easier to categorize than his novel. These days, he's best known for his work with Canadian artists as museum director, curator, and consultant who recently organized the retrospective exhibition of the works of sculptor Joe Fafard and wrote his biography. He's also biographer of the painter Ernest Lindner, author of four books of poetry (co-authored with the late Anne Szumigalski), and a fiction writer whose first book, *The Truth and Other Stories* (1972) exerted enormous influence on younger prairie writers. He's a Regina-born historian with a doctorate from Oxford with an extraordinary feel for the religious and political forces that have always linked grassroots Canadians to worlds far beyond narrowly conceived self-interest. Heath reanimates our past as few do because he understands that the triggers and expressions of emotion alter over generations. Wherever Margaret Cannon finds "clunky dialogue" and "Stalinist blather," I hear the adult voices of Heath's childhood and my own speaking in an English they never quite owned as they struggled awkwardly to articulate what the ruling class was so eager to suppress with the velvet gloves of correct grammar, proper accent, and positivist logic within the iron fist of a red-coated police state.

~

JOSEF ŠKVORECKÝ

The Engineer of Human Souls (1984)

Edenvale College stands in a wilderness. In a few years, the nearby town of Mississauga is expected to swell and envelop the campus with more variety and colour, but for the time being the college stands ... two and a half miles from the nearest housing development. The houses there are no longer all alike; people have learned something since George F. Babbitt's time. Perhaps it was literature that taught them. Now there are at least four different kinds of bungalow spaced at irregular intervals so that the housing development looks like a Swiss village in one of those highly stylized paintings. It is pretty to look at.... Often, as my thoughts flow, I conjure up again the wonderful things I have seen in this country of cities with no past. Like the Toronto skyline with its black and white skyscrapers, some plated with golden mirrors, thrusting their peaks in to the haze, glowing like burnished chessboards against the evening twilight above the flat Ontario land-scape, and beyond them a sun as large as Jupiter and as red as an aniline ruby sinking into the green dusk.... There is beauty everywhere on earth, but there is greater beauty in those places where one feels that sense of ease which comes from no longer having to put off one's dreams until some improbable future.... I feel utterly and dangerously wonderful in this wilderness land.

Josef Stalin had such high regard for writers — he allegedly called them "the engineers of human souls" — that some youngsters within the USSR came to the unintended conclusion that words were powerful enough to undermine the New World for New Men by returning readers to the pre-Stalinist world by constructing diversions that are, as Škvorecký subtitles his masterpiece, "An entertainment on the Old Themes of Life, Women, Fate, Dreams, The Working Class, Secret Agents, Love, and Death."

The Engineer of Human Souls is part of a cycle of works that construct, deconstruct, and reconstruct the life of Danny Smiricky, an artist throwing spanners into Stalinist workshops of every sort. The series encompasses five decades, several novels — *The Cowards* (1970), *The Miracle Game* (1980), *The Republic of Whores* (1994) and stories *The Swell Season* (1982) — written originally in Czech and, after Škvorecký's arrival in Canada in 1968, translated by Paul Wilson. Wilson's translation of *Ordinary Lives* (2008) brings the sequence to a close with Danny's graduating class's fiftieth reunion set in 1993.

Reviewing *Ordinary Lives*, the poet Ken Babstock listed some of the things he's learned from reading Škvorecký: "jazz and its place in wartime and postwar Prague culture (note: hip-hop in the Balkans), the heartbreaking thaws and freezes in postwar Czechoslovak politics, tragicomedy under Stalinism, the Prague Spring, literary modernism, moral ambiguity under tyranny, romantic love and its discontents, an exile's life in Canada and, most memorably, the enduring role art can play in a life otherwise drenched in stupidity, brutality, absurdity and hopelessness." And, yes, Dvorak as well.

Danny and his friends are self-elected members of a "second government" (the phrase is Solzhenitsyn's) — people who find in whatever artistry enters their lives a way of recognizing and celebrating dignity, freedom, and the fundamental values of friendship joy, comfort, knowledge, religion, and love. Love invariably gets Danny in trouble and inevitably aroused the Offended Police against his author so it was courageous for the jury of the Governor General's Literary Award in Fiction of 1984 to ignore not only on-campus custodians of the politically correct but the "This is an English Language Award" chatterers and bestow the prize where its merits placed it.

A complex, challenging analysis of contemporary politics and society, The Engineer of Human Souls *will become a milestone in the evolution of world literature.*

QUILL & QUIRE, MAY 1984

A funny, despairing, satirical, compassionate, sprawling, gloomy, provocative, prophetic, angry, and entertaining book. One of the most important novels ever written in Canada.

CANADIAN FORUM, AUGUST 1984

In *Engineer,* Danny, is exiled in Toronto, working as a university lecturer, and writing:

My novels, published here in Czech by Mrs. Santner's shoestring operation, are widely read by my fellow Czechs but hardly ever reviewed, because there is no one to review them. There are those two or three grateful laymen who lavish praises on them in the émigré press, their flatteries sandwiched between harvest supper announcements and ads for Bohemian tripe soup; they are literate, but they do not understand literature. Then there is Professor Koupelna in Saskatchewan. Every once in a while Passer's mail-order firm in Chicago sends him one of my books as a free gift along with his order of homemade jelly and Prague ham. The book arouses a savage and instinctive outrage in the good professor which he mistakes for the spirit of criticism and he fires off a broadside to the journal of the Czechoslovak Society for Arts and Sciences in America.

What seems a meandering stream of memory and reflection among broken dreams isn't: acts of bravery and cowardice are microscopically examined as Danny's generation takes issue with itself and with the young. The result is a book full of joy that feeds on contradictions that can't be engineered out of life.

Škvorecký and his wife, writer and actress Zdena Salivarová, founded '68 Publishers in 1971, which, over the next twenty years, published banned Czech and Slovak books. The imprint became an important mouthpiece for dissident writers, such as Václav Havel, Milan Kundera, and Ludvík Vaculík, among many others. For providing this critical literary outlet, the president of post-Communist Czechoslovakia, Václav Havel awarded the couple the Order of the White Lion. The award was presented to them as *Canadians*.

～○

MORDECAI RICHLER

Barney's Version (1997), *Solomon Gursky Was Here* (1989)

... the true function of a writer is to produce a masterpiece ...
no other function is of any consequence.

CYRIL CONNOLLY

Barney's Version (1997)

Barney's Version is so effortless to read that it's easy to fall into the trap of thinking it's simpler than it is: I did (in an embarrassing essay that I'd suppress if I could) and should have known better because I'd caught both allusions in the title — the purple dinosaur of children's television and *Roger's Version*, John Updike's novel about a divinity professor's determination to destroy a whiz kid's attempt to prove the existence of God on his computer. It's one of Updike's funnier fictions and Richler had once cited oh-so-serious Canadian reviews of it as yet further examples of humourlessness in our literary character. Like Updike's, Richler's novel is about one man's attempts to short circuit another's creative work but Richler replaces Updike's Christian Trinity with a more primitively potent one of his own — Barney Panofsky's three wives who incarnate the major Hindu goddesses: Clara, the first Mrs. Panofsky is creative and self-destructive; the Second (nameless) Mrs. Panofsky is self-regarding and creatively destructive; Miriam, the third, is compassionate and nurturing. This makes it much more interesting and existentially anguished than I first realized. Stupid me! Brilliant Richler!

Richler was single-minded in his pursuits: he'd grasped a few truths early in life and never tired of them. He was a conservative moralist, the grandson of a rabbi, who wrote as a commentator — a secular Talmudist — on wisdom ignored and values mocked by the incurious and unobservant. To honour what was true and good, he skewered whoever was silly and self-serving. He could be comically Borsht Belt but he was as serious and witheringly sarcastic as any of the Biblical prophets. After his return to Montreal in 1971, Evelyn Waugh's influence waned. Perhaps it had to do with the books he was selecting for the Book-of-the-Month Club or people like Wilfrid Sheed whom he schmoozed with on his monthly trips to New York but he began to measure his work by new standards, particularly ones set by Joseph Heller: both take the side of uncommon common men to make cases against the imbecilities of North American ruling elites and the sheep-like instincts and cravings of the middle classes. *Solomon Gursky Was Here*, Richler's masterpiece, is as dark, audacious, and deft a skewering of the realities of corporate rule and self-inflating mythology as any non-war novel has been in the wake of *Catch-22*. After its narrative complexities, linguistic dexterities, and utterly delicious parodies, I was expecting as powerful a fusillade against the prevailing myths of our national consciousness as Heller's sequel to *Catch-22*, *Closing Time*, is to those of the USA. But Richler had something else on his mind and I failed to get it until Mavis Gallant spoke plainly about her old friend's new work: "It's an existential novel." And a peculiarly Canadian voyage into postwar Paris.

Panofsky definitely isn't Richler. Roughly the same age and from the same St. Urbain neighbourhood, Barney's world and Richler's world bump up against each other in the thinly disguised portraits of several of Richler's drinking buddies. But Barney has set himself a task Richler never faced: with memory loss and little literary ability, Panofsky is writing a defence of himself against what he takes to be various libels perpetuated against him by Terry McIver, a hack who alleges that Barney murdered Bernard (Boogie) Moscovitch, a failed writer of great promise. McIver is a catchall and a catcall against arts-council-subsidized writers. Barney is a ranter and his storytelling is as motivated by self-justification and revenge as McIver's.

As writer and moralizer, Barney is clumsier than Richler. If Richler hadn't shared with Barney his pitch perfect ear for catching people revealing themselves in bits of unguarded dialogue, *Barney's Version* would fail as Barney fails. But here's Barney describing his second wife coaching him before his first meeting with her parents:

> "You are not to order more than one drink at the table before lunch."
>
> "Right."
>
> "And whatever you do, no whistling at the table. *Absolutely no whistling at the table.* She can't stand it."
>
> "But I've never whistled at the table in my life."

Barney's Version became Richler's most popular success at home and abroad. As Richler promoted *Barney's Version*, he repeatedly told radio and TV audiences, "Like every writer, you hope you've done something that will last — and once you've done that, it's time to quit. I don't think I've done that yet." Well, actually, he did make some books that last and he died too soon to add another but was less honoured and respected for it in this country than many now care to know or remember. This may have been a sorrow but certainly was no surprise to him: as Barney says,

> I've never known a writer or painter anywhere who wasn't a self-promoter, a braggart, and a paid liar of a coward, driven by avarice and desperate for fame.

～◦

Solomon Gursky Was Here (1989)

Richler won the Giller Prize for *Barney's Version*: it was the first time since *St. Urbain's Horseman* won the Governor General's Literary Award in Fiction in 1971 that Richler had been up for a major Canadian literary award. *Barney's Version* wasn't shortlisted for a GG, nor were his two previous novels — *Joshua Then and Now* (1980) and *Solomon Gursky Was Here*. It was the neglect of *Gursky* by the GG jury that propelled the Giller Prize into existence. Doris Giller, then Books Editor at the Montreal *Gazette*, was absolutely furious that the 1989 prize went to Paul Quarrington's *Whale Music* — the work of a professional musician but hobbyist writer. Raised in the same neighbourhood as Richler and his contemporary, Giller loved to read. "And since she had nobody to guide her reading, no university professor or mentor, she developed her own views about books that were very personal and honest," her husband Jack Rabinovitch told *Toronto Life*. "When she saw shit, she said shit." Rabinovitch gave her the revenge she wanted on shit-readers by setting up the prize in her honour a few months after her death and celebrating her legendary sense of fun by making the Giller Gala the literary social event of the year. One can only wonder how many times Rabinovitch has said "shit" on her behalf as winners have collected their cheques.

Public places weren't widely tagged by graffiti artists through most of the twentieth century: the most common mark inside toilet stalls, on railway underpasses, inside school desks took the form: X was here, as in the world famous "Kilroy was here" that GIs left behind in all the theatres of World War II. Name, location: a simple assertion of existence that rooted in the depths of human history that leaves passersby wondering, "Whatever happened to?"

Richler's protagonist Moses Berger, the writer-boozer son of a failed poet, is obsessed with Solomon, the black sheep of the Gursky dynasty, whose history parallels that of Canada. Solomon disappeared on a solo flight just as his family's business was shifting from Prohibition-era bootlegging to a legit multinational distillery. Did Solomon decide to leave his brothers Bernard the schemer and Morrie the bumbler to do what they wanted to do without him? Or was he murdered by Bernard? Or has he returned to the high Arctic, the land of his grandfather Ephraim? Moses works out an answer by tracing Gursky history from Victorian England to contemporary Montreal and points in between in a gut-busting sprawl of continents, characters, and contagious misbehaviour that eviscerates the pretentious, the religious, and the avaricious in a novel that proclaims from sea to sea to sea, "Richler was here."

In *Mordecai Richler* (2009), M. G. Vassanji writes that *Gursky* is "his most ambitious and riskiest book, linking his personally staked-out space of Jewish Montreal with the Canadian North, the rituals of Judaism with the rituals of the Inuit, the history of Canada with the history of the Jews. Daring and brilliant in its conception, it is in a sense a Jewish and personal appropriation of Canada" that "broadened the cultural scope of Canadian fiction" by bringing to it "an exuberance it had not seen, with his vernacular, his wit, his indomitable though often tortured characters."

Richler was a *wisdom* writer, as old as King Solomon, as dark as the writer of Ecclesiastes, and as rich in loyalty to all that he loved as the singer of The Song of Songs. If Richler doesn't convince you the Bible is epic storytelling not proto-history, no one will.

~

EMMA RICHLER

Feed My Dear Dogs (2005)

Any reader of *Saint Urbain's Horseman, Joshua, Then and Now*, and the *Jacob Two-Two* books has met some near relations of the Weiss family of *Feed My Dear Dogs* — a mechanically maladroit father with unruly hair and rumpled clothes who writes for a living, cares passionately about professional sports and classic movies, smokes small cigars, drinks single malt, jokes with his children, and adores his wife — a beautiful former model who inspires awe with uncanny, conjuring abilities as gardener, cook, mum — and their handful of perceptive children who are obsessive and impulsive in various artistically anarchical ways.

So why read Emma Richler? Well, the characters may be familiar but her point of view is fresh and funny, smart and startling. She may be her father's daughter (and that's no bad thing) but she's an accomplished writer in her own right.

Like her creator, Jemima (Jem) Weiss is the middle of five children. She has two older brothers — Ben and Jude — a younger sister, Harriet, and a younger brother, Gus. Jem's voice is one not often heard in fiction these days, the voice of the sibling most enmeshed within a family's collective life — the one who collects and recollects the responses of the others to all the rules, rituals, celebrations, and shared experiences that knit them together and set them apart. Because dad is Jewish and conflicted, mum Protestant and calming, the daughters nun-influenced products of convent schools, the eldest son a musical and bookish child of Gothic sensibility, and everyone has been uprooted from England and transplanted to the father's hometown of Montreal, life among the Weiss is as crazy-quilted with colours, tastes, flavours, myths, legends, longings, and emotional resonances as a delicatessen window. Jem finds refuge in her brother Jude:

> Jude and I are only fifteen months apart, and in spite of ourselves, I guess, we have a twin mentality, which time and distance cannot take away.... I have doubts about many things but I am absolutely sure that I was born out of love, despite my affinity for wartime.
>
> Jude and I were steeped in World War II, although we were born some fifteen years after it ended. Knowing about the war gave me a sense of distinction, as if I, too, had suffered and overcome, emerging with my own badge of courage.... But what do I know about war? ... In grown-up life, there are few demarcations. It is a great battlefield with constantly shifting fronts, that's how I see it. Where, for instance, do I end and Jude begin? When does childhood end?

Unable to create a sense of herself as bold and courageous as she was as a child, separated from Jude who has become an actual war correspondent, and from the rest of her family who have made lives for themselves in Canada, Jem lives alone in London, sifts through memories, and watches old films: "I have just seen a film which I think is pretty important viewing if you are inclined toward a love encounter with a person who is not a member of your family. Most people are, including some nuns I have known." The film is *Un homme et une femme* from 1966 and it elicits flashbacks to Ben's and Jude's adolescent girlfriends and then to the ways the parents love one another before segueing to a meditation on her "date with Jude" after eight months of separation.

Feed My Dear Dogs is a whopping 502 pages in smaller than usual typeface. Is it too big for itself? John Updike wrote of J. D. Salinger: "the refusal to rest content, the willingness to risk excess on behalf of one's obsessions, is what distinguishes artists from entertainers, and what makes some artists adventurers on behalf of us all." That fits Emma Richler who is following in Salinger's footsteps as much as her father's. "Forgetting is exile. I remember everything. I will not be a stranger in a strange land," Jem says. Like Salinger in his Glass family stories, Emma Richler uses familiar settings and colloquial speech to create a realistic surface that masks a fantasy as rich as myths about return from the underworld or fairy tale escapes from forests and monsters. Readers know and don't know where we are: everything is over-observed, over-the-top, larger than life by being as specific as Cinderella's slipper.

Shoe rules: Do not wear plimsolls outdoors. Even in sports. Do not wear Clarks Commandos indoors. Do not wear indoor shoes in gym (unless you have forgotten your plimsolls) and definitely not outdoors where they will get ruined and become perplexing, unfit for indoors or out. Nowhere shoes. If you have the wrong shoes, a nun will get flustered and usually call upon Mean Nun to sort out the bad situation of the wrong shoes. Mean Nun has an eye out for crime.

Dogs surpasses Mary McCarthy's *Memories of a Catholic Girlhood* in the passion of its summoning up of a life shaped by convent school. What one reviewer called "over-layered clutter" in the text is in fact controlled patterns of literary allusion — *Le petit prince*, Sherlock Holmes, *Oliver Twist*, Torah, *The Wizard of Oz*, *The Lives of the Saints*, *Ben Hur*, *Le Morte d'Arthur*, Blake, Shakespeare, Shackleton among others — articulated by Jem as jokes, facts, dialogues, tags, aphorisms, quotations. They're there to catapult readers beyond pieties about family values and the reduction of feminism to reaction to victimization. Jude implores her "to stop making everything to do with us ... the Weiss family are not the world ... you can't stay in your family forever." Emma Richler made her way out of her family and into the world as an actor in theatre, film, television drama, and BBC radio before taking up her father's business. Does her indebtedness to Kafka come from him or through Salinger or through her own reading? Does it matter when she turns the Kafkaesque into something inextricably female?

~

RICK SALUTIN

The Womanizer (2002)

Rick Salutin has become so adept, incisive, and skilled at eviscerating incivility-as-default-setting-neo-con-nonsense on the Op-Ed of *The Globe and Mail* that it's easy to forget that the best columnist in the country is also a novelist and playwright. Salutin won the *Books in Canada* First Novel Award in 1988 for *A Man of Little Faith* (long out of print but deserving a reissue given the current disintegration of political pluralism in Israel) whose protagonist's ironic position as a Jewish religious educator makes him as extraordinary and lovable as any character in Canadian literature.

Max, the title character of *The Womanizer*, is a "Casanova with a guilty conscience, which is no Casanova at all" as one of his more than 150 lovers ruefully admits. There's little plot — just anonymous narration of Max's sexual exploits with interpolations from the more important of his lovers. What's important is the chronicling of five decades of shifting attitudes among men and women against a political and philosophical background as the reader tries to understand Max and Max seeks to understand gender and generational shifts through an exegesis of desire. Max is a walker in the city and his turf is

Toronto's Euclid Avenue in Little Italy as it gets gentrified. Max likes Euclid for these associations:

> Greece, democracy, reason, science; unlike the many streets in the area that recall Olde Englande (Markham) or a cabinet minister from the Napoleonic Wars (Palmerston). Euclid, now there was a numbers man from an era when quantification didn't exclude moral valuation.

The Womanizer is never all about him. He wants to understand everything happening around him but not exclusively to him. Max's mind is as capacious and freewheeling as his sexual appetite: only in the final chapter and only with skepticism does he embrace the smaller world of a wife and a son. Before that happens, readers get a crash course in mindsets from the fifties to the nineties in Toronto, London, and Paris. According to some observers of the Toronto media scene, the novel is "a thinly disguised autobiographical work." Maybe so, but there's much to be gained in reading it as a neo-Proustian *roman à these* rather than a Philip Roth-like *roman à clef*: to get past the whiff of stale scandal, keep in mind this bit of critical advice from Salutin's column of January 30, 2009:

> Blinding moments of insight often come in asides, parentheses or (among academics) footnotes; what seems overbold gets slipped past fast.

~⌒

KEATH FRASER

Popular Anatomy (1995)

Popular Anatomy won the Chapters/*Books in Canada* First Novel Award and was hailed by the judges as a "grand, erudite, complex, passionate, cerebral, multi-layered, rewarding book." Surprisingly, it sold extremely well for a couple of years before becoming more talked about than read: it is outsize — nearly six hundred pages and weird. For Fraser, "good fiction is common knowledge uncommonly held." By that, he means among other things (and with Fraser as with *Tristram Shandy*, one is always in the midst of many *other* things):

> Illusion creates the uncommonness. I suppose you could say this illusion becomes unimportant when the common knowledge is common. Untransformed by any illusion or magic. Journalism? Nothing the matter with good journalism, and I love essays. But since we're talking about fiction maybe it's worth being obvious and mentioning that dubious fiction lacks magic. It's genetically predictable.... I do know whenever I'm trying to deploy uncommon knowledge — examining the nuances of homoeopathy or the lines of Nazca, a baritone's technique or a Club Med's routine — it takes me a long time to ensure this knowledge, such as it is, arises from a character's perception and not mine, that it isn't literary or obviously mugged up.... God may be in the details, but the way to heaven depends on how these details are shaped by narrative.... For the novelist, minding his own business is really listening to everyone else's illusions, as a way to arrive at some illusive and elusive truth. A coherence, if you like, a vision or glimpse of something larger than self.

Popular Anatomy is composed of three interconnected "books" — *Against Nature, The Life of a Tuxedo, Bones* — that span three centuries (including the late twenty-first) but centre on a four year period in the recessionary/inflationary 1980s in Vancouver and the lives of Dwight Irving, owner of Herodotus Travel and husband of Reesa Potts, a TV personality; their chiropractic housemate Bartlett Day; and Aloysius, Dwight's punk rock foster-charge from the streets of Bombay. Fraser says:

> I had become determined to explore what I believed fiction to be, which was popular anatomy of no less than the world. I wanted to know

this world to its bones.... I've always been stunned by the variety of the world — both man-made and natural — by the endless possibilities of beginnings. In this way I've never really grown up. In middle age a sense of wonder is a little naive and often suspect. But I think I also have an abiding elegiac sense.... I [keep] Proust's little dictum in mind: "We must never be afraid to go too far, because the truth lies beyond." ... I think Oscar Wilde was very thoughtless not to have said that art is the tip one leaves behind for the meal one makes of life.

Popular Anatomy is a spendthrift's tip and one even more attuned to the economic crises of the present than to Vancouver's real estate boom years.

In 2002, Fraser published *The Voice Gallery: Travels with a Glass Throat*. For most of his literary life, Keath Fraser's speech was strangulated and nearly unintelligible — the result of *spasmodic dysphonia*, a misfiring of the vocal chords caused by faulty transmitters in the brain and not, as he'd been told for twenty years, psychosomatic. Recovering a more or less normal speaking voice with botox injections, Fraser travelled to New Zealand, Australia, South Africa, Great Britain, Ireland, the US, India, and Sri Lanka collecting stories of fellow sufferers, social outcasts who lost careers and spouses, endured depression, quackery, and electric shock therapy and who remain terrified of everyday conversation and social situations. Fraser's ear for voices — not only those of the similarly afflicted but also the cadences of singers, voice teachers, and actors — and playfulness as a traveller provide both insights into the magnificence of oral communication and open new avenues into the pun-filled, teasing, bouncy wordscape of his fiction. If *Popular Anatomy* seems too daunting an introduction to one of our most intelligent writers, try *Thirteen Ways of Listening to a Stranger: The Best Stories of Keath Fraser* (2005).

~⌒

DARREN GREER

Still Life with June (2003)

In a contemporary Ottawa rendered socially unresponsive by corporate greed in bed with government and haunted by AIDS, Cameron lives downtown with a Humane Society tabby on Lime Street above the Blue Moon, a Filipino grocery store, and works at "the Sally Ann Cocaine Corral" (a.k.a. the Salvation Army Drug and Alcohol Treatment Centre). He's gay, thirty, and his hairline is receding half an inch every six months: he figures he'll be "bald as a hard-boiled egg" by forty. More a "story thief" than the writer he aspires to be, Cameron noses his way into confidential client files, attends a weekly writing group at a big box bookstore, cruises gay bars in search of the saddest stories of the saddest boys, earns an extra one hundred dollars a week by spying on the comings and goings of his upstairs cokehead neighbour at the behest of the guy's sister, and visits June on his days off. June has Down's syndrome complicated by Becker's muscular dystrophy and is a long-term resident of a home operated by the Sisters Who Gave Good Hope. In order to obtain visiting privileges and gain access to medical records that provide more stolen stories, Cameron claims to be her brother Darrell, a former inmate of the Cocaine Corral.

What's compelling in all of this is Greer's position that "nobody is who they say they are" and his construction of a novel as 217 fragments that range from a single sentence to a couple of pages that include emails, stolen stories, imaginary ones, spy reports, lists, and vignettes of his encounters with June. *Still Life with June* is a story you've never read before told in a voice more acerbic and poignant than you've ever heard unless you cruise gay bars and encounter more bad stories than good sex (or so I've been told by people who do).

∽

ANNALS OF OURLIT V

DARREN GREER'S

Strange Ghosts (2006)

Still Life with June attracted the minor ReLit Award, a listing among *NOW* magazine's "10 Best Books of the Year," and a couple of the dumbest book reviews of recent years. Greer's essays, *Strange Ghosts* (2006), ought to have attracted the notice of the Taylor Prize and the jurors of the Governor General's Literary Award for Non-fiction.

The best of the sixteen essays speak publicly about the private matters hinted at in *Still Life*: like Cameron, his fictional protagonist, Darren Greer is gay, HIV-positive, and intimately acquainted with drug and alcohol rehabilitation centres, but coke-free: he's also joyously alive, vibrant. Greer exults in craft and constructs a compulsive, appealing mix of memoir, travelogue, polemics, politics, and aesthetics that covers a lot of geographical, artistic, and emotional territory: Paris, Baghdad, Venice, Bangkok, New York, Ottawa, Toronto, Tennessee Williams' novel *Moise and the World*, Felix Partz of General Idea, Marcel Duchamp, Oscar Wilde, his own novels and plays, growing up gay in Greenfield, Nova Scotia with a non-accepting father, dealing with addictions, coping with being HIV-positive, bonding with cats, dogs, lovers, baseball fans. When Greer is writing at the height of his skill, as in "Remembering Felix Partz," he stuns:

> I chose to stay in treatment, despite the HIV diagnosis. A few weeks later, I found myself, on a Sunday afternoon, in the National Gallery of Canada once again, looking at one particular exhibit. That was the year Felix Partz and the Canadian art-making team General Idea placed three gigantic AZT capsules on the floor of one room of the gallery. On the walls of the room were glued smaller replicas of the capsules —

they were about the size of footballs, dissected and arranged in the pattern of days in the month on a calendrical page — one page of capsules for each month of the year. There had been some public furor about the cost of this exhibit. I agreed the first time I saw it. I might have been gay, but I didn't think much about AIDS then. Half a million dollars for this? This time, however, things were different. My doctor had started me on a regimen of AZT. I stood in that room of giant capsules and cried. I got it. Boy, did I get it. Modern art had spoken to me, in an awfully narrow, shared band of experience — not one that everyone would want to share.

Greer creates hilarious, redemptive examinations of lost, out-of-kilter characters whose lives offer glimpses into their notions of paradise. He's smart enough to know when to be ironic and when to play it straight. At this writing, his demons have gotten the better of him. Fingers crossed for him making it back, strengthened not diminished by his ordeals.

COLIN McADAM

Some Great Thing (2004)

What do you need to know about the writer before you pick up a first novel? Not much, usually. So many fiction writers begin their careers knowing little other than themselves and their family mythology, and then show rather than tell dysfunctionality in unambitious prose. What you get on the page is pretty much who you find lurking behind it. Not here. If you didn't discover from the cover copy that McAdam is the son of a Canadian diplomat, has lived in Hong Kong, Denmark, England, and Barbados as well as studied at the University of Toronto and McGill and holds a Ph.D. in English literature from Cambridge University, you wouldn't guess it from the first hundred pages of *Some Great Thing* as Jerry McGuinty is telling his story. We could be in any doughnut shop in this country any morning of the week when any self-made man with a pickup truck parked outside is motor-mouthing his way through a profanity-laced success story for any audience he can find:

> Thirteen neighbourhoods, five thousand roofs, thirty thousand outside walls, and a rock-hard pair of hands. That is what I have built. I have laid iron, I have laid iron mesh, I have breathed more iron filings than the men who built the railroads. And I have plastered ... and I am the best.... I own my own company. I have heard and told 10,000 filthy jokes.... When I was in the middle of it I didn't realize what I was in the middle of. It took me a few years, a few sleepless smelly years, to realize it was the greatest boom this land has ever seen.... We couldn't help but make a fortune.

If McAdam's debut contained nothing but this hyper-realistic and rueful tale of a plasterer turned developer who is devoted to creating suburban neighbourhoods and filling them with quality houses, it would still be special:

I have missed more nails than you have opportunities, and I haven't missed a nail in thirty-one years. Frostbite has whitened both my earlobes and sunburn has turned my forearms to suede. Before steel soles, I stepped on five nails and after hard hats I missed death twice.

But alongside McGuinty's, there's another story from further up Ottawa's social scale: Simon Struthers is the son of an MP, a career civil servant with the National Capital Division, the federal agency responsible for planning Canada's capital, a developer's worst nightmare. Simon's name carries weight but inspires distrust: He knows success "in the public service was achieved by saying nothing to the right people" and "true power ... was not just in a name, but in one's knowledge of one's colleagues." As Simon gets to know his colleagues (and his knowledge of the women among them is as carnal as he can persuade them to be astride his desk) and exercises bureaucracy-run-wild power over land use in the name of heritage and culture through "the memo, the oldest and noblest form of official advice," his story intersects with McGuinty's. Both spiral to unpredictable endings.

Beware — there's a false start that makes the first twenty pages dispensable and there are *longeurs* in Struther's amatory adventures but *Some Great Thing* is smart, wickedly funny, and McGuinty is as oddly endearing as Richler's Barney Panofsky: hard-handed, heavy-hearted men (and the women who love them) are going to enjoy his madly energetic company.

~

ANDRÉ ALEXIS

Asylum (2008)

If you listened to *Skylarking*, novelist and playwright André Alexis's Sunday-afternoon CBC Radio 2 show before its cancellation, you soon learned that his taste in storytelling and music is sly, playful, and appealing in the quirkiness, unlikeliness, and outright oddity of its juxtapositions. What holds it all together is the host's geniality in fooling around — "scuffing," he calls it — and his dance to his own drummers. He never misses a beat as he brings it all back home with Dylan rubbing shoulders with Dante and the Ramones roughing it up with Ravel.

In Alexis's three published fictions for adults (he's also a playwright and children's author) — *Despair and Other Stories of Ottawa* (1994), *Childhood* (1998), and *Asylum* (2008) — home is forever Ottawa. In *Childhood*, a debut that is widely regarded as one of the most accomplished first novels of the past quarter century, Thomas MacMillan is out of touch with himself and with much of the world but he is enamoured with Ottawa:

> ... there are two strands of the city in my imagination. There's the city I walk in: the smell of summer on MacLaren as I pass Dundonald Park and hear the trees whisper ... an inch of snow on the black railing beside the canal ... inside the old Elgin Cinema down to the front row.... Then there's the city I negotiate in dreams and daydreams. They aren't entirely distinct, of course. Ottawa feeds the city of my dreams, and the city of my dreams is a dimension of the city itself.

In *Asylum*, a decade-in-the-making second novel, Ottawa is a city seriously off-kilter and out-of-touch, as both daydream and nightmare asylum.

It's 2003, and Mark, the narrator, is living in Italy at Santa Maddalena, a Gregorian monastery. Monastic life has been good for him: he wakes early and spends his days gardening, beekeeping, churning butter, praying, meditating, worshipping, reading, and translating German texts before early evening bedtime. Suddenly, after fourteen years away from his birthplace, Mark's feelings shift: he longs for Ottawa with heartfelt anguish, not mere nostalgia. Fra Phillipo, his spiritual adviser, urges him to drown his memories in more work, deeper prayer, but Mark chooses instead "to meet them head-on, to write them down, faithfully for as long as it takes."

Mark takes a year and "three Hilroy notebooks (blue, red, blue)" to work his way forward from 1983 through two decades, filling lined pages with "yearnings, losses, bereavement, and changes of fortune" that recreate "the shuttle and shunt of various lives." In doing so, he describes his own soul, the inner life that is "both everywhere and nowhere" in the lines of Rilke that close the book:

> He who has no house will not build one now.
> He who is alone will be alone for some time,
> Will be wakeful, will read, will write long letters ...

Mark is neither poet nor conventional memoirist: life at the monastery has erased the context of his last years in Ottawa, and he realizes that he must invent as much as he remembers if he is to get beyond "nothing but detail, detail, fact and detail." The schoolboy notebooks transmute into a novel of a kind now out of fashion except among those who still read Proust, Flaubert, Joyce, and Henry James as if they were our contemporaries: thoughts and emotions trump external action. Such Edwardian novels of character and ideas need to be wordy and aren't served by the Creative Writing 101 mantra of "show, don't tell." Looking backward to late-nineteenth-century narrative traditions (formal diction, Latinate vocabulary, and a penchant for classical allusions), Mark acknowledges twentieth-century stylistic conventions only through European cinema's "voiceover." Through his protagonist, Alexis steps boldly forward to a time when the force of literary fiction might be less hobbled by Planet Holly-wood "values" and academic "correctness."

At odds with family and contemporaries because he "thought too much ... wondered about every little thing," Mark, in his mid-twenties during the Mulroney years, lives alone, works in a bookstore, and centres his social life on the Fortnightly Club, a group that meets to discuss philosophy and ideas. They're assorted civil servants, academics, and business people under the informal direction of Professor Walter Barnes, a sociologist and man of many women who is currently at the end of an affair with a member whose husband has his suspicions. At the heart of the group, and Mark's storytelling, is Franklin Dupuis, an ideologue and a strong supporter of the Mulroney government. As Mark interweaves their stories, he struggles to reveal both the higher motives and baser betrayals in the lives they're leading inside and outside the club.

This is all much more compulsively readable than even the comic possibilities suggested by the main plot device, Franklin's attempts to persuade the Mulroney cabinet to build a new federal prison according to the precepts of classical architecture, on the grounds that prisoners can best be reformed by "the idea of order" — a social experiment drenched in an idealism not much in evidence in either the Prime Minister or his ministers. Much of what makes *Asylum* dryly humorous is the contrast between Mark's inflated high-Tory rhetoric and the reality of the Conservative regime of the Mulroney years. Alongside sexual and financial shenanigans of several sorts, there's a brilliantly executed scene in which a disgraced cabinet minister submits his resignation to the Great Muldoon himself.

Asylum is conjured from the same aesthetic intelligence as *Childhood* (the character Henry Wing appears in both), but the pattern is more intricate, the vision fuller, deeper, as Alexis continues the serious writer's magical business of making it possible for readers to lose themselves and find themselves in another's words — "losing and finding," as Mark says, "being the heart of whatever the journey of this life is." In his review of *Childhood*, Neil Bissoondath noted that the brilliance of Alexis's writing is that "it examines lives in ways so subtle that they defy analysis — not that they cannot be analyzed ... but that to analyze them is to do an injustice to that subtlety" and elegant comedy.

～

AUSTIN CLARKE

The Polished Hoe (2002), *More* (2008)

The Polished Hoe (2002)

Austin Clarke is uncompromising: He assumes readers are literate, acquainted with Greek and Latin classics, and holds fast to Mark Twain's dictum that schooling should never get in the way of education. He understands that *eros* begins with a love of human skin and requires mouths that are neither polite nor

politically "corrected." In quality of prose, depth of humanity, acuteness of sexual awareness, importance of the political issues, social range, and maturity of
vision, Austin Clarke's collected works (sixteen books prior to *The Polished Hoe*)
outstrip the *ouevres* of the late Timothy Findley or Robertson Davies by a country mile: he's in the front row of our living novelists alongside Josef Škvorecký.

The Polished Hoe (the *double entendre* intentional) is a conversation between
two characters that alters their present and perceptions of the past. It's 1952 in
the fictional West Indian island of Bimshire and we're eavesdropping on Miss
Mary Gertrude Mathilda Paul as she gives her statement regarding the murder
of Mr. Bellfeels to Crown Sergeant Percy DaCosta Benjamin Stuart. Mary
Mathilda has known Sergeant Percy all her life. They grew up together but, as
adults, they have only ever observed one another at a distance, kept apart by the
fact that Mary Mathilda was the mistress of Bellfeels, their village's plantation
manager, for over thirty years. She is also the mother of Wilberforce Bellfeels,
an Oxbridge-educated doctor of tropical medicine, who is Mr. Bellfeels's only
son and has been accepted as such within Bimshire society.

Conversation between the overlord's kept woman and the village's policeman
encompasses the crime that has been committed as well as a half-century of race
and gender relationships on Bimshire. They talk all through the night and Clarke
reports it in something very like real time. Read *The Polished Hoe* at roughly
the speed of actual speech and spend at least fifteen hours over it or you'll miss
not just the musicality of the Bimshire vernacular but also the delicacy of the
relationship between this "loose" woman and this "upright" man. The overall
effect is less like reading a novel — even such a novel as James Joyce's *Ulysses* —
as it is to listening to an uncut production of Eugene O'Neill's *Mourning Becomes
Electra*.

Mary Mathilda owes something to Joyce's Molly Bloom and something to
Homer's Penelope but she's in a direct line of descent from Aeschylus and the
women of his *Oresteia* — Clytemnestra, Cassandra, Electra, and the Furies. Like
O'Neill before him, Clarke brings elements of a terrible ancient myth to
the New World and makes of it something historical, stunning, heart-rending
and so unnerving that to read it is to be morally challenged by a vision of evil
we have never before encountered in such a mask and an ideal of goodness we

thought beyond human embracing. *The Polished Hoe* is both a prologue to all else that Austin Clarke has written and the beginning of a greater summing-up. It's an extraordinary and thoroughly compelling tragedy of Shakespearean scope and poetic intensity wrapped within a metaphorical history of slavery in the West Indies.

More (2008)

When Idora Morrison learns of her son, BJ's, involvement in crime and gang warfare, she recoils from a world that stretches from Cabbagetown to Kensington Market (and not much further) and unwinds her life in a spiral of words spoken within the walls of her basement apartment over four days and nights. Idora's story is of present-day Toronto as a Waspish enclave of genteel racism against which women of colour struggle day after day to find the strength to live with dignity and courage. Once again, Clarke expects readers to adjust to the pace of lived experience. Time and memory move more quickly here than in *Hoe* but only barely as he plays out and reels in plotlines with the nonchalance of a fisherman with eternity in his hands.

On a wintry Thursday morning, Idora finds herself unable to get up and go to work one more time. Under bedclothes, neither her body nor mind find rest: she feels overwhelmed by fellow commuters who turn away from her skin, her deadbeat husband, Bertram, who rejects her deeper substance, and television and newspapers that rebuff BJ, the flesh of her flesh, and all other young black fatherless men as dead-end dunderheads whose own mothers live in fear of the guns that define their status and the shootings that rend their own communities. Sonnet L'Abbé wrote in her review in *The Globe and Mail*,

> It is in Clarke's ability to capture the interior tumult of a strong mind alone, alive, grasping at threads of sanity and virtue when all other resources of cultural and social capital are closed to her, that we feel the powerful fit of Clarke's poetic monologue to the mundane reality of racialized urban existence. In the midst of her waking nightmare, Idora steers herself again and again toward her desire to speak at her church

and her moments of satisfaction in sensual pleasures. Her Thursday-to-Sunday journey is an internal, personal Triduum, beginning with betrayal and agony in her little garden, to walks through Toronto bearing her many crosses, to a bloody, strangely joyful resurrection.

~⌒

TOMSON HIGHWAY

Kiss of the Fur Queen (1998)

In 1951, Abraham Okimasis, a Cree from northern Manitoba, wins a World Championship Dog Derby. Part of his prize for being the world's best dogsledder is a kiss from the young white Fur Queen, winner of a Northern beauty pageant. The father's touch of lips with white culture stains the lives of his sons — Champion and Ooneemeetoo Okimasis are soon taken from their family and placed in a residential school in Manitoba. Forbidden use of their mother tongue and renamed Jeremiah and Gabriel, the boys are de-cultured, re-educated, and sexually abused by Catholic priests. Despite all this (and Highway spares no details), the brothers place themselves under the protection of a trickster-like mythologized Fur Queen who helps them embrace white, European artistic traditions without rejecting Native influences.

Like his creator, Jeremiah is drawn to the piano, and the art of the concert pianist while Gabriel (like Tomson Highway's late brother Rene) leaps and bounds into the world of contemporary dance and choreography. Both are openly gay but only Gabriel becomes HIV positive and is drawn into the horrors of AIDS when treatment and life expectancy wasn't as it is now.

Given the rawness of material and underlying autobiographical reality of the lives these brothers live, *Kiss of the Fur Queen* dances, sings, breaks your heart, and renews your gratitude to be alive and capable of reading it with its utterly distinctive fusion of European tragedy and Cree humour. Interviewed in 1998, Tomson Highway said, "I didn't have a choice. I had to write this book. It came screaming out because this story needed desperately to be told. Writing it hit me hard in terms of my health. So I went to a medicine man who helped me defeat the monster. We lanced the boil and cured the illness." He also said:

> There's a major fault in Western society. It makes room for only one god, and in only one gender. There's no balance, no co-existence, no partnership. We must restore the idea of Earth as mother. My brother's death — all these diseases like AIDS — are just a reflection of what we're doing to the Earth, of what we're doing to women. We must restore the balance or reap the consequences. In *Kiss of the Fur Queen*, I try to restore the goddess to her rightful place. It's the only way I can make a contribution to change.

~

THOMAS KING

Green Grass, Running Water (1993)

How's this for a plot device? Four very old Indians — called Ishmael, Hawkeye, Robinson Crusoe, and the Lone Ranger — escape from a mental hospital and insinuate themselves into the lives of five members of a Canadian Blackfoot clan — Uncle Eli Stands Alone, Charlie Looking Bear, Alberta Frank, Lionel Red Dog, and his sister Latisha. The old men are very, very old — they might be the last of the Indians interned at Fort Marion in Florida in the nineteenth century or, maybe, the first human beings of their tribe's creation myths — and difficult to keep institutionalized. They've escaped captivity thirty-seven times and each breakout coincided with a man-made or natural catastrophe: the stock market crash of 1929 or the eruption of Mount St. Helens, for instance. Uncle Eli Stands Alone is a former university professor who is determined to prevent a damming of a river on Indian land and Charlie Looking Bear is a lawyer working for the other side in the dispute. Alberta Frank, who wants a baby, dates both of them but wants more than sperm donation.

This barely hints at the complex stories told and the good humour pervading a melange of traditional realism, mythopoetic surrealism, literary gamesmanship, slapstick, stand-up improv in a reinvention of the world that fuses the Book of Genesis with oral traditions.

"Everybody makes mistakes," the Lone Ranger says.
"Best not to make them with stories," Ishmael replies.

Thomas King doesn't.

Son of a Greek mother and a Cherokee father, King was born in California, educated in Utah, worked in Australia, and has lived in Canada for most of his adult life. He's a professor of Native American studies, a photojournalist, anthologist, novelist, storyteller, children's writer, host of CBC Radio's *The Dead Dog Café*, film director, and erstwhile NDP candidate for Guelph. *Green Grass, Running Water* amazes and delights wherever you open it up.

~⌒

BRIAN MOORE

Black Robe (1985)

If you've never seen Bruce Beresford's 1991 film adaptation or it isn't fresh in your memory, rent the DVD: the movie has its own virtues (especially Lothaire Bluteau in the lead) but Moore wrote the screenplay in a way that complements (while excluding much of the obscene bantering) and visually completes a book that is radically unlike most "historical fiction." More alien than SF portraits of extraterrestrial cultures, there's a sense in which it can be described as *A Clockwork Orange* retrofitted to the seventeenth century.

Father Laforgue, a French Jesuit priest, and his young companion travel upriver in late fall with Algonquins, across what is now Quebec, to find a distant mission in a Huron village. Their escorts desert them, under the impression that Laforgue is a demon, and return only to be captured by a party of Iroquois. The Algonkian (friendly) and Iroquois (unfriendly) ways of life are frighteningly unlike our modern Western culture that descends from France and Christianity. Incomprehension of customs and thinking is mutual and much harder to overcome than languages (the film includes authentic dialogue in Cree, English, Mohawk, Algonquin, and Latin).

Inspired by one of Graham Greene's essays, Moore draws his descriptions from the *Relations*, the actual letters the Jesuits sent back to their superiors in France. Greene's concision is always close to Moore's fingertips:

> The day passed. The sun, high in the sky, dipped until it barely cleared the tops of the trees. A wind rippled the water into waves, a wind which numbed Laforgue's cheeks. He remembered what Father Bourque had told him of a second false summer which came in mid-October, bringing a few days of heat at the end of the autumnal season. That false summer was ending. Winter was near.

Moore does a particularly fine job of balancing distinct spiritual worlds: the *dieu* to whom Laforgue prays is no less plausible for much that happens to him than a sorcerer or chance. The prolonged tortures and ritual cannibalism of the Iroquois makes "the violence in the book ... shocking, more graphic than anything in Cormac McCarthy" as Colm Tóibín and Carmen Callil note in *The 200 Best Novels in English since 1950*.

The question of crumbling ideals is central to the fiction of Brian Moore. How his characters respond to it makes him as relevant in post-Bush America as ever in his lifetime. When challenged to our core, do we abandon principles or do we, as Father Laforgue does, open ourselves to the possibility that in order to move on and live by the essence of what those ideals are really all about, we must be willing to be change just as strongly as we desire to change the world? Moore once said (in an interview quoted by *The Irish Post* in its obituary of January 23, 1999):

> I discovered when I was writing novels that I was very interested in people who believe in something. All of us when we're young want to have some ideal in life which makes it worth doing what we're doing. For most of us we're disappointed, disillusioned at a fairly early age, but I find that if you write about a political loss of belief in 1960, by 1990 no one will remember what it was all about, whereas if I write about a loss of religious belief, people will identify with that and that's probably the main reason I do it.

~

FRED STENSON

Lightning (2003)

Lightning, Fred Stenson's fourth novel, squeezed between *The Trade* (2000) — nominated for the Giller and the IMPAC Dublin — and the Governor General's shortlisted *The Great Karoo* (2008), received less attention than either. That's a shame because it's more substantial than first appears. I'd completely overlooked it until Marina Endicott recommended it.

It's 1881 and cowboys herd cattle over vast spreads from Texas to Alberta. Settlements are few, far between, and mostly housed under canvas. Cheyenne, for instance, is "proof almost anything can be done in a tent. Hotel tents, whore tents, drinking tents, food tents. Whatever there was of Cheyenne at the beginning of the day, there would be more by day's end." Doc Windham is a vertically challenged, forty-year-old Texan on a drive from Dillon, Montana to Cochrane in what will become Alberta. A peculiar sort — his interests include phrenology, Walt Whitman, Dickens's *Great Expectations*, the Masons, reading the philosopher Seneca in Latin, the new sport of bowling — Doc's a worrier with problems worth losing sleep over. Cattle are prone to stampede, other cowboys to fits of sulkiness and surliness, and Doc is being stalked by Ivan Overcross, a crazed killer with less than a full head thanks to one of Doc's rare shootouts. Doc's more talker than gunslinger.

Lightning's narrative shifts between the 1881 cattle drive and Doc's life fifteen years earlier when he travelled town to town with a hustler named Pearl and discovered religion in the form of the Masons. Although violence and brutality flare up, this is the Wild West as reflected by tamer Canadian history and Stenson isn't a genre-writer although he can impersonate one when it suits him. Here his purpose is carrying forward what he began in *The Trade* and "write between the known lines" by excluding the religiosity that has misshaped the telling of our stories from the Jesuit *Relations* to Rudy Wiebe. Stenson's Canada isn't God's Country and never was but it doesn't lack moral fibre and common decency. Doc Windham is Everyman (not Pilgrim) on a quest that's never as simple as Disney or evangelical Christianity make it out to be and more spiritual than either imagine. David Adams Richards regards Fred Stenson as "one of Canada's greatest living writers." He's also one of our most subversive.

∽

GUY VANDERHAEGHE

The Last Crossing (2002), *The Englishman's Boy* (1996)

The Last Crossing (2002)

If you're prairie-born and a guy of Guy Vanderhaeghe's (b. 1951) generation, chances are that as you hurtled through *The Last Crossing* (2002), you might have overlooked the fact that it is a lot more than a wonderful whoop-it-up Western "history" of the kind movies and television gave us when we learned to "talk slow, talk low, and don't say too much" watching John Wayne in *The Searchers* and Clint Eastwood in *Rawhide*. *The Last Crossing* isn't just a rattling good page-turner, it's a gem of a book, one of the best Canadian novels of the last half-century, and Vanderhaeghe's masterpiece. It's also a story that more urban and urbane, more sensitive (male or female) partners and friends are just as likely to be enthralled by as we are but for somewhat different reasons. The first person to sing its praises within earshot was Barbara Gowdy, the most unfailingly honest writer in this country. Before it had been reviewed anywhere, she spoke to me of its mastery of wrapping stories within stories and its tragic sense of female memory and male forgetfulness.

What Gowdy praised in it was amplified by Annie Proulx (author of numerous Wyoming stories including the one that became *Brokeback Mountain*) in her publication day review for *The Globe and Mail* (September 26, 2002). Calling it "a feast of a book ... *The Last Crossing* is like a *rijsttafel* of highly seasoned main dishes with innumerable saucers and side-plates of toothsome relishes," Proulx makes the case for sensual, emotionally intelligent, dominantly *theatrical* reasons for being enthralled by *The Last Crossing*. Proulx realizes that "Characters appear in scenes as on a stage. The cast is packed with sharply drawn cameos and caricatures of frontier and English types." What does Proulx mean by *stage characters* in "cameos and caricatures"? Just this: Vanderhaeghe's tale provides the proscenium upon which several quests twist and turn and intertwine as farce, as comedy, and as tragedy by travelling players in a road show. The major performers are Charles Gaunt and his elder brother Addington as they search for Simon, their missing brother, in 1871 in the North American Midwest — modern-day Montana, Saskatchewan, and Alberta — in the company of Custis Straw, Jerry Potts, and Mrs. Lucy Stoveall (whose sister's fatal rape provides as much of the initial narrative impulse as Simon's disappearance). And what caricatures these characters are! Proulx sums up Charles Gaunt as "a cynical portrait painter with a streak of kindness"; Addington as "a syphilitic egoist with a habit of stealing women's garments"; Simon as "credulous and vulnerable (or, according to Addington, a 'little, pecksniffing, pious ass')"; Lucy as "handsome but tough ... vengeful"; Custis as a "decent horse-trader"; Caleb Ayto as a "horrible, vulgar American" newspaper reporter who becomes Addington Gaunt's sycophant, intent on writing a book about the audacious Addington as "a master of martial arts." Cameos are played by "the loathsome Kelso brothers ... the obsessive con-man preacher Witherspoon; trading post factors; Talks Different, the Crow who rescues Simon; Miss Venables, a believer in romantic chivalry; various hard cases, and barflies; Crows and Piegans; military men; soiled doves." As a cast of theatricals, they don't speak a common parlance: their tongues wag and wiggle and stick in cheeks in idioms and invectives as sonically textured as John Ford's classic western "soundscapes" as Vanderhaeghe sometimes reconstructs, sometimes invents both patois and frontier talk of the late nineteenth century that switch back and forth from cultivated English characters to American wranglers to Scots-Canadian settlers to his Yankee newsman.

Theatrical as it is, *The Last Crossing* won't be easy to transfer to the screen, like Vanderhaeghe's big-budget miniseries *The Englishman's Boy*, without enormous loss of complexity: Whenever the *mise en scène* starts to become overly familiar and starts tipping into the stereotypical, Vanderhaeghe dives and dips between first and third-person narratives, flops and flips between present tense and flashbacks in ways that surprise and delight by presenting fresh opportunities for humour and comedy. Some of this novel's best moments are based upon the manipulation of metaphor. Proulx particularly likes Oxford being said to have "ripened more mush-headed fruit than the rest of England's orchards put together," a would-be dandy observed "wearing a white shirt with ratty ruffles like weeviled-out cotton bolls all down its front, a shirt so threadbare you can see his nipples right through the cloth, brown as pennies" and a wagon that laboured with "wheels crusted thickly with mud ... that un-wound in long bandages of greasy clay to the accompaniment of the low groans of the wagon box."

At the end of her review, Proulx wrote, "*The Last Crossing* deserves honours and the widest readership. Guy Vanderhaeghe, one of North America's best writers, is at the top of his form." That view was seconded a week later in the *National Post* (October 3, 2002) by Noah Richler's review headed "Search for the best is over: Guy Vanderhaeghe's *The Last Crossing* is a masterpiece": "What is so utterly remarkable about Vanderhaeghe's novel, what convinces me that it is a masterpiece, is the author's uncanny immersion into this story. And the novel is so consistently vivid, the storytelling so magnificent, that I cannot attribute to it, as is the fashion these days, the moniker 'historical.' Vanderhaeghe's Midwest is no more distant a time and place than McEwan's Dunkirk is in *Atonement*. Better to say that *The Last Crossing* is a novel of the historical present, even if the story is set in what is constitutionally our past." For Richler, Vanderhaeghe's uncanny ability to identify himself and his contemporaries within his frontier characters makes them "formative, Canadian." Our capacity for "understanding them will play no small part in determining just how we see ourselves and get along today." Or, to use the term Richler employs in *This is My Country, What's Yours?* (2006), *The Last Crossing* can and should be read as "psycho-geography" — that is, the transformation of raw landscape into places that have character and exert forces upon people that can, if we're attentive, restore humility and mystery to our lives and transform us.

This way of looking at *The Last Crossing* adds and doesn't subtract from the gut power of a story that can be heard, seen, smelled, felt in the rawness of muscle and the ache of bones as you read Vanderhaeghe's tale of the Gaunt brothers and their followers on the trail from Fort Benton, Montana (where Simon, Charles' twin, was last seen trying to bring religion to the "heathen" Indians) to wherever their guide, Jerry Potts, leads them. Potts (a historical personage, the Piegan-Scot who played an important role in assisting the North West Mounted Police in the clean-up of Fort Whoop-Up) is himself both guide and seeker as he tracks the whereabouts of his estranged Crow wife and their son. Lucy Stoveall forces herself upon their search party as she seeks to avenge her sister by confronting and killing the Kelso brothers who have fled Fort Benton for Saskatchewan. Custis Straw, a man oddly broken and poorly knit back together by the Civil War and its aftermath, follows Lucy, whom he loves, and is followed by his friend Dooley who wants to protect Custis from his excesses of good and bad temper. In Vanderhaeghe's hands, all this tale telling is as intricately plotted and compulsive reading as any Elmore Leonard "Western" with a similar emphasis on dialogue to pinpoint racial and social frictions as each character speaks in character. As in Leonard's novels, as Margaret Atwood noticed, the good cuss differently from the bad. It's a fine distinction because lines between law-abiders and law-breakers aren't altogether firm wherever racial and social injustice prevails.

The Last Crossing found the wider readership Proulx had predicted by hand-selling in independent bookstores, by word of mouth among readers, and then by being selected their favourite novel by CBC Radio's Canada Reads panellists of 2004 just as it was released simultaneously in Britain and the United States. In England, *The Guardian*'s Clive Sinclair compared Vanderhaeghe's "larger than life" characters and ever-twisting plot to such "unputdownables as Rider Haggard's *King Solomon's Mines* and Lionel Davidson's *The Rose of Tibet*" at one end of the scale and a grander mentor at the other — Charles Dickens ("he has Dickens's chutzpah when it comes to coincidences"). As Sinclair points out "one of the great advantages of the [Dickensian] missing sibling plot is that it leaves room for romance. Another is that it makes the picaresque seem necessary rather than arbitrary, gives it a proper structure." Sinclair paid particular attention to the reason why Simon Gaunt is missing:

> He went west with a crooked preacher named Obadiah Witherspoon. Their purpose? To convert the "Red Indians". The reason? Witherspoon's Church of Christian Israel proposes that the Native Americans are in reality a lost tribe of Israel, whose conversion will facilitate the Second Coming.
>
> Vanderhaeghe is not making this up. No less a personage than General Custer was persuaded that "the Indians are the descendants of the tribes of Israel that were led captive into Assyria". Moreover, he had observed that many of the "Indian customs and religious rites closely resemble those of the Israelites". Though Custer is never mentioned in the text, he remains an important off-stage presence; nemesis of the Sioux, the Cheyenne and the Blackfoot, seducer of the Crow, destroyer of the way of life Charles encounters on his first crossing from England in 1871.

For American reviewers, the fictional territory that came quickest to mind was Larry McMurtry's *Lonesome Dove* and the newer and raunchier television series *Deadwood*. It was left to Marina Endicott (another fine writer currently at the top of her form) to place Vanderhaeghe alongside Cormac McCarthy in her online review for *Arts & Opinion*:

> As Cormac McCarthy created a passionate tribute to the frontier between the U.S. and Mexico, Vanderhaeghe is in the process of developing an

equally important "Border" work that looks at the idea of the 49th.... Vanderhaeghe's border lies between old and new world, white and Indian, the love and hatred between brothers, sisters, husband and wife, and particularly the impassable wall between the English and the white North Americans, so briefly removed from England in time but so far removed by landscape.... Vanderhaeghe gives us the nineteenth century, and the distance between that world and ours, in the weakness of the body: the vile ailments and viler medicines of that time.... The desperate remedies, the drink, the ferocity, are not sovereign against this appalling life, but they serve.

Sexuality drenches the book, both hideous and virtuous, lit brighter in the new world under the dazzling sky. But it is darkened, as is every other element of the book, by the harder tin-cut shadows that Charles finds under the new light.... Turned poet in middle age, Charles Gaunt tells a young man, "The praise my verse has won is not due to its excellence as poetry, but rather because of the genuine passion it so awkwardly expresses."

Genuine passion fills this great book, but it is deftly revealed and expressed. It is the authenticity of that passion that makes *The Last Crossing* "the kind of literature that reminds other writers of why they want to create, and convinces readers that the world is a vast and mythic enterprise, larger than our individual crises or triumphs" for Endicott every bit as much as for Proulx, Richler and a host of others.

The Last Crossing unites and unifies in one place all the things that make Guy Vanderhaeghe's vision of life so broad, so deep, so disturbing in its rejection of comfortable answers to the human predicament. In his world, to live is to suffer humiliation — that's the premise from which all else flows: self-protection demands caginess in childhood; distrust, suspicion, sarcasm in adolescence; scorn, disdain, derision in adulthood; and a sense of the ridiculous as fuel for comical inventiveness in old age — especially from males. All appeals to higher authorities — doctors, lawyers, politicians, priests of any and all persuasions (Freudians and Marxists included) — are unreasonable, absurd, futile, and ludicrous because the powerful are always corrupt and corrosive, driven by vanity to sacrifice all vestiges of dignity in the poor and powerless to gratify their own pretentiousness. It's only when this realization takes root, that self-protection can morph into something like salvation.

In his earlier works, Vanderhaeghe, as fiction writer, is very close to Clint Eastwood, as film director, in his fascination with the solitary who live by a simple code, men whose emotional range runs from bad-tempered to elegiac. The differences? Vanderhaeghe is almost always more extravagant in his comedy and more driven to Gothic depictions of grotesque disfigurements of flesh and spirit. As he has matured as an artist, Vanderhaeghe has discovered deeper and deeper reserves of dignity in his heroes: they do not become more powerful, they become more compassionate and as they do so, the world of his writing gets larger and the women within play less passive roles.

The Englishman's Boy (1996)

The Englishman's Boy intertwines fewer narratives than *The Last Crossing*: three stories criss-cross. In Saskatoon in 1953, Harry Vincent, a movie theatre operator, recollects in the present tense his brief career as a Hollywood screenwriter thirty years earlier. Back then, he's sketching in the scenario for a Homeric Western movie of the silent era, an American *Odyssey*. Part of his job is to track down Shorty McAdoo, an old film extra, an "oater" cowboy whose real life adventures include participation in the notorious Cypress Hills Massacre of 1873 when a mixed group of American wolf hunters, American and Canadian whiskey traders, and Métis cargo haulers opened fire on a camp of Nakoda (or Assiniboine) in the Battle Creek valley, slaying twenty-three Nakoda while suffering a single casualty. More outraged by the trespass on sovereignty than by the Nakoda deaths, Prime Minister John A. Macdonald's government created the North West Mounted Police who established dominion in the Cypress Hills by arresting the Americans and putting them on trial. In a judicial decision that set a sad and sorry precedent in the weighing of "red" against "white" deaths within jurisdictions policed by the Mounties, none was convicted. This is just one of the many Canadian "complicities" in the mythologizing of America that dominate the storytelling and subversively satirize it. Disgusted and dismayed by the consequences of his meddling with history while servicing Hollywood's demands during the era of Senator Joseph McCarthy and the Congressional Committee investigating Un-American Activities, Harry Vincent returns to Saskatoon. The joke — and it's a huge one — is that he then spends the rest of his life in a movie theatre, "selling" American dreams.

The Englishman's Boy is more emotionally intelligent than any of Vander-haeghe's earlier writings: its rigorous concern with integrity leaves no room for sentimentality. It's a book you feel in the solar plexus — not the tear ducts. Like his earlier works, it's larded with detail. Vanderhaeghe has rarely left any fragment of his research unused and *The Englishman's Boy* is jam-packed with Hollywood trivia. Here it serves a larger purpose by effectively highlighting the complicity of moviegoers in manufacturing filmdom's deceitful self-portraits. And in doing that, Vanderhaeghe's facts, facts, facts break their tethers and his imagination begins to soar far above the prairies and sail westward to the shoreline of California, making room for broader, deeper discomforts and humiliations as Harry's story builds to its own bloody shootout. Good as it is, *The Englishman's Boy* isn't quite as deft at revealing or expressing the passions that fill it as *The Last Crossing* because it takes fewer sexual gambles and so offers fewer opportunities for both the greatest humiliations and the finest jokes in life.

Guy Vanderhaeghe became one of Mordecai Richler's favourite younger writers early on and it's dead easy to grasp why: in *The Englishman's Boy*, a character speaks for the author when he says, "The truth of small things leads to confidence in the truth of large things." Richler frequently said and wrote that Montreal's St. Urbain Street was "my time, my place, and I have elected myself to get it right." Having learned from his favourite author Samuel Johnson about the truth of small things as the gateway to good behaviour in bad times, Richler understood that the second half of the twentieth century, the sequel to the Holocaust and so much else, required writers to be *honest witnesses* to their times, their places, and the mythologies that rule them if we were ever to get to the larger truths about a century of whopping untruths. In this sense, it's as impossible to imagine *The Englishman's Boy* being written in a world where Richler's *St. Urbain's Horseman* and *Cocksure* don't exist as to try to imagine *The*

Last Crossing in a world bereft of *Solomon Gursky Was Here*. But no matter how much writers like Vanderhaeghe and Richler draw inspiration from older writers, it's competition from contemporaries that keeps them focused on seeing just how good they can get. If *The Last Crossing* is bettered by Vanderhaeghe's next novel (a difficult feat to imagine), Fred Stenson will deserve more than a little credit for goading him on with *The Trade* (2000), *Lightning* (2003), and *The Great Karoo* (2008). Between them, they are not simply challenging preconceptions about the psycho-geography of the West in radical ways, they're subverting the sense of *history* in the historical novel as no one has attempted since Rudy Wiebe wrote *The Temptations of Big Bear* (1973) and *The Scorched-Wood People* (1977) nearly a generation ago. Where both Stenson and Vanderhaeghe surpass Wiebe is in their capacities to combine tragedy, epic, history, and religious fervour with every bit as much creative audacity but without becoming didactic and humourless.

On the last page of *The Last Crossing*, a man at the foot of a staircase "takes one step, then a second, then a third. He lacks the courage to look up during his slow ascent, afraid to see...." Whatever is happening to whoever this is, Vanderhaeghe isn't offering us a self-portrait; he's wide-eyed, he's fast, he's as courageous a male writer as we have.

ANNALS OF OURLIT VI

TWO ATLASES — NOAH RICHLER'S QUEST:

This Is My Country, What's Yours? (2006)

Writing in the *Toronto Star* on November 24, 1990, on the state of Canadian fiction, I noted that "despite indifference in the reading public, inattention in the academic community, governmental and bureaucratic mean-spiritedness in funding of the Canada Council, precarious finances in the publishing industry," wonderful writers kept emerging and important books got printed. I listed some of the English fiction writers who emerged in the eighties, already mattered, and were only beginning to attract the attention they deserved: "Brian Fawcett, M. T. Kelly, Gail Scott, Ann Diamond, Barbara Gowdy, Douglas Glover, Diane Schoemperlen, Nancy Bauer, Wayne Tefs, Peter Behrens, F. G. Paci, J. J. Steinfeld, and Wayne Johnston." What attracted me to these writers more than others of the time was their capacity to write of marginalized places and their inhabitants in cosmopolitan ways that placed their works closer to Josef Škvorecký and Mavis Gallant than to W. O. Mitchell and Margaret Laurence. Another development in the latter half of the eighties had been the emergence of youngish writers such as "Nino Ricci, Sarah Sheard, Steven Heighton and Patrick Roscoe" who were bringing homegrown sensibilities to bear on faraway places without becoming neo-colonialist *romanciers*.

Written just before the GST was introduced on January 1, 1991, I worried about the effects of the new tax on book sales (which had previously been sales-tax exempt) and predicted "fewer fiction titles from fewer publishers sold in many fewer independent bookstores" and fewer translations from the French into English. The all-too-true rumour that month was the next publishing house to collapse in English Canada would be Lester & Orpen Dennys, which had just published François Gravel's *Benito* in its International Fiction List. *Benito* is a droll contemporary fable from Quebec, a kind of book that rarely gets written in English, its nearest relative being Jerzy Kosinski's *Being There*. Thanks to his blankness, others pour out their innermost thoughts to Benito. What makes this more than a pleasant diversion is that Gravel understands that the road from kindness to political consciousness has a million mischievous twists and turns. It seemed to me that the writers I'd mentioned had much in common with Gravel and others on the Lester & Orpen Dennys list in terms of political awareness and literary complexity.

What also had me worried was that the kinds of literary activity these authors espoused would be driven further to the edges of a collapsing marketplace by the emergence of "Harlowquins" (a coinage of Sheila Fischman's, translator of *Benito*) in "honour" of Professor Robert Harlow of UBC's MFA writing program. Harlow was infamous at the time for being one of the two university teachers who'd judged Mordecai Richler's *Solomon Gursky* inferior to *Whale Music*, Paul Quarrington's cover of the life of The Beach Boys' Brian Wilson that won that year's Governor General's Literary Award for Fiction.

Having first espoused Surrealism and then metafiction as the paths for students to follow at UBC, Harlow was now encouraging them to snuffle and root among international headlines, new or old, for storylines to personalize — a project never to be confused with Conrad's, D. H. Lawrence's, and Thomas Mann's characterizing of settings out of which headlines erupt. The "Harlowquin" was represented on 1990s fall fiction list by Doubleday's publication of *Noble Sanctuary* by Scot Morrison, Harlow's protégé, in which a disaffected yuppie real estate salesman in Vancouver meets an exotic woman out jogging and (despite the fact that she is intelligent, highly educated, politically aware, and he is none of these things) they fall in love and he follows her back to a Palestinian refugee camp in Lebanon and makes love to her in the ruins and she gets killed in the general carnage of the civil war. The sufferings of multitudes become a vehicle for self-awareness and elevate puny insights into a picayune life to something as worth considering as the shattered lives of refugees.

Those observations formed the template for the *Atlas of Canadian Literature* I'd already begun to rough out. Ten years later, in the spring of 2000, I finally forwarded a formal proposal to Louise Dennys, who had become head of Knopf Canada. It didn't take much discussion for us to realize that what was needed to do justice to our best authors and their works was beyond our resources — that it was the kind of book that ought to be a companion to a documentary television series along the lines of projects Karen Armstrong was doing on world religions in England, that left to my two hands it would be under-muscled. My *Star* piece of 1990 had opened with the observation that thirty years earlier "all the important novelists and short story writers in Canada could have squeezed into a limousine" and that "these days, they'd have to be shoehorned into a bus." A decade later, the bus was at least an Airbus A320 — a 150-seater.

You can't copyright a title and I've never asked the mutual friend who would know the answer if any part of my Knopf proposal filtered down to Noah Richler. Richler wrote a very different book than I'd imagined — a book for radio's ear not television's eye and one driven by a different ardour and intelligence than mine. Here's the epigraph from Jorges Luis Borges that he chose for *This Is My Country, What's Yours? A Literary Atlas of Canada*:

A man sets out to draw the world. As the years go by, he peoples a space with images of provinces, kingdoms, mountains, bays, ships, islands, fishes, rooms, instruments, stars, horses, and individuals. A short time before he dies, he discovers that the patient labyrinth of lines traces the lineaments of his own face.

Atlas or *Odyssey?* It's difficult not to see something of Homer and Joyce at work here — of Telemachus and Stephen Dedalus, of Odysseus and Leopold Bloom, of a father beholding a son beholding a father, of Noah and Mordecai, of the final stanza of Joyce's "Ecce Puer":

A child is sleeping:
An old man gone.
O, father forsaken,
Forgive your son!

Noah Richler returned to Canada in 1998 from London, England, where he'd been a producer and presenter of BBC radio documentaries for fourteen years. He came back because he knew that Canada was home in a way Britain could never be, echoing what his father had said when *he* returned in 1972. As a younger man, Noah prospected in the Yukon, walked the Prairies as part of a seismic oil exploration crew, laboured in an iron mine in Labrador, stage managed a theatre company in the Rockies, and developed an affinity for all three coasts of Canada's physical margins but especially the northernmost one. At first, he thought he'd rediscover Canada's present and his past by writing a book about what it is to *work* here. Then, after his father died in 2001, it became "a book about the country through the work that storytellers do."

Richler criss-crossed the country for two years and interviewed a hundred authors (from Robert Arthur Alexie through an alphabet of all the usual suspects and numerous unusual ones down to Alissa York) about places and ideas most meaningful in their work. His *Atlas* isn't intended as a reference book but it is excellent for those who want to hear our storytellers in sometimes cantankerous, unpopular, engaged arguments with one another and with Richler (who serves as a curious, critical bystander with ideas of his own) about this country of ours as a place of new beginnings and erasures of the past. Early on, he quotes Jane Urquhart saying, "Here, nobody has explained away the country's magic yet." Richler's achievement is that he conjures the magic and allows the explanations to defeat themselves — including his own attempt to make the unruliness of his project cohere by dividing his book into three metahistorical constructs — The Age of Invention, The Age of Mapping, and The Age of Argument.

> What is it that stories do? We accept that stories reflect the way we see the world back to ourselves, but what if they do more than that? What if stories are not innocent but sometimes aggressive rivals locked in an evolutionary struggle? ... In Canada, the young country, all sorts of story forms vie for our attention. Creation myths and cautionary tales compete with novels and epic stories, and somewhere in this imbroglio the idea of a nation is taking shape.... The novelist acts as conduit and occasionally as seer, a storyteller standing on the cusp of human experience — much as, in the First Nation cultures, the shaman did. The writer occupies a middle space between the world as it is and as it ends up being represented by the work.

Someone still ought to make a television series in which as many of our writers as possible take viewers into the Sundays of their creative lives — the places where they feel at home in this country, starting with one of the essential authors Richler overlooked: Don Akenson, a storyteller who could have told him more than anyone else about every place in Canada that the Irish and the Bible have ever been, starting with a stroll through Susanna Moodie's backyard.

⌇

DON AKENSON

At Face Value (1990), *An Irish History of Civilization* (2005)

At Face Value (1990)

In 1990, *At Face Value* made the front pages of eight prominent daily news-papers, all subscribers to the Southam News Service, as "news" of a rather odd kind: in his "biography" of John White, a true blue Tory backbencher repre-senting East Hastings from 1871 to 1887, Akenson "unmasked" White as Eliza McCormack, an Irish immigrant, a prostitute, and a cross-dresser. The story had "legs" because it coincided with the newly minted postage stamp honouring Agnes Campbell McPhail as our first female MP.

As the author later wrote in "My Tory Transvestite," dealing with the Southam syndicate and assorted television interviewers was "a bit like trying to discuss neurosurgery with a bunch of axe murderers." Akenson had actually written a postmodern, post-feminist, historically grounded fictional elaboration of cul-tural depth, political importance, and literary delight — a hoax, a ruse, a joke, a prank but neither fraud nor swindle: a great "what if?"

The trickery wasn't difficult to see through: whenever Donald Harman Akenson, Douglas Professor of Canadian and Colonial History, Queen's Univer-sity, the world's pre-eminent historian of the Irish diaspora (*Conor: A Biography of Conor Cruise O'Brien*; *God's Peoples: Covenant and Land in South Africa, Israel and Ulster* and a dozen more), and provocative biblical scholar (*Surpassing Wonder: The Invention of the Bible and the Talmuds*; *Saint Saul: a Skeleton Key to the Historical Jesus*) turns from strictly scholarly pursuits to fiction, he abbreviates his name on the title page to Don Akenson. He'd done this four times in the years leading up to *At Face Value* with books that include another buried trea-sure, *The Orangeman: The Life and Times of Ogle Gowan* (1986), the most brutal and liveliest portrayal of nineteenth-century Upper Canada's scandalous politics ever written. But what's even more transparently fictional in Akenson's merging of Eliza McCormack/John White's identities are implicit parallels to *Moll Flanders* and explicit references to Daniel Defoe, its author.

Akenson puts Defoe in plain enough sight: Eliza is moved by his writings on female pirates and *At Face Value* includes reproductions of engravings from Defoe of bare-breasted Mary Read with cutlass in hand and Anne Bonny with pistol drawn that lead Eliza to seductively wooing and successfully winning Esther Johnson as wife and, with help from the local Mohawk band, mother to their daughters and son. *At Face Value* covers some of the same boggy ground and bedroom misbehaviour as *The Orangeman* (Eliza McCormack appears in the earlier book and Ogle Gowan in the later one) but takes a more sexually ambiguous and domestic view of political *parvenus* on the loose in Susanna Moodie's backyard (Eliza/John and Esther White with their many children are near-neighbours). As John White, Eliza is not only successful as a Tory but also self-empowering as a subversive anarchist.

Akenson demonstrates "that gender prejudice is not only rampant, but damned silly, and that the assumptions we make about human beings when we pin a gender label on them are so big that we never thereafter have an open mind about his, her, or their life." *At Face Value* asks,

> How would my view ... change if, in an effort to escape gender bias, I assumed that he is actually a woman, or she a man? ... Was John White really a woman? That is a question from male history and an inherently, if unconsciously, hostile one. The known facts of White's life fit the hypothesis, but the reality can never be known and that is just the point: in a culture where most historical records have been made and preserved by males it is very difficult to get at the true stories about women's lives.

Akenson writes in his endnotes that this is peculiarly true wherever transvestism is more severely ostracized and criminalized than romantic love between women. Because of its unnerving threat to male domination, the blurring of gender is one of our most pervasive fears, one that will take much more than a fashionable "boyfriend look" to conquer. Having seen and heard what happened to Hillary Clinton in her quest for the presidential nomination, imagine what would happen to all the short fuses at Fox News if Michelle Obama bobbed her hair and pulled on her husband's white shirts and dark suits!

The late George Woodcock was among those who got Akenson's point on first reading: "rarely have I seen a better exemplification of the relationship between real fiction and the necessary fictions of history." *At Face Value* was shortlisted for the Trillium Prize, losing out to Alice Munro's *Friend of My Youth*. Since then, it seems to have fallen below the radar of even those who circulate top-20 lists of literary hoaxes on the Internet where it ought to be "canonized" in the way Alan Sokol's "Transgressing the Boundaries: Toward a Transformative Hermeneutics of Quantum Gravity" (1996) has been but, more to the point, it ought to be read for wit and cunning that rivals Anthony Burgess's.

An Irish History of Civilization (2005)

As Donald Harman Akenson's scholarly reputation and works on the Irish and the Bible went global in the nineties, Don Akenson dropped further and further from view until the volcanic eruption of *An Irish History of Civilization* in 2005, 1524 pages spread over two volumes of what the author describes as "a micro-Talmud of humankind: for, ultimately, we are all of the one stock, and what we learn of one of us tells us something about each of us."

> Dublin, November 1902: Battle of the Network Stars
> Near the entrance to the National Library occurred the most mythol-ogized intersection in Irish literary history since Gráinne's head met the rock.
> Neither genius remembered accurately anything the other said. And each several times re-invented his own words.
> Yeats and Joyce were awkward acquaintances not only because of their age difference — seventeen years — but because they repaired to a Harcourt Street café and ordered chocolate and sticky buns, an aesthetic mistake. The treacly icing on the buns made little crumbs of bran stick to the fingers. Yeats kept wiping his hands with his pocket handkerchief, as if he had recently been in a particularly nasty public

lavatory. Joyce let the crumbs and icing accumulate and looked long-ingly at them. He had not had breakfast and if he were alone he would have licked his fingers.

While moving their lips in discussion of serious matters, each lets his mind wander:

> — *How can anyone have such long and filthy fingernails?*
> — *Christ, I wouldn't even want to be hanged in such a silly-looking tie.*

They agree to keep in touch.

Brian Fawcett provides an eminently useful synopsis and a penetrating analysis at www.dooneyscafe.com: "Akenson gives us drama, deadly accurate social history, character portraits of the two greatest Irish writers — and some delicious slapstick. What more could be asked a 180 word vignette?" By way of answer, Fawcett notes, "he does this with nearly equal economy and penetration three or four hundred times through the two volumes" of what is "a major work of [Canadian] literature" and "a global classic, even if no one figures it out for a decade or so."

My own judgment predates publication and found its way to the back cover:

> If James Joyce had studied the Talmud as assiduously as the Odyssey and been as enamoured of Saint Paul and Saint Patrick as he was of Nora Barnacle, he might have produced as overwhelmingly mordant a work ... but only if he'd had Conor Cruise O'Brian and Roddy Doyle as rewrite men. Don Akenson has one-upped Joyce and forged the con-sciousness of a race.

Two volumes divide into four books that move from the adolescence of Saul who becomes Paul the Apostle to a private chat (tape-recorded for posterity) in the Oval Office between Richard Nixon, H. R. Haldeman, and Billy Graham in February 1972 — a trio who discuss "Jewish control of the media" and why Nixon needs to be re-elected. Akenson dedicates his work to Sir Walter Raleigh, author of a five-volume *History of the World*, who "should have known better" and Eduardo Galeano, author of the three-volume *Memory of Fire* (1985), who "certainly does."

Don Akenson as Donald Harman Akenson is so innovative a scholar on the subject of the birth of the Bible and the Talmuds that Harold Bloom reveres the breadth and depth of his reading and the acuity of his insights. *An Irish History of Civilization* owes its basic literary strategies the Talmud's mélange of rabbinical stories, legends, history, and witticisms and to Galeano's stretchy groupings of vignettes, tableaus, prose poems but adds twists of its own; twists that place the work firmly in the tradition of the novel that starts from *Don Quixote*, runs through *Tristram Shandy* and incorporates Joyce's *Ulysses* and Anthony Burgess's *Earthly Powers* — works that demonstrate that the novel is capable of anything, including the negation of itself as a "mystical" creation, the offspring of muse and genius. Here's how Fawcett puts it:

> Akenson, I think, doesn't believe in either the mystical formalities of fiction that, at its best, simplifies human reality into an essentialized coherence, and at worst, separates historical figures and events from recognizable motives — and thus makes both history and literature uninteresting and/or incomprehensible to non-specialists or non-acolytes.

What Akenson does believe in is:

> "fact" — which he handles as if it were a whisk and not a sledgehammer, and then there is the fantastication of fact: sometimes self-serving embroidery on what is known and knowable, and sometimes — more rarely — true flight of imagination that enlarges and illuminates factation without falsifying it. He doesn't, in other words, think that the 12 disciples of Jesus after the crucifixion were much different as a group or as individual beings than a hockey team in a locker-room after a game, or a group of professors meeting in a faculty committee room

after a government budget cut. All are going to be doing the same things: trying to construct an understanding of the process they're inside, but also worrying over their private concerns, being hungry, thinking about their girlfriends or boyfriends, and needing to go to the washroom.

We're all in this together and none of us is more than a banana skin short of a pratfall. Or, to quote Cervantes as Donald Harman Akenson does at the close of *Some Family: The Mormons and How Humanity Keeps Track of Itself* (2007):

> Sancho, I want you to know that there are two kinds of lineage in the world: those of persons who trace and derive their ancestry from kings and princes of the sort that time has gradually undone. In the end, they end-up in a point, thusly; a pyramid turned upside down. Others have their origin in low-born ancestors, but they have risen by degrees until they have become great lords. The difference between them is that some were and are no longer — and others that once were, now are not. (translated by George Lovell)

If that isn't the trajectory of a novel, what is?

ALICE MUNRO

The View from Castle Rock (2006)

Given the infrequency of interviews and the questions left unanswered, Alice Munro's approach to reading is better known than her methods as a writer. Writing about Matt Cohen's *The Sweet Second Summer of Kitty Malone*, for instance, she says she has read it "several times, but not front to back or beginning to end." She dips into things, establishes her own beginnings and endings and, in comments on her own books, encourages her readers to do the same. She's much the same in conversation: wickedly playful but always, seemingly inadvertently, to some larger purpose. Her talk, her writing, and one suspects her reading follow flights of ancient lineage, arcs more common among novelists rooted in Cervantes than modernist short story writers. Anthony Burgess blew a lovely raspberry at aesthetic proponents of the short story as a separate and higher art form by stating, bluntly, in his introduction to *99 Novels* that the distinction is "a matter of convention only" and one settled, not by critics, but by "the publishers, printers and binders who process a manuscript into printed copy dressed in an overcoat."

> If a work of fiction can be bound in hard covers, its pages stitched and not stapled (as a pamphlet is), we had better accept that it is a novel.

To be such (how many of Munro's stories are of sufficient length to qualify if published separately?) in a *good* way, it has to have a peculiar shape, the parabola of lives lived not sliced and diced: it must, Burgess says, "leave in the reader's mind a sort of philosophical residue" a view of life indirectly propounded that's *new, surprising, clarifying*. By that standard, *The View from Castle Rock* is an excellent novel even if the author insists on calling it "stories," then undercuts the transparency of the claim in the opening piece, "No Advantages."

Unless you've read Akenson's *An Irish History of Civilization*, Munro's *View* will be unlike any historical fiction or autobiographical fiction that you've encountered since Burgess's *Big God and Little Wilson*. As Deborah Isenberg wrote in *The Atlantic Monthly* (December 2006), Munro's work

> is more on the order of a flowing exploration, which begins in obscurity, brings vividly into the light assorted pioneers and settlers of the author's family, and then weaves itself into various circumstances of Munro's own life, probing possibilities and happening upon continuities. The book looks simultaneously back and forward, even beyond the confines of its own end, seeking to divine the place and internal experience of certain individuals, including the author herself, within history and passing time. To read this book is to experience oneself speculatively, too — to sense acutely the properties and capacities of a mortal existence as the future streams toward us.

If you have read Akenson, you might feel tempted to think of *Castle* as "A Scottish History of an Odd Corner of North America" and cast Munro as Virginia Woolf to his James Joyce. Munro is Munro and Akenson is Akenson and neither has to bask in any other author's reflected glory. Readers familiar with the joys of Munro's writing — what Isenberg specifies as

> the breathtaking accuracy of observation; the apparently casual narrative that turns out to have led inexorably to some inescapable juncture; the disarming directness of expression; the author's ability to captivate us immediately and draw us gradually into strange, intense, lingering states of mind; the flashes of deadpan satire; the penetrating social vision; the inimitable blend of cool scrutiny and profound empathy

will find *The View from Castle Rock* "not only every bit as beautiful and substantial a work as [they] might hope for" but also "a work of dizzying originality."

As *The Observer* wrote,

Munro refers to the "glacial geography" of Canada and the existence of maps that show how the Ice Ages shaped the landscape. She is undertaking something similar on the level of culture, charting the remains and the permanent scouring effects of the retreating glacier known as Presbyterianism

as she follows her family history back to the Ettrick Valley, fifty miles south of Edinburgh and thirty miles north of the English border, which her great-great-great-grandfather James Laidlaw and his family left in 1818. The Laidlaws "seemed to produce somebody who went in for writing long, outspoken, sometimes outrageous letters and detailed recollections" in every generation and Munro shifts from their voices to her own, the places they once knew and she now knows.

What Canadian reviewers by and large missed is what's new or, at least, vitally renewed in Munro's artistry: the first stories, the old stories, are an important late development in her work as she invents backwards from ends to counter-intuitive beginnings, insisting all the while that carriers of stories are as vulnerable to them as Don Quixote is to his legend within the second part of his adventures. Then, as she moves forward to the "real life misadventures" — father's fox farm, mother's illness, her affair with a religious boy, her summer job as a maid — that recur within *The New Yorker* stories, there's not just the surprise of encountering wonderful material that's not been used elsewhere but a carrying away of the reader to a new kind of responsiveness to what Henry James calls the "visitable past" — the "world we may reach over to as by making a long arm we grasp an object at the other end of our own table." Like Robbie Burns (to whom she has never seemed closer), Munro is witnessing to the importance of the vanishing:

Much that I saw that night was going to disappear. The cupola, the hand-lifted ladles, the killing dust.... Many particular skills and dangers were going to go. Many everyday risks, along with much foolhardy pride, and random ingenuity and improvisation. The processes I saw were probably closer to those of the Middle Ages than to those of today.

And I imagine that the special character of the men who worked in the Foundry was going to change, as the processes of the work changed.

Tessa Hadley explicates the novelty of Munro's work, brilliantly and at length, in the *London Review of Books* (January 25, 2007):

> Transposing her own sensibility backwards, Munro opens a door for us into a strange place, enabling us to read its signs, fill the gaps between its codes with familiar flesh, the familiar flashes of appeal and repulsion between individuals pressed up close together in families. She never tries to give us an exhaustive picture of the past moment, any more than she would want to be exhaustive if she were writing about her own time; she moves intuitively around, putting out her words to catch its essential elements. Capturing the far past, if one can only do it, turns out to involve very much the same act of imagining as capturing the present: and that's just where its special difficulty lies. These ... stories in *The View from Castle Rock* are an important addition to Munro's work, something new, full of interest and mystery ...

and a radical departure for a writer who previously has adhered so closely, Hadley argues, to Henry James's advice in the preface to *The Aspern Papers* to write only of the "visitable past," the world within living memory, the world "we may reach over to as by making a long arm we grasp an object at the other end of our own table" and can "access as easily as looking over a garden wall into another garden." Beyond that, James insisted, "even by use of our longest ladder we are baffled and bewildered — the view is mainly a view of barriers." But not Munro's. Not here.

READING SOME OF "THE TALENTED WOMEN WHO WRITE TODAY"

Novels of Comfort and Love?

ANNALS OF OURLIT VII

A Night at Quincy's; Midnight at Banff Hot Springs

The room was Quincy's on 7th in Calgary on a Friday night, mid-October 2000, and it looked a lot like nightclubs in prewar Hollywood musicals where Fred Astaire might tap, sing, and twirl Ginger Rogers out the door — except that there wasn't a dinner jacket in sight. Right ambience, wrong era — the end of the last millennium or the start of this one — another little triumph of irony as Catherine Bush, Lynn Coady, and Eden Robinson got jammed up against the back wall on my right; Elizabeth Hay and Anita Rau Badami on my left.

PanCanadian WordFest brought many writers to town and hundreds of people (including everybody else who was anybody in Calgary's literary scene) was at Quincy's for *Out Loud Live*, a fusion of poetry and jazz with Clifton Joseph, Sheri-D Wilson, Paul Dutton, Fortner Anderson, Bob Holman, and Joolz Denby playing leads and the Tommy Banks Quintet backing them.

As spoken-word events go, this one was better rehearsed than most. Even so, too much sound assaulted ears that aren't what they were when I was in my twenties and could take in everything that happened on stage and scope a room at the same time. Voices swooped and leapt as Dutton got half-Tibetan, half-Innu and all-his-own sounds out of his throat and chest and guts while Wilson, author of *Girl's Guide to Giving Head*, erupted from inside a little black dress that every woman (and some men) in the room would like to be able to wear at least once with such in-your-face insouciance. *There's talent in this room!!!*

The words formed in my head and I lost the plot of *Out Loud Live*: writers born on the far shore of the mid-twentieth-century can't use the words *talent* and *room* in the same phrase without recalling Norman Mailer's essay "Evaluations: Quick and Expensive Comments on the Talent in the Room." Published in 1959 among his *Advertisements for Myself*, Mailer sized up American writers in this order: James Jones, William Styron, Truman Capote, Jack Kerouac, Saul Bellow, Nelson Algren, J. D. Salinger, Paul Bowles, Vance Bourjaily,

Chandler Brossard, Gore Vidal, Anatole Broyard, Myron S. Kaufman, Calder Willingham, Ralph Ellison, James Baldwin, Herbert Gold, William Burroughs, and — "the talented women who write today" — Mary McCarthy, Jean Stafford, and Carson McCullers. Mailer sized them up and found them (with the exception of Broyard and Burroughs) lacking the ability to write "the big one."

"The big one."

Inside Quincy's on that night a decade ago, I asked myself which of the *many* talented women who write today dreamed of writing "the big one" — a novel that confronts the taboo, looks into the heart of darkness, alters cultural climates as radically and explosively as a hydrogen bomb upsets the environment. And my answer was no one — female or male.

In 1959, the year Mailer published *Advertisements for Myself*, schoolchildren rehearsed air raids by holding heads under desks as shelter against the A-bomb. *The big one.* Five decades later, most writers, even Maileresque alphas, have learned a little humility: literature is only marginal in the lives of a minority and totally absent elsewhere. The words of even the best of the best work the edges of human consciousness.

Mailer wasn't much dumber than Arthur C. Clarke a decade later. Everything happening in Quincy's that October night in 2000 was of our moment, and none of it had much of anything to do with *2001: A Space Odyssey*. Our world remains obdurately more liveable than the one that Clarke imagined. But Clarke wasn't really interested in prediction: he was advocating "the big story" that obsessed an entire generation of SF writers. Welcoming a reissue of Clarke's 1968 novelization of the screenplay of *2001* in the pages of the *Independent on Sunday* on December 31, 2000, John Clute, author of the *Encyclopedia of Science Fiction*, neatly encapsulated "the big story" — a tale of destiny:

> We of the human race are destined to continue forging the tools — creating the greater technologies — that will enable us to continue to rise towards the planets and the stars. It is our nature to rise. And rise we must ... through the manly use of big tools.

What Clarke missed in 1968, not through stupidity, but because he wanted something else was:

information, which is another way of saying he missed the Internet. He missed the explosion in the complexity of our perceptions of how the world — our bodies, our minds, our environments, our global opportunistic diseases, our politics, our weather — actually works. We now know infinitely more about everything; and we know that almost everything is infinitely harder to understand than we thought it would be.

Of the writers *in that room* at Quincy's a decade ago, I thought it was Catherine Bush who had gotten more of this more wonderfully right than anyone else. Widening my line of vision to take in all of the country, I ranked only Janette Turner Hospital and Carole Corbeil her equals with Barbara Gowdy and Margaret Atwood higher on the scale. I paused to wonder what Lynn Coady, Eden Robinson, Elizabeth Hay, and Anita Rau Badami might contribute to the complexity of our perceptions.

At the end of *Out Loud Live*, moving toward Quincy's exit alongside Dennis Lee and Louise Dennys, Catherine Bush and Eden Robinson were two steps in front of us. Dennis and Louise were reminiscing about 1950s poetry — Gregory Corso's "Bomb" in the shape of a mushroom cloud, recitations in coffeehouses with bebop saxophonists back before The Beatles launched their first LP. When we exited on 7th, Catherine and Eden were half a block ahead. Bush is a dancer and Robinson sings and whatever they were saying to one another caused Eden to whoop and Catherine to pirouette.

During WordFest, Carole Corbeil died in Toronto after a lengthy illness and I mourned. I knew her only a little but I knew her two novels intimately. Was there a third in her desk drawer? Not likely. She'd been in poor health, fought a lot of pain. There were powerful male voices — notably Mordecai Richler and Ian Rankin — to be heard in Calgary and Banff, WordFest's secondary locale, but Corbeil's death drew me to women's voices. Listening to what they said when they talked about the when, where, why, and how of what they wrote,

I heard about writing as a small tool for finding comfort and making sense of love in a world made uncomfortable and unlovely by very big tools, including the cranes wherever one looked downtown and the earth movers corralled at the outskirts of Calgary that were destined for the tar sands.

Catherine Bush and I went walking and talking in the mountains and afterwards joined others in a taxi to the hot springs, donned 1920s striped woollen swimwear, and floated under a clear sky and midnight stars. Lying back, beyond the edge of their conversation, in a swoon of moonshine, my line of sight crossed hairs with somebody else's idea of rhapsody: three *très petite* Asian women emerged from the bathhouse, wrapped necks to ankles in oversize beach towels. As they stepped into the pool, the towels dropped and billowed into the waters behind them. Definitely not three little maids from school, they wore itsy-bitsy black vinyl bikinis and began walking toward me. Mid-pool, they turned slowly and turning, exposed dragon heads breathing flames tattooed on their right shoulders. The tattoos extended down their backs in wings, torsos, and tails. Even before turning my head and seeing a group of Asian men in dark suits, white shirts, and sunglasses glinting with starlight behind me I knew that none of this display was for the benefit of visiting writers. As dragon tails wriggled back to the bathhouse, I wondered if I'd been looking into a geisha-like past or a post-feminist future. What was written on their bodies was more startling then than now when so many women have surrendered so much public flesh to the tattooist's pen with such bravado. Mailer had bravado. A man as stupid as he was about women couldn't survive without it.

But was Mailer brave or merely foolhardy? He confronted taboos and looked into the heart of darkness. Did he face up to the true test, the question that haunts Achilles in his encounters with his mother, Thetis: How does one continue to live while tormented daily by grief? Among the many talented women who write today we find some of our bravest warriors in wars worth winning. Here are some Amazons and a quartet of male writers who are accurate geographers of major battlefields.

∿

CAROLE CORBEIL

Voice-Over (1992), *In the Wings* (1997)

Voice-Over (1992)

In April 1992, Carole Corbeil was on a triumphal trip back to her old hometown of Montreal as a literary celebrity. Her first novel, *Voice-Over*, was on Canadian bestseller lists and she was having more fun than serious writers are supposed to have when they have just broken into print. The response to *Voice-Over* had been phenomenal. On sale barely a month, it was already being called a "classic" by credible reviewers. Carole Corbeil was receiving the kind of media coverage that's usually reserved only for well-established award-winners.

She'd already given five or six interviews that day and was struggling to catch her breath and collect her thoughts but she was smiling as she said, "All this attention! It's like going from famine to feast. You're alone for so long and then whoosh, you're out of the gate."

And leading the pack from an odd position: *Voice-Over* doesn't have what one generally expects to find in a book that captures the public imagination — a strong plot. What it does have is an emotional trajectory that sweeps readers up into the world of Claudine Beaulieu, an angry Québécoise documentary filmmaker, and the WASP literary con man in her life in Toronto in the mid-eighties. "I found that I had to be really true to those characters and their emotional states. My biggest discovery was that emotional honesty has a narrative drive in itself because this is actually quite a fragmented book. There is something about it like a broken mirror and all the pieces are reflecting one another. It amazes me that people read it through and get into it despite the lack of any real plot."

Voice-Over does what very good novels always do: it gives new and specific insights into a small story that throws unexpected light upon larger issues. The setting is the summer of 1984 and Claudine Beaulieu's films of women at the margins of society — prostitutes, prison inmates — have earned her a middle-of-the-political-spectrum reputation in the Toronto arts community but her personal life is as fragmented, torn-up, and wasted as clips of film on the editing room floor. She's in a relationship with a punk poet, a *poseur* such as only Upper Canada College can produce. They live together without sharing any kind of life beyond that one fuelled by cocaine, booze, and jealousy. Together, they are vile in more ways than they could ever manage on their own. What gives Claudine's life any interest beyond voyeurism are the tenuous connections she maintains with Janine, her sister, a suburban housewife married to a house renovator, and with their divorced mother — Odette — who remarried into Westmount money and privilege, carrying her daughters with her, losing language, gaining golf.

The relationship between Claudine on cocaine and her poet on booze neatly skewers all such relationships. After closing this book, no reader should be able to look at a guy with a bunch of poems stuffed inside his black leather jacket quite as romantically as before. The relationship between Claudine and her sister is done as well as sisters have been done in this country since Barbara Gowdy's *Falling Angels* in 1989. *Voice-Over* smartens us up while moving us deeply and it does it with more French dialogue than most Toronto publishers were willing to risk even in the early nineties.

In the Wings (1997)

Voice-Over not only stayed on the bestseller lists for many weeks but was also shortlisted for the W. H. Smith First Novel Award, and the Trillium Book Award and won the City of Toronto Book Award. *In the Wings*, more accomplished and complex, chased Mordecai Richler's *Barney's Version* down to the Caribbean for the regional final of the Commonwealth Prize but failed to make an impact on the juries for either the Governor General's Literary Award for Fiction or the Giller Prize or on the public via bestseller status. The publisher did the book no favour by featuring a cherub and human skull on a sepia dust jacket and promoting it in terms that tiredly convey something less than the heart of a vital book that has nothing in common with a soap opera:

Allan O'Reilly is a young actor on the cusp of a brilliant career when he meets Alice Riverton on the set of a forgettable movie. Alice, almost 40, almost successful, had escaped to Los Angeles after a disastrous affair with a married man, but her mother's sudden death brings her back to Toronto. Scheduled to play Gertrude in an upcoming production of *Hamlet*, Alice falls in love with Allan and sweeps him into her world ... [and] shifts calamitously when Allan is cast as Hamlet. Carole Corbeil's new novel is a passionate and lyrical exploration of how art informs life — how a script as ancient as *Hamlet* can haunt those who set about to revive and relive it.

Compare that with this sample of Corbeil's own prose. Here is Allan, depressed, riding the King streetcar from the corner of Parliament:

... as the doors fold behind him, sees himself as if he were watching the streetcar from outside, a dark figure lunging about in a bright tube.

Sitting down, he looks at the fine veins of his wrists.

White light on his wrists. Smell of wet wool. Ads with beautiful women licking their lips. Outside, old territory clattering by. Used to walk here with his father when Nate and he were boys. His father had this drill when they were walking. He'd say, where are we, boys? Look around you. Where are we? On this old street that was once close to the lake they'd say, York, sir. Muddy York.

Peel it back, boys, King Street is an old Indian trail.

The Mississauga tribe sold a hundred thousand hectares of this land for ten shillings to the government of Upper Canada.

And what's a shilling, Dad, one of them would ask.

Pocket change.... It's not just history that's under there, but a whole way of life. They paved a whole way of life....

His wrists ache. He thinks of what it would be like to cut them. Cut sideways, not across.

In the Wings revolves around a down-to-the-last-of-its-funding Toronto theatre company's attempt to save itself from ruin by staging William Shakespeare's *Hamlet*. Corbeil interweaves three characters haunted by loving relationships they have lost. Allan, cast as Hamlet, comes by his depression genetically: his father, recently deceased, was bipolar. Alice, as Queen Gertrude, has returned to Toronto from Los Angeles for the funeral of her mother. Pullwarden, the drama critic for Toronto's largest newspaper, is separated from a wife who has moved to Vancouver to maximize the distance between him and his beloved infant son. Pullwarden is mad with lust for Louise, a much-too-young-for-him actress. Alice is failing to stay free of men who do her no good. Allan is feeding his manic side and staving off depression as best he can by using women and being used by them. Their struggles are framed in prologue and epilogue by the child of Allan and Alice summoning their ghosts back to the stage in a narrative device that brings to *In the Wings* the device of play within play that rivals the complexities of trial within trial in Mordecai Richler's *St. Urbain's Horseman*. Like Richler at his best, Corbeil can comment on eroticism, domesticity, loneliness, obsessiveness, aging, religion, writing, reviewing, and Canadianism without knocking her novel out of shape.

Corbeil knew the theatre world and Toronto's actors at least as well as Richler knew the world of scriptwriters and Canadian expatriates in London. Everything feels authentic. Her dialogue is spare but effective. She isn't a satirist — that's not her métier — but she can be richly comic. Here's Pullwarden the critic interviewing Allan the actor:

> "You were," Pullwarden says, looking out the front window at the painted brick houses across the road, "very good in that dog thing. Not a very good play, but you gave a lambent performance. The friend I was with at the time was very taken. We all were."
>
> "Thank you."
>
> "Yes, a very vital performance."
>
> "It was a good experience. I usually hoard myself until there's an audience. It tends to freak out directors who want it right away, you know what I mean. But here, it's the weirdest thing. I got it almost

right away, and then working out the bits, it's kind of ... It's just so huge. It requires so much muscle of every kind. It's ..."

"I collect Hamlets, Allan," Pullwarden interrupts. He is still staring at the brick house across the street. "And my collection is extensive, it dates back twenty years, to when I saw Ian McKellen playing it in Cardiff. I've seen the very greatest, and the not so greats, and the lost. When you see the lost playing it, it's like seeing a horse with dropped reins — whereas you've seen others run with a speech, they're chewing at it like nettles by the side of the road."

Corbeil is also humorous in a larger-hearted way that's difficult to capture with a few lines: what she nets through subtle shifts in the tone of utterances and reflections as one scene is played off against others is self-mockery. Its absence makes Pullwarden awful and its presence makes Alice appealing and more typical of Canadian women who are really good at their jobs than female leads in too many other novels.

Corbeil's young men no less than her mature women force themselves and their lovers out of the wings and into the central dramas of their own lives by taking risks and enduring the harsh illuminations of self-consciousness and then the consciousness beyond self-consciousness that is moral judgment. This is the way that Shakespeare resonates in this novel. The joinery between the tales told in *Hamlet* and those *In the Wings* aren't made by connecting dots. By making Allan something less than the fully articulated self-consciousness and genius in expressiveness that is Hamlet and by dozens of smaller strokes, she offers Allan and her other players the opportunity of following Shakespeare's script or their own. Because choices are made that reflect and refract *Hamlet*, the play becomes a thing in which the consciences of a theatre company are captured. For those of us who read Shakespeare as Samuel Johnson did "[t]he better to enjoy life, or the better to endure it," *In the Wings* is committed to clarifying what is to be enjoyed, what is to be endured, and what ought to be altered in the ways we live now. It's the seriousness and sympathy Corbeil brings to sexual tensions and their resolution that was the freshest and most refreshing mark of her writing. She found a way to describe the intimacies between lovers in her work without being exploitative and to show how sex can affect the whole of a life and do it in a way that elicits sympathy for both lovers simultaneously without canting or becoming corny.

In the week following her death, Susan G. Cole wrote this of Carole Corbeil in a tribute in *NOW* magazine:

> She was so awestruck by the appalling powers invested in arts reviewers that she couldn't help but take on those issues in her second novel, *In The Wings*. Robert Pullwarden, the theatre critic she creates, is a cautionary portrait — power-hungry, manipulative, vengeful. Everything Corbeil wasn't.
>
> She was, instead, a study in understated grace. I learned the virtues of this quality when I participated with her on a panel alongside Gloria Steinem at the Stratford Festival in the early 90s.... But it was Corbeil whom everybody noticed.
>
> In her brief but deft remarks she recalled the nuns who taught her, not as mindless victims but as strong women trying to come to terms with their faith. It was a humbling experience to be sitting beside her at that moment, a lesson in how the workings of a supple mind and a subtle intellect will always triumph over flash and trash.

~‿◦

CATHERINE BUSH

Minus Time (1993), *Claire's Head* (2004/6)

Minus Time (1993)

In "A Conversation between Lynn Coady and Catherine Bush" in the November 2000 issue of *LRC: Literary Review of Canada*, Bush says:

> I am from a very female household, the oldest of three daughters. We were encouraged to do what we wanted to do in a very individualistic

fashion. I do not think any parent really encourages you to become a writer, but my sense of writing was always that it was something that women did. I read Alice Munro, Margaret Atwood, Margaret Laurence. My mother's name is Margaret, so there was an association and a sense of writing as part of a female genealogy. My father is a scientist, so if I try to wed the two parts of my family, it is in writing.

Minus Time (1993) begins on the shoulder of a Florida highway where Helen and Paul Urie, twenty-year-old siblings from Toronto, are watching the launch of a space shuttle. "Minus time" is countdown to launch but also, their mother says, it's when what you choose "makes a difference, becomes a kind of demarcation of choice, the infinitesimal division of worlds." Barbara Urie is the first Canadian mother in space on a mission to establish a new record for time in orbit. Her children ought to be at the launch site, but they refuse to have their reactions broadcast around the world. Later, watching a replay in a roadside restaurant, they discover that as far as the world is concerned, they weren't absent: the space agency provided look-alike stand-ins for them and for their estranged father. A mother in outer space, circling five hundred kilometres over-head, connected to her family by a special television channel and from any telephone on the planet, is wonderfully bizarre, a ghastly image of the fragmentation of family life by technology. Physical separateness and electronic intimacy between Helen and her mother prefigure middle-class experience in our era of ubiquitous cellphones and webcams.

Minus Time alternates between third-person narrative and Helen's first-person account of childhood, adolescence, and inner life. Helen's identity is shaky and she wants "a little autonomy, a little time, a sense of private space in a world where every ninety minutes her mother circled the sky above her head" while millions gawk.

A University of Toronto freshman dropout, Helen gets around town by bicycle, subway, and foot. Her feet on pedals, platforms, and pavement are plugged into "the complexity of our perceptions of how the world — our bodies, our minds, our environments, our global opportunistic diseases, our politics, our weather — actually works." At a supermarket, Helen spots Foster slapping

"EAT THIS AND YOU'RE DEAD MEAT" stickers on packages in the refrigerators. With his friend Elena, the three become a single cell of an animal rights group. Helen is welcomed because she has access to her mother's Volvo and tactics require fast anonymous forays with posters, spray cans, and stickers into the suburbs.

Bush is too bright, too engaged with the world, to fall into the trap of seeing rural life as intimate and city life as disconnected. She told Lynn Coady:

> For me, cities are both a place of obvious disconnection and a place
> of an intimacy, a charged intimacy just because you are living with so
> many people.... I am always surprised when people describe cities as
> being large, impersonal spaces. I have never experienced them that way.
> At a certain point I wanted to write about the place of all these weird
> collisions.

Minus Time has the sense of unpredictable lighting shining out of a greater darkness. Bush's Toronto contains both corruption and innocence but it is never pure hell or paradise because it enfolds all sorts of contrary impulses. To mark the six-month anniversary of Barbara's ascent into space, the City of Toronto decides to turn off power for five seconds so that the astronaut can see her city disappear and reappear in a flash. Helen is taken to the CN Tower's observation platform for her own view of the spectacle:

> The ride in the elevator up the side of the Tower was very quick, crush
> of bodies, scent of perfume, smell of sweat.... Windows ran in a circle
> around the exterior of the observation level, floor to ceiling.... Outside,
> the sky was dark, except for a pale turquoise line in the west. Helen
> worked her way between people, didn't care if they stared at her now
> in annoyance, until she was standing where she wanted to be, facing
> north towards the bulk of the city and the blinking lights along King
> Street West, the steak restaurant and Chinese restaurant and theater all
> owned by Honest Ed. Beyond this block of light-bulb-ring billboards,

like among star cluster in the distance, she could see the faint blinking at the heart of his empire: Honest Ed's itself.... The lights touched her, like a child, in a way the daytime view never had, filling her with wonder, a lake of light.

Whole floors of Bay Street bank towers, the curved, scintillating walls of the Roy Thomson concert hall went dark as if at the flick of a switch. Billboards, pixelboards, the garish block of lightbulbs, dots that had been houses disappeared, everything swallowed up, consumed, leaving just a brown glare, a trace among the wavering outlines of streets and hospitals lit by their own generators, all so that her mother could see it. It seemed like such an effortless, American kind of power.

Bush's characters are recognizable. What's harder to grasp is the author's emotional intelligence, the ways she gets under the surface and shakes apart the conventions of the "loss of mommy" novel to say something different about the relationship between mothers and daughters than what gets said in Bonnie Burnard's *A Good House* or Elizabeth Hay's *A Student of Weather*. Helen is unhappy and cut adrift by Barbara's success. She feels abandoned and neglected, but Bush isn't applying for membership in some Generation X backlash against the careerism of first-generation feminists. What is at issue between Helen and Barbara is not ambition but obsession and the dishonesty it breeds.

As the child of work-obsessed parents, Helen has grown up unconventionally and oddly. Reflecting on how she appeared to a boy whom she met during the summer holiday just before her mother joined the space program, Helen says of herself,

He didn't know I was an expert on thawing times, that I could tell how long it took to thaw a package of ground chuck or chicken legs just by looking at it, and could identify the food my family ate even when it was covered in tinfoil in the freezer, or that I found it impossible to think about the future.... I was a girl in shorts and a blue T-shirt walking along a dirt road in Muskoka.

Helen's triumph in the novel is that she does find it possible to begin to think about the future and to think about it elastically once she and her mother begin speaking truthfully to one another.

It's taken several readings over a decade to grasp the peculiar braininess of a book as sure-footed in each of its particulars and as perfect in its way of capturing a young person at a crossroads as Leonard Cohen's *The Favourite Game*. Are there high school teachers confident enough to offer students the eminently worthwhile challenge of confronting Bush? What little sex there is in *Minus Time* is all safe. When Helen has intercourse with Trig, her high school boyfriend, and then with Foster, condoms are always readied and used. If she and her partner have orgasms, they aren't recorded.

Claire's Head (2005)

On a mid-October Friday in 2004, Catherine Bush is on a book tour for her third novel, *Claire's Head*, and pleased to see me. A month earlier, I'd told *The Globe and Mail* readers that her new novel was an emotionally compelling and intellectually enthralling love story that is as much of our world as an MRI brain scan and as timeless as the Buddha. I also wrote that it confirms what readers of her earlier fictions suspected and what Barbara Gowdy succinctly asserts on the dust jacket: Catherine Bush is not only "clear, humane, gripping and unfailingly intelligent" but also "one of our finest writers." Bush has paid close attention and is one of the few writers around who recognize and respond to the ways in which Gowdy has increased both the difficulties and the rewards of making novels out of the experiences of sisters.

Rachel Barber is a walking headache — literally and figuratively. Chronic migraines have so discombobulated her that she can't hold down a full time job nor maintain an intimate relationship nor raise her daughter as a single parent. When Rachel (who makes ends barely meet as a freelance medical journalist) disappears after visiting the Montreal Neurological Institute to interview researchers studying the cause of migraines, it's up to Rachel's younger sister Allison to continue making a home for Rachel's daughter, Star, and for Claire, the youngest of the three, to find Rachel. This thrusts her into a journey through downtown Toronto, Lower Manhattan's East Village, Montreal, Amsterdam, Frankfurt, Paris, a Tuscan health spa, Las Vegas, Mexico — and inward.

The Barber sisters are third generation *migraineuses*. As girls, they had mother and grandmother as models of how to live with chronic neurological pain. As adults, they've absorbed different lessons and follow distinct and unusual paths: Allison is the most domestic with a husband and children and so nurturing that she works with the orangutans at the Toronto Zoo. Claire is tidy, systematic, controlled, a cartographer working for the city of Toronto mapping changes in its wetlands while Stefan, her partner, maps cancer cells. Claire is cautious in every choice from what to eat and which pill to take next out of the pharmacopoeia in her handbag (Zomig, Imitrex, Tylenol 3s, 292s, Epival, Elavil, Sandomigran) to the largest question looming over her life — does she or doesn't she stop taking her meds and have a child with Stefan? "This me you love and want to have a baby with, this is me on drugs."

Travelling out of her safety zone and into hazardous ones where Rachel has been sighted (Las Vegas is particularly risky for a *migraineuse*), Claire becomes reckless as she takes train, plane, and automobile trips that put her into proximity with perfumed people, newspaper ink, smoke, alcohol, conditioned air, new carpets, jet fuels, car exhausts, bleach, disinfectants, dry-cleaning fluids, onions, fluorescent lights, and dozens of other "triggers" for migraines. Few writers evoke nasty sensations and negative atmospheres as accurately as Bush and she does not cheat her characters or her readers and use pain as a jagged big symbol. Suffering here is a fact of life that is as much a mystery to be meditated upon as a problem to be solved.

Bush is unapologetically well read: Proust washes over the pages of a pain diary that Rachel hides (and Claire finds) — a sustained piece of writing as exact in its articulation of the processes at work in an obsession as anything anyone is likely to find anywhere. Bush's characters might be as gloomy as the anxiety-prone in Proust but they aren't doom-laden: there's more buoyancy, a greater sense of the inclusivity of love and consequently the possibility for growth, change, redemption. She's as open-hearted and even-handed as the wise old gambler in that classic old Kenny Rogers song as she prompts her protagonists to learn when to hold, when to fold, when to walk away, and when to run.

Claire's Head is filled with incidents that are cinematic in a European manner, reminiscent of Michelangelo Antonioni and Lina Wertmüller. Wertmüller? Catherine Bush's surreal sense of humour turns on incongruities, is attuned to oddity, and is sly, subtle, brainy, deadpan. Bush is comparable to Joseph Conrad in the way that she's drawn to the edges of consciousness as it tries to make sense of collisions between the familiar and the less so as the globe shrinks. Such novels as Conrad wrote and Bush writes used to be called "poetic" before that term got hooked up with "mythic" and hijacked as a catchphrase for the overwrought musings and amusements of Ondaatje and his imitators. Bush's continuity with Conrad goes beyond testing the limits of a metaphor at book length: she's also testing the limits of morality in the absence of God. None of her characters talks about God and the silence is intentional. Her plots are driven by synchronicity and not by coincidence, chance, or fate. Everything follows clearly defined rules of engagement with modernism. The exchanges between mother and daughter in *Minus Time* aren't as over the top and tin-eared as they're sometimes made out to be: Bush's prosody in these passages echoes the musicality of D. H. Lawrence, which is — do readers really need to be reminded of this? — in continuity with the King James Bible, the *Common Book of Prayer*, and English as it is still spoken among those who have sat through private-school assemblies and been bathed in the words of anglophile headmistresses and headmasters in Toronto.

In January 2006, *Claire's Head* was issued in a trade paperback with extensive revisions that elaborate Rachel's and Claire's views on motherhood. That's the definitive version.

~‿o

EDEN ROBINSON

Monkey Beach (2000), *Blood Sports* (2006)

Monkey Beach (2000)

Eden Robinson is Aboriginal, born of a Haisla mother and a Heiltsuk father, and niece of Gordon Robinson, author of *Tales of the Kitamaat* (1956) and the first Haisla ever published. She grew up near Kitamaat Village and returned to live there after many years in Vancouver. This first *novel* to be published by a Haisla, *Monkey Beach* celebrates life in Kitamaat.

Opening on the morning after Jimmy, the narrator's brother and an Olympic swimming prospect, is missing at sea, Lisamarie Hill faces the possibility that he's dead. Robinson employs elements of Haisla storytelling (dreams, relationships between humans and animals), provides details of Haisla rituals, and demystifies the beliefs of her people to summon up lives that include encounters with b'wus (the sasquatch) and other characters from the Haisla spirit world in believable ways. Robinson believes guardian spirits speak to her much as they speak to her narrator. "I had one [guardian spirit] poke me in the butt," she told an interviewer. "Another was just so pissed at me — yelled and shouted. Gave me nasty dreams all night.... There are some places that are not for me to go ... I'm not that brave! It's one thing to have some psycho stalking you, and quite another to have them around." *Monkey Beach* introduces readers to unknown fictional territory and nudges a coming-of-age novel in new directions.

The language of *Monkey Beach* (it's a particular and peculiar fusion of wry, raw, muscular, urgent humour that is shockingly, bloodily funny with transcendent lyricism that's simple, bold, vivid, vital, and moody) splendidly celebrates indeterminacy, ambiguity, and generates non-random multiplied meanings on repeated readings. In his essay "Why the Novel Matters" in *Phoenix*, D. H. Lawrence wrote:

> The novel is the one bright book of life. Books are not life. They are only tremulations on the ether. But the novel as a tremulation can

make the whole man alive tremble. Which is more than poetry, philosophy, science or any other book-tremulation can do.... [Novels] in their wholeness affect the whole man alive, which is the man himself beyond any part of him. They set the whole tree trembling with a new access of life, they do not just stimulate growth in one direction.

It's this capacity to expose discrepancies between what human beings are and what they ought to be that rescues novels from sloppy sentimentality and enables them to become Lawrence's "perfect medium for revealing to us the changing rainbow of our living relationships." Robinson's conflicting styles make reading *Monkey Beach*'s cracked and splintered narratives spellbinding and addictive.

Blood Sports (2006)

Robinson's fiction has two distinct wellsprings — the Kitamaat world and the world she made for herself as an adult in East Vancouver before returning to her ancestral village. Both rely on Robinson's ability to borrow from the conventions of social realism in order to create "dark fantasy." But they have something else going for them — the trickster within her. Robinson has one of the most uproarious and infectious laughs in Canadian literature, a great Falstaffian full-bellied chortle that begins as a bass and rises to soprano that I could hear in my head as my jaw dropped to the floor in the final pages of *Blood Sports* (2006) when a couple of carefully placed sentences turned her second novel inside out and upside down. The sting catches a reader off-guard in much the same way that Alice Munro does whenever she reveals capriciousness in the more virtuous of her characters.

Eden Robinson is not usually mentioned in the same sentence with Alice Munro because her most obvious influence when she writes of East Vancouver is Stephen King of thirty years ago. *Blood Sports* is violent and its violence is twisted and explicit as it assaults the sensibilities of anyone not given to shooting, knifing, chopping, dicing, exploding video games. Living and dead bodies are abused in ruthlessly shocking ways: worse still, death is never the final indignity for many of them. As in *Monkey Beach*, Robinson combines conflicting styles with such technical virtuosity until the final pay-off causes a loop back to the first page to try to catch what one missed.

On first reading, *Blood Sports* seems to be about the nicest introduction any warm body seated in a comfy chair can reasonably expect to the radical acts of dysfunctionality that pass themselves off as ordinary human behaviour among sadistic drug dealers and masochistic users in East Vancouver. Tom Bauer is a twenty-something epileptic who medicates himself with marijuana as he tries to break free of the abuse that links him to his alcoholic mother and his psychopathic coke-snorting cousin Jeremy. Tom's pothead way out is to father a daughter with Paulina, his cousin's ex-junkie girlfriend, and establish some kind of family life at the edges of Grandview Park amid "anarchists and activists, blue-collar families and immigrants ... hippies who couldn't afford Kitsilano [and] ... new condo owners." Tom supplements his earnings from the night shift at Lucky Lou's corner store with irregular withdrawals from a briefcase stash of cash and drugs that Jeremy left behind when he went to prison. When Jeremy is released, the past reasserts itself and Tom, Paulie, and their baby become hostages to other people's missing fortunes.

Blood Sports follows the action by way of video-plays, letters, and emails that strategically intercut a clear, clean riveting *noir* narrative that opens on June 22, 1998, and closes on July 10, 1998. The story of Tom and Jeremy and the relationships that link them to people and places in and beyond Downtown Eastside Vancouver opens up into a greater darkness than the underside of family life without loss of devastating domestic impact. In an endnote, Robinson writes that *Blood Sports* is "a homage to the original 'Hansel and Gretel,' the version where Hansel uses a finger bone from a previous victim to convince the witch he's still too skinny to eat." That's the version where the storyteller concludes, "My tale is done, there runs a mouse, whosoever catches it, may make himself a big fur cap out of it." Robinson's story has a forest in common with the Grimms' "Hansel and Gretel" with a house in the woods that has a cage attached, but the boy and girl are man and wife, their parents are missing, there's no witch enticing them, no clever stratagems of escape, and no great riches at the end. The affinities and continuities are psychological: Tom and Paulie have been left to shift for themselves in a world of emotional deprivation and starvation where porn passes for sex, neighbourliness means coordinating stereos to drive bad neighbours out by playing Céline Dion at the max, and family life is built around rehab programs that sometimes succeed.

~~○

CAROLINE ADDERSON

Sitting Practice (2003)

Caroline Adderson isn't timid when it comes of subject matter: her first novel, *A History of Forgetting* (1999) tackles living with a loved one drifting away into dementia but is more transgressive than Michael Ignatieff's *Scar Tissue* — her lovers are a gay hairdresser and his partner. In *Sitting Practice*, she takes on heterosexuals living with a major physical disability and she's as good as Joan Barfoot in *Critical Injuries* while tackling very different characters.

Ross Alexander is newly married to Iliana when a car accident leaves her paralyzed from the waist down. The novel follows them as they abandon Vancouver for Duncan on Vancouver Island and open an organic vegetarian café. The title isn't just Iliana in her wheelchair; it's also Ross's initiation into Buddhism. Charlie Lee-Potter in *The Independent on Sunday* (September 14, 2003) under the head "Buddhism and the art of bicycle maintenance" speculates that Adderson might just have come up with the definitive assignment for would-be creative writing students: "Write an explicit, funny and touching passage in which a paralysed woman has a passionate affair with a spotty youth, while her husband wrestles with his Buddhist beliefs and falls off his bicycle."

Ross is cuddly ("a finger poked in anywhere on him would sink to the second knuckle"), affable, self-absorbed but sociable. Iliana, the daughter of fundamentalist parents, is sinewy, athletic, and hungry for affection. Mere weeks into the novelty of marriage, they have to sort out a whole new set of rules of engagement with one another as sex withers. After Ross asks his twin Bonnie and her boy to move in with them, they face further catastrophes.

Adderson says in interviews that she dislikes plot synopses, thinking (rightly) that it makes her works sound more depressing than they are. Spinal cord injury isn't the worst thing that can happen to a person: the loss of all sense of humour ranks higher and Adderson's writing is about the joy that erupts in unlovely situations among genuinely affectionate people. As novelist, Adderson has a smaller reputation than as the short story writer who first attracted attention with *Bad Imaginings* (1993), a finalist for the Governor General's Award, and more recently *Pleased to Meet You* (2006), longlisted for the Giller and the subject of a column in *The Globe and Mail* (June 12, 2008) by Russell Smith that begins:

> Reading Caroline Adderson's prose after wading through the leaden, child-pleasing stories of our prize-winners (not mentioning any [Vincent Lam] names) is like being let through the door from the grey IKEA-furnished nursery into a sunlit garden full of adults. One lets out a happy sigh, loosens one's tie and accepts an intriguing and unusual drink. I could stay in her world all weekend. In fact, I just did.... *Pleased to Meet You* ... is my favourite book of the year so far; my favourite Canadian book of the past five.

Smith calls it "fiction of startling images made by metaphors and insights, as dense as poetry" and says, "when she creates her narratives she is more guided by the explosions of language in her brain than by any preconceived story: The language that comes to her will actually lead the story. This might explain more than anything why short stories seem more difficult than novels, and also why they are, like poetry, where the unexpected and unformulaic tend to happen." He's spot on. This approach does cause structural problems in both novels but they deserve the recognition they've gotten in the United Kingdom and missed here.

~∽

LYNN COADY

Mean Boy (2006)

Some reviewers delight in examining Lynn Coady's novels as "either/or" — as in *the funniest* OR *the most depressing*. In an interview with *The Danforth Review*'s Michael Bryson, she addressed this:

> With regard to those "dark and depressing complaints" — to me this exemplifies one problem with Canadian book culture right off the bat.... It's really, really middle-class.... The feeling I got from those who felt the darkness of *Strange Heaven* (1998) was gratuitous was that they simply resented the idea that people like this could exist ... because they can't understand how anyone could end up in such a situation and, more importantly, they can't understand the way it shapes people. They know that poverty sucks because you can't afford to buy stuff, but they don't understand that it doesn't make you noble or strong as a result, it doesn't build character. On the contrary, it makes you petty and hostile and small-minded unless you have supernatural reserves of personal integrity, or else someone in your life who actively works to counter such influences.... The positive thing about the Canadian corner of the literary debate is that we seem to have an easier time talking about class in this country. We're not saturated in its influence the way Britain is, and we're not as in denial about it as the United States.

Larry Campbell, the protagonist of her third novel, *Mean Boy*, isn't very mean but is painfully self-conscious in a "university novel" that can be mentioned in the same sentence as Kingsley Amis's *Lucky Jim* without overinflating Coady or downgrading Amis. Larry, who wants the world to know him as Lawrence, is a second-year, inarticulate, undergraduate English student in an unnamed small-town university in New Brunswick in 1975. Larry wants to be a poet like Jim Arsenault, his work-shirted, shit-booted, alcohol-fuelled professor, a self-absorbed manic-depressive whose failure to obtain tenure drives the plot forward. Hilarity arises from the fact that everyone, except Arsenault, is so very, very normal. Coady adapts some Amis set pieces to her own design — the generation gaps revealed at family festive gatherings; the classroom as home turf of the portentous; drunkenness as the trigger of confusions that worry the day-lights out of the hung-over. Coady adds weight and balance by making Arsenault a competent poet and an inspired literary critic with a genius for self-destruction.

Although Larry is from Summerside, PEI, not the Miramichi, and his family runs a motel and mini-golf course, not a movie theatre, and the campus has more in common physically with Mount Allison than Saint Thomas at UNB, and it's set a decade later, this is the world from which David Adams Richards (one of Coady's strongest influences) emerged and *Mean Boy* is worth reading as an *homage-à-clef*. But, it's more than honouring a mentor! Coady has the gift of swinging a character from depths to heights with the deftness of Tiger Woods going from rough to green and it's nowhere better displayed than in Larry's perambulations through this rotting apple orchard of academe. Larry becoming Lawrence is awkward and endearing: Coady emerging from Maritime regionalism and becoming a major novelist with daring parodies and brilliant satire is, as Aritha van Herk says, a *tour de force*. Van Herk knows the world of creative writing programs as student and teacher to depths most of us don't. Here's part of what she wrote in *The Globe and Mail* (March 4, 2006):

> I would not dare to gesture toward any actual persons, living or dead, on whom the character of Arsenault, his black despair, his drinking, his manipulation of students, might be modelled.... Coady's portrayal of the jealous tenuousness of friendship, the in-fighting and fierce competitions of the literary world is daring and brilliant.... Poetry as high art, the calling of intellectual priests, is shredded. The whole of *Mean Boy* seems intent on proving that poets are born, not made.... What is funniest of all is that those who would be *poètes maudits* end up being poetasters, and poetic licence is trumped by poetic justice.

MARINA ENDICOTT

Good to a Fault (2008), *Open Arms* (2001)

Thinking about herself and the state of her soul, Clara Purdy drove to the bank one hot Friday in July. The other car came from nowhere, speeding through on the yellow, going so fast it was almost safely past when Clara's car caught it. She was pushing on the brake, a ballet move, graceful — pulling back on the wheel with both arms as she rose, her foot standing on the brake — and then a terrible crash, a painful extended rending sound, when the metals met.

Does any reader need more encouragement than this to pick up a copy of *Good to a Fault* to find out what happens next? Endicott was not nearly as well known as she ought to have been and Freehand Books was the newest Canadian publisher on the block when the book was published in spring 2008. Making the Giller shortlist and various bestseller lists changed all that and — happily — changed my idea of listing her as the best unknown novelist in the country.

Endicott's debut *Open Arms* (now reprinted thanks to Freehand) was shortlisted for the Amazon.ca/*Books in Canada* First Novel Award of 2001 but was overshadowed (in the eyes of *this* jury member) by Michael Redhill's winner *Martin Sloane* and Dennis Bock's runner-up *The Ash Garden*. Eight years later, more characters and scenes from *Open Arms* are lodged in memory with greater vividness and involvement than from the others. And more laughter: Endicott is really funny, a sweet-natured but sharp-eyed and quick-tongued social observer in the Jane Austen–Barbara Pym–Anne Tyler tradition who can wring love, revulsion, and hilarity from readers in a single page. *Open Arms* was out of print for too long: among other things, it makes high comedy out of the low morals of poets whose cosmic sense of self-entitlement exempts them from loyalty to anything but their own "genius."

The wrong-turn crash that opens *Good to a Fault* causes Clara Purdy's solid sense of everyday morality to take wing and soar beyond previous experiences. Clara has been living a small, quiet, and affluent life but is "in a state of mild despair, forty-three and nothing to show for it." Once married, briefly and stupidly, she's spent most of her life working for an insurance company, caring for sick parents until their recent deaths, gardening, housekeeping, reading books on spirituality, and attending her local Anglican church. The people in the other car — parents, three children, grandmother — come from a very different world. Lorraine and Clayton Gage together with Darlene and Trevor and baby Pearce and Old Mrs. Pell, Lorraine's mother, are virtually homeless when Clara dreamily bumps into them on a Saskatoon street. They've been drifting from town to town, living in an ancient Dodge Dart junked by the accident, and ailing internally — Lorraine is dying, cancer-ridden with late stage lymphoma and Clayton is messed up inside in other ways.

Speaking to her priest after the accident, Clara, a fine and fastidious example of Barbara Pym's "good woman of the parish" at cross-purposes with her conscience, tells Father Tippett that she sees what this family needs but doesn't know if she can do what she thinks ought to be done. More alive to the parable of the Good Samaritan and the teachings of Jesus than this seemingly stony man and his arid sermons, Clara rejects his advice and takes the Gage family into her house and starts to share her life with them. As she does, she finds herself dealing with consequences that include exhaustion, rage, merriment, love, and the intense scrutiny of her own motives in offering hospitality to strangers: is she acting out of guilt, out of goodness, or out of the selfish desire to become a mother without the bother of a partner and pregnancies?

Until her recent success, Endicott was better known in the Canadian theatre world than the literary one. She's worked as an actor, director, and dramaturge and has written three plays — stage experiences that pay off in writing that is tight and compelling. *Good to a Fault* has the same kind of relentless, unstoppable expectancy as Barbara Gowdy's *Helpless* (and once again, many will read the end in order to get past the middle). What's almost singular to Endicott are flashes of hard-won wisdom reminiscent of Leonard Cohen's at his most self-deprecating. Or Thomas Merton's. This bit of Merton comes out of the mouth of Clara's Anglican priest, "Suddenly there is a point where religion becomes laughable. Then you decide that you are nevertheless religious."

DONNA MORRISSEY

Downhill Chance (2002) and Duet: *Sylvanus Now* (2005) & *What They Wanted* (2008)

Downhill Chance (2002)

In 2002, *Kit's Law* was the most visible Canadian book in Dublin's bookstores where it was stacked beside Annie Proulx's *The Shipping News* and piled as high. Back home in Newfoundland (where it's set), Nova Scotia (where Morrissey lives), and odd corners of elsewhere, *Kit's Law* amassed impressive sales since publication in 1999 — mostly by word of mouth as befits a work that, as Thomas Keneally, the author of *Schindler's List*, says, "exists in a valley of its own saying."

Kit's Law was a precursor to Lisa Moore's *Alligator* as far as North Atlantic Gothic and as unpredictable in its high spirits and comic ingenuity. *Downhill Chance* is broader and sharper. It begins in the pre-Confederation years surrounding WWII with an adolescent Clair Gale pursuing truth and justice within the closed world of two outports and two families. Then, years later, ten-year-old daughter Hannah is her mother's daughter as she tries to understand her grandfather's death and her mother's teenage self while making a place for herself in a world full of new roads and government jobs. As Hannah and Clair combine forces to unlock wartime secrets that were buried at Monte Casino, Morrissey eschews ingenuous plotting in order to enlarge the sense of character she shares with Thomas Hardy. Her people, female and male, old and young, have been to church but are not stupefied by the pursuit of salvation and are rich in traits that are not moral at all. They can be loved without their behaviour being approved of, sided with, or otherwise countenanced.

Donna Morrissey was born in 1956 at The Beaches, an outport on the northwest arm of Newfoundland, and writes dialogue as if she'd been reared a generation earlier and never left that coastline. Her work stands outside her own university-educated life and current living space in Halifax in much the same way that Hardy sustained Wessex into the twentieth century or Faulkner carried Yoknapatawpha County, Mississippi with him to Los Angeles. The comparison to Hardy is more apt (and made by Irish reviewers) because the people who populate Morrissey's imagined seaside villages are Old World in their attitudes and un-Americanized in everything except the rawness of their moonshine and the campfire locales of their drinking sprees.

Duet: *Sylvanus Now* (2005) & *What They Wanted* (2008)

Thomas Hardy classified the works for which he's now best known as "Novels of Character and Environment" and in *Sylvanus Now* and *What They Wanted* the environment takes on an ever-expanding character of its own as the social effects of Canada's resource-based economy are microscoped through the changing fortunes of the Now family. Morrissey is more original, more daring with each book, less bound by regionalism, more attuned to distinctly Canadian experience in the latter part of the twentieth century and the start of the twenty-first.

Even among the unusually dynamic and perceptive writers emerging on the East Coast, Morrissey is in a league of her own in terms of an ability as a woman to create fathers and sons every bit as vivid as her mothers and daughters in both their physicality and interiority. Her men are truer to their male selves than most male novelists allow them to be.

Sylvanus (Syllie) Now, a young man of charm and strength, is as determined as any character in all of Hardy to live life in the old ways, to fish for cod as his ancestors did — out of his own port in his own boat with a wife who bears his babies and works alongside the other women "on the flakes" of Cooney Arm, salt drying fresh cod. He courts Addie, the beauty from the neighbouring outport, and beguiles her into seeing him as a refuge from her isolation: "She pasted life around her as if it were wallpaper, but then had scrambled into hiding after it started crimping and peeling and falling in strips around her."

When Joey Smallwood's government turns against the outports, Syllie and Addie have nowhere to go but to one another as the life he loves is replaced by fishing trawlers and fish factories. The "progress" of industrialized fishing and the dispersal of families to towns and cities and, inescapably, the mainland is the only predictable thing about this book and its successor, *What They Wanted,* which carries the Now story forward into the next generation and out to the oil-fields of Alberta.

Both stories are straightforward and fairly uncomplicated. "What is complex," as Lewis DeSoto puts it in his review of the later volume for *The Globe and Mail*, "what is intricate and convoluted and often tortuous, are the emotions that attract, repel and ultimately bind the characters to each other." Here, from the Prologue to *What They Wanted*:

> I remember clear as yesterday those last days in Cooney Arm, the sea dying around us and taking Father's spirit with it ...
>
> For months we all watched him — me, Mother, Chris, Kyle, Gran. We watched as he sat at the table looking out to sea, his head turned from Mother's hands as she fussed with his tea and biscuits and scolded him for distressing his poor old mother, Gran, who was forever standing on her stoop watching over him as he rotted within himself, along with his stage and his flakes and his boat.... It was always Mother's job to worry the most, and for months she'd been lamenting Father's fate, lamenting her own need of wanting him out of this darkness, this terrible, terrible darkness he was sinking into, wanting him back in his boat with the sun colouring his face and the wind brimming his eyes and that awful, awful smell of sickness washed off him. But the fish were gone, sucked into the bowels of a thousand foreign factory ships, leaving Father, and a few other struggling inshore fishermen, sitting weighted at their kitchen table, staring out the window at their languishing boats.

Morrissey's works are almost-oral folk epics. The nearness to conversation is a major source of the energy and transport of imagination that sweeps readers along. Pages get turned quickly as one book closes and the other opens. Syllie and Addie's lives of complicated births, arduous existences, and matter-of-fact deaths are carried forward into their daughter, Sylvie's. She's a university student and bar worker, a good daughter and perhaps an even better sister.

A philosophy major, she understands implicitly that her life, like Augustine's or Rousseau's, is a problem of interesting complexity and historical importance. At the end of his review, DeSoto, writes:

> Readers familiar with Morrissey's other novels will know that she writes of the Newfoundland landscape with the lyricism of a poet. It will come as no surprise then, but perhaps with greater impact, to find that when she turns her attention to Alberta's oil rigs, she conjures up a Dantesque inferno of mud, dirt, stench and darkness, where the men take on the aspect of demons.... If at times I blinked away tears while reading this book, there were other occasions when I gasped for air as I felt myself choking on mud and gas. I swear she must have worked on an oil rig herself, so convincing are these sections.... Read this book.

When Virginia Woolf visited Thomas Hardy, who had endured more abuse from critics and greater neglect by the book-buying public than even she thought had befallen her own works, Woolf was astonished by his calm indifference to literary reputation and by his assurance that to be sociable and a poet at the same time requires only *physical strength*. Donna Morrissey has a similar capacity to astonish those for whom the literary life is less a question of being a prize winner than living the only life she wants to know.

∽

MARY LAWSON

Crow Lake (2002)

Many readers surrendered themselves to the magic of *Crow Lake*; it and Miriam Toews's *A Complicated Kindness* are among the bestselling Canadian novels of the decade. Long before that happened, David Macfarlane had written, "I didn't read *Crow Lake* so much as I fell in love with it. This is one beautiful book." So too had publishers in England, the United States, and half a dozen other countries.

> My great-grandmother Morrison fixed a book rest to her spinning wheel so that she could read while she was spinning, or so the story goes. And one Saturday evening she became so absorbed in her book that when she looked up, she found that it was half past midnight and she had spun for half an hour on the Sabbath day. Back then, that counted as a major sin.

At the end of a first novel that feels as real as a long-time companion speaking dreams, hopes, and fears across a breakfast table, Mary Lawson writes in an author's note that "*Crow Lake* is a work of fiction, but two things in it are not 'figments of ... imagination.'" One is the book rest on great-grandmother's spinning wheel and the second is Lawson's younger sister "whose infant self was the model for Bo." Bo, at eighteen months, is the youngest character in *Crow Lake* — "small and round and had a fine, fair fluff of hair that stood straight out from her head as if she'd been struck by lightning" and so alive in all her pot-banging, fractured sentences, fingers in the food, food not quite in the mouth, diaper-sagging self that she becomes the force of nature who keeps disbelief suspended, persuades us that all of this happened exactly as it is said to happen.

There's very little that a reader really needs to know in advance about the things that do happen in *Crow Lake*. Kate Morrison, the narrator, is in her late twenties and an Assistant Professor of invertebrate ecology in the department of zoology at the University of Toronto. She's reached the point in her relationship with Daniel, a full professor in her department, when it's time to introduce him to her family back in Crow Lake, a farming community four hundred miles north of Yonge and Bloor. The prospect of bringing Daniel home for her nephew's eighteenth birthday fills Kate with fear and summons up detailed memories of the year she turned eight, the year when both her parents were killed by a logging truck and her two teenage brothers (Luke was nineteen, Matt was seventeen) refused to see themselves and their siblings scattered among relatives and set about raising Kate and their baby sister (the eighteen-month-old Bo) on their own.

In *Crow Lake*, Mary Lawson assesses what gets knotted up and what comes undone in the relationships between brothers and sisters when degrees of higher education physically separate, intellectually invert, and emotionally contort the bonds of childhood. It's Matt who is Kate's hero and guide. It's Matt who is the brilliant one in the family, the one who shares his passion for "the ponds, a mile or two across the railroad tracks" with her. It is Matt who teaches her to lie perfectly still "gazing into the dark water, waiting to see what we would see ... drifting out from under rocks and shadows and showing themselves." But it's Kate who goes to university and becomes the expert biologist.

Lawson moved to England in 1968, where she married, raised a family, and worked as a behavioural scientist before turning novelist in her mid-fifties. At first glance, the Canada of Crow Lake and the Morrisons and their neighbours may seem locked in the same sort of time warp that afflicted CBC's *Morningside*, a vast northerly place less varied in its inhabitants, less urban, than the spaces we actually inhabit (as Peter Gzowski acknowledged in his last interviews). And anyone who wants to indulge themselves (at this late date) in further contemplation of the themes too long considered central to Canadian literature, *Crow Lake* is reducible to the tensions between ties to the land and tribe versus faith in a higher power and the self. But, then again, so is the whole of the Bible. Those readers who don't want entire generations to pass in a paragraph, readers as patient as a child gazing into the dark green mirror of a pond soon discover that Kate Morrison's voice makes everything fresher, larger, livelier than it first appears. Kate is not "into" her narcissistic self: she's a trained observer, a good-humoured ecologist who records the ways in which all forms of life, no matter how disparate, are forced to accommodate one another in a common environment, forced to change or perish.

FRANCES ITANI

Deafening (2003)

Taken aback where? Where had she been taken?

Grania had never asked. It was one more mystery to add to the others she carried inside her. Years later, at school, when the words finally tumbled out, it was Miss Marks who intercepted and explained.

"Put an *a* before *back* and the meaning changes," she said. "To be taken aback is to be surprised — by something unexpected."

Pre-publication acclaim for *Deafening* was extremely loud. Sold to twenty markets (the American, British, and Japanese publishers were particularly ear-popping in their auction bids), *Deafening* made Frances Itani a millionaire. That's success for any literary author and not expected for a first-time Canadian novelist. The last time anything like this happened (albeit with a quieter opening chorus) to as good a book and as deserving an author, readers were rewarded with Mary Lawson's *Crow Lake. Deafening* provides more varied pleasures just as flawlessly: a movie version will get made if Meryl Streep's agents get it to her — she's the perfect Mamo, the grandmother who saves Grania O'Neill from living the smaller, shallower, more closeted life that deafness seems ready to impose. As a five-year-old in 1902, Grania is struck deaf by scarlet fever. "Your name," Mamo says in the book's opening sentence. "This is the important word. If you can say your name, you can tell the world who you are." Grania can only say "Graw" and begins to say more because Mamo rises above the hopelessness the rest of her family feels, and teaches her enough words and phrases to navigate neighbourhood life in Deseronto, Ontario, a prospering timber port on the Bay of Quinte.

Convinced that their younger daughter deserves more than living at home can give her, Grania's parents send her to the Ontario School for the Deaf in Belleville where she spends seven years in segregated schooling (the deaf are returned to the hearing world only for summer vacations). It's there that she meets Jim (her beloved "Chim"), the hearing assistant to the school's doctor. They marry before he departs for the Great War to serve as a stretcher-bearer in France and Belgium.

Frances Itani was a nurse in an intensive-care unit before she became the author of the eight collections of poetry and short stories that led up to her "overnight success" in her third decade as a writer. She's married to an official of the International Committee of the Red Cross and has lived in war zones including Croatia during the Bosnian conflict. When she shows readers the wounds Jim and his companions deal with every day, we see, smell, and touch exactly what is unavoidable for front line medical workers when limbs, eyes, ears, and minds are shattered by bullets and flesh is torn apart and scattered by bombs and life is violently sucked out of bodies amid the mortars, minefields, and madness of military combat. It would be unendurable if it wasn't so necessary to Itani's purposes. Compared to Ondaatje and Findley, Itani as an anti-war writer is more precise, knowledgeable, and honest and less given to drawing attention to the art embedded in the writing. A speaker of English, French, German, some Japanese, Spanish, and sign language, she's developed an unadorned English prose that is Zen-like in its both suggested lyricism and suppressed theatricality.

Technically a "historical novel," *Deafening* has an overwhelming sense of immediacy. Grania, Itani has said, is modelled on her own grandmother Gertrude Freeman Stoliker (1898–1987), the Deseronto hotel the O'Neill family operates is based on a great-grandfather's, the Ontario School for the Deaf is itself, and its school newspaper *The Canadian* is quoted to excellent effect. The emotional intimacy that flows between the different generations of O'Neills makes you feel that what exists between Mamo and Grania is carried forward to Itani and will be passed on to her own children's children. A neighbour says of Mamo, "Did you see the way she looked at that child? Oh, the love on her face when she looked at that ... child."

Itani keeps the uncommon lives of common people in wartime in full view without succumbing to Hollywood's narrow conventions about who is heroic and who is not. Her soldiers are any and all of us and the sound of war is the real enemy. "Sound knocks us all over," Jim writes to Grania from the front, "blocks all thought, seeps into the body like deadly gas." Those who vanquish it differ from those who are vanquished by it by learning what Grania can teach about "tuning out" and finding complex but necessary routes between the roar of experience and the silence of understanding.

∼

SUSAN SWAN

The Wives of Bath (1993)

The Susan Swan book most often discussed among writers is *The Biggest Modern Woman of the World* (1983), the story of a real-life 7′6″, 413-pound Nova Scotian giantess, Anna Swan, who weighed eighteen pounds at birth in 1846 and was awarded that title by P. T. Barnum at his freak show. In search of a larger life than Barnum offered, Anna Swan travelled from New York to Europe, returned, and built an oversize farmhouse in the American Midwest, where she attempted to live the rest of her life like a Victorian lady. Swan's account of her ancestor mingles truth and legend in ways that still startle. Alberto Manguel, one of its earliest fans, has written of Swan's work:

> Susan Swan creates myth to lend a story to the problems of our time, a time which has lost touch with its own stories and mythical vocabularies. Swan uses classical modes of story-telling but distorts these modes in order to fit the voice of her time.
>
> Her work is a subversion of both the historical and documentary voice which she believes operates under the pretense of being factual.... In subverting these voices, she forces us to look at another reality, a deeper reality which is rooted in something archetypical. Her interest in freaks, in the gothic, in the apocalyptic, are all ways of lending a narration to contemporary myths.

There's never been a novel quite like it.

For readers who aren't writers, Susan Swan is better known as the author of *The Wives of Bath*, which Lea Pool (working from a script by Judith Thompson) transformed into the 2001 film *Lost and Delirious*, starring Piper Perabo, Jessica Paré, and Mischa Barton. *Lost and Delirious* (and Swan's novel) strike some viewers/readers as nothing more than a tale of steamy lesbian sex in a girls' boarding school. Pity them because to see/read it in such a limited way is to forget what it once was and still is to be an adolescent gripped by a fine madness, transcendent in its idealism and topsy-turvy in its expression of desires.

In the book, it's 1963 and Mary "Mouse" Bradford is sent off to board at Toronto's Bath Ladies College by an insensitive father and invidious stepmother. She meets Paulie Sykes — a prototypical rebel *grrrl* — and they try to figure out what really separates men from women in a closed society where (like Chaucer's Wife) they can live by their own rules. Paulie tests Mouse to prove that she can *be a boy* in small ways — eating six bowls of tapioca pudding without vomiting, letting a match burn to the skin without crying, and managing to urinate whilst standing up — and larger ones that include cross-dressing, fighting, and seduction. That's as far as plot revelations goes: rent the movie, read the book, compare and contrast, and try to remember (if you're in the September of life) what it was to feel that Shakespeare had you and the girl who obsessed you in mind when he wrote *Antony and Cleopatra*. Be prepared to laugh as you read: Mouse's delicious and delirious streaming consciousness is funnier and more complex than any movie can depict in detailing the jokes gender plays with all of us.

❧

JANICE KULYK KEEFER

Thieves (2004), *The Ladies' Lending Library* (2006)

Thieves (2004)

Janice Kulyk Keefer's publisher targeted *Thieves* at readers who adored A. S. Byatt's *Possession* and Michael Cunningham's *The Hours* as another contemporary tale that unravels an unsolved mystery connected with a major literary figure of the past with a third narrative strand in the middle distance. It's an elegant formula for exploring evolving sexual and social relationships between literate women and men from late Victorian times to the present.

Like Byatt and Cunningham, Kulyk Keefer is both literary scholar and novelist — smart, well-informed, imaginative, and nuanced when it comes to bringing inner worlds to life on the page: she more than holds her own in their company. Kulyk Keefer is immersed in Mavis Gallant, Elizabeth Bowen, Virginia Woolf, and Katherine Mansfield and is adroit capturing the jumble, snarl, muddle, bungle, and disarray that fuels the restlessness of young people abroad. *Thieves* moves from New Zealand to England, through Europe to America, and ends up in Windsor, Ontario.

It's 1988, the centenary of the birth of Katherine Mansfield (1888–1928), New Zealand's most famous writer — a woman whose creative years were burdened by alienation from her family, jealousies between lovers and friends, venereal disease, tuberculosis, and an ineffectual husband. All are reflected in her depiction of middle-class married and family life in the short stories upon which Mansfield's reputation rests. Virginia Woolf edited and published her and famously said, "She is the only writer I have ever been jealous of."

Montgomery (Monty) Mills, the Kiwi protagonist of *Thieves*, has spent years trying to draw attention to this rivalry/jealousy. While a doctoral student in English at the University of London, Monty presented a paper to a seminar in the very room that served Woolf as a bedroom in her youth, asserting that Woolf had "stolen the bones of her best fiction" from Mansfield.

Woolf hadn't borrowed mere themes or subject matter.... No, what Woolf had stolen from Mansfield had been a technique for singling out, intensifying the small, seemingly shallow things in life — a woman combing her hair, a child playing with a bowl of porridge.... Compare ... Woolf's often stilted sentences and cumbrous similes with her rival's fresh, arresting images and fluid prose. Surely these different styles have something to do with the writers' differing perceptions of their bodies? Woolf's dismissal of her own sexuality was widely known; why not read in that context her remark about Mansfield smelling like a civet cat that had taken to street-walking?

Monty's colonial thumb in the imperial eye destroyed his academic future before it started. Back in Wellington, teaching at "the boys' school nearest the South Pole," Monty lets go of his academic dreams only to have Mansfield return and reconfigure his future. A letter intended for his writer-father (who is also a Mansfield scholar) sends Monty to a major Mansfield archive in Chicago where an encounter with a collector of Mansfieldiana leads him to Windsor, the long-time home of Garnet Trowell, a music teacher, who was Mansfield's lover when they were both twenty and the cause of her only — miscarried — pregnancy. By finding lost letters and discovering what happened to Garnet after his parting from Katherine, Monty comes to a new and better understanding of the differences between imagining and becoming:

> This life of ours that we think of as a journey, with a marked road to follow and a destination to achieve, is really a random leaping back and forth.... An opal thrown like a skipping stone, light to light across the dark.

In the sixties, so many undergrads were drawn to Mansfield and her writings by her tubercular afflictions, her bisexuality, her promiscuity, and her unconventional marriage that the poster corner of university bookstores featured her face at least as prominently as Woolf's before she fell out of fashion (along with her friend D. H. Lawrence) in a way Woolf never has. To read *Thieves* is to discover Mansfield as a fierce and forceful woman who, in death as in life, has a remarkable ability to see what everyone else misses, no matter how painful it gets.

The Ladies' Lending Library (2006)

> Sexual intercourse began
> In nineteen sixty-three
> (Which was rather late for me) —
> Between the end of the *Chatterley* ban
> And the Beatles' first LP

So Philip Larkin wrote in "Annus Mirabilis." That's an owlish middle-class university-educated Englishman for you! For the group of first-generation Ukrainian women who summer with their children at Kalyna Beach on Georgian Bay — the "Ladies" of *The Ladies' Lending Library* — the summer of 1963 includes *Lady Chatterley's Lover* but also *Valley of the Dolls, The World of Suzie Wong, The Carpetbaggers, Fanny Hill*, and books such as *Portrait of the Artist as a Young Man* "that Sasha Plotsky's come across doing courses at the university." But the books are the excuse to meet "for gin and gossip at Sasha's cottage every Friday afternoon, as their husbands are starting the long drive up from the city" and "give them a way of feeling sophisticated and daring: women of a wider world."

> About sex, the Ladies already know everything. Almost all of them married young; they had their children right away, there's never been any time to wonder if things could have worked out differently. Sex and haste and exhaustion, sex and the fear of kids barging into the bedroom at all and any hours of the night. Never, ever sex in the morning, sex in the afternoon.

Larkin's sex as

> A sort of bargaining,
> A wrangle for a ring,

has become sex that "takes forever, like being in a lineup at the checkout counter at the supermarket" until

> ... finally you feel the one sensation you are guaranteed: your husband's body crumpling in your arms, for all the world like a baby that's drunk its fill at your breast.... And the awful remarkable thing is this: the women aren't really resentful, most of them; they know they'd have much more trouble surviving if they had to make room, find the time — that's always it, the time — for any slower kind of sex than what they're used to.

Apart from Sasha who is willing to challenge traditional community values, the ladies resent Darka Marchuk, sixteen-year-old babysitter-in-residence. Darka, who bleaches her hair the day she arrives, "alarms and irritates" them because "the girl parades the softness and fullness of her body, the obvious pleasure she takes in the bounce of breasts and bum" in a two-piece bathing suit that is her everyday uniform. The idea of physical passion that Darka represents — "of becoming a prisoner, not to a lover so much as to your own body" and "feeling so intense that *pleasure* seems too mild a word for it" — excites fear and curiosity, makes them "dying to know, what happens, how and why" to those "who give way, as the saying goes, to passion."

When sex "breaks out like some contagious disease" and changes everything among them, it isn't a book but the film *Cleopatra* and "its aftermath, the outrageous, irresistible love affair between Elizabeth Taylor and Richard Burton" that becomes "the subject they discuss" as they try to understand that "you don't have to be Elizabeth Taylor to give way, to give yourself away. That it can happen in Hamilton as well as Hollywood. That you can make it happen."

As advertised, this is "a story for anyone who has longed for the sweet and heady days of bygone summers and the risky promises of change" but it's also deeper. Kulyk Keefer isn't simply a writer who was lucky enough to spend summers in a childhood paradise on Georgian Bay and be blessed with a capacity to recreate that past with no more than trivial memory lapses. In her "Acknowledgements" she writes, "Readers of ... Mansfield will recognize the debt ... to the author of "At the Bay." "Mansfield was expert at writing short episodes that gradually intertwine to reveal the complexity and fragility of social situations. Her great theme is that to live is to yearn most strongly for that which is seldom possible. *The Ladies' Lending Library* is subtler and more substantial a work of art than any tale turning on Elizabeth Taylor's *Cleopatra* has any right to be.

~⁀⊃

JEAN McNEIL

Private View (2002)

Born in Cape Breton, Jean McNeil worked in publishing in Toronto before leaving for England in 1991 in high dudgeon after the collapse of Lester & Orpen Dennys. Her London years have been interrupted by lengthy travels in Latin America. McNeil is, among other things, the author of the *Rough Guide to Costa Rica* and a contributor to the *Rough Guide to Central America*.

Private View, her second novel, is set in Shoreditch, an East End enclave of artists and galleries less than a mile west of Brick Lane that's begun to draw gentrifiers. As artistic values are carried off by inflationary real estate, Alex and Conrad, odder than the original *Odd Couple*, try to figure out what's next. Sole survivor of a plane crash in the Amazonian jungle, Alex is a young woman who has lost the ability to remember Ben, the lover with whom she was travelling, and the power to make art. Conrad, Ben's bisexual friend from New Brunswick, is mid-thirties, mid-career, and troubled by manias that make art possible but threaten to destroy him.

Private View allows Conrad to talk and Alex to reflect on what it means to live with possibilities that don't present themselves to most people most of the time — living without memory, loving without being distracted by gender:

> Eventually, through twenty minutes conversation about nothing — the area they lived in, house prices, how long Alex has been in London, why Bethnal Green tube station is a little too far for daily commuting — she realized that Conrad's new lover ... was one of those shockingly beautiful people who make you inadvertently hold your breath while you are talking to them ... it came from the place in everyone that is instantly moved by symmetry.

McNeil can be hot in the way that D. H. Lawrence is tropically lyrical and as cool at introspection as Virginia Woolf without making a mess of conflicting modernisms. Remarkably, she makes something new that is satirical, sensitive, fresh, and vibrant in its exploration of the sexual muddles of artists living at a similar distance from Puccini's "Bohemians" as a Turner Prize winner is from a Turner painting.

~

DIANE SCHOEMPERLEN

In the Language of Love (1994)

Caroline Adderson says Diane Schoemperlen is "one of the most consistently innovative writers in Canadian fiction." She's that and more. Author of six story collections and three novels, Schoemperlen delivers the unexpected alongside what readers have come to take for granted in her work — likeable characters, everyday predicaments, realistic dialogue in familiar settings, wit, and chortling humour. Her protagonists are women writers or artists, living in cities that seem a lot like her adopted Kingston, who are the kind of people other women like to befriend. When Schoemperlen reads her work in public, there's intense and immediate intimacy between her and women of every age that doesn't exclude young men. Whatever else is going to happen in the next hour, her audience senses shared confidences and gossip.

Her stories, as Adderson says, are as old as Jane Austen's — of "women's friendships and how fine a line there is between offering support, collaborating in a delusion, and even being complicit in deceit." Where she adds something remarkably new is in finding unusual forms of storytelling that build upon her secondary career as a collage artist. As Nikki Abraham says, she "can take an old tune and play with it — twist it, bend it, loop it back on itself, turn it upside down, appear to abandon it completely and then, with a sly flourish, return it to you fresh, new, still itself but transformed now into a thing with possibilities."

Schoemperlen's first novel, *In the Language of Love*, employs one hundred words from a 1910 word association test (words like *table, dark, loud, ocean, anger*) as seeds for one hundred vignettes. Each word association takes readers further into Joanna's awkwardness: she's a collage artist, an improviser forced to tackle pregnancy and motherhood innovatively. As Chris Sinha noted in a recent letter to *The London Review of Books* (February 21, 2008), none of the leading proponents of the Frankfurt school of psychology (Max Wertheimer, Max Horkheimer, Theodor Adorno, Kurt Koffka, Kurt Lewin) with its dominant emphasis on Gestalt and related anti-positivist approaches to cognition ever had access to research resources in the USA equivalent to those they were forced to abandon in Germany after the collapse of the Weimar republic. The work of these men prefigure many ideas current in modern cognitive science and in the work of a writer like Schoemperlen who blends images with texts in ways that satisfy unspoken longings.

The title story of her *Red Plaid Shirt: Stories New and Selected* (2002), a second-person singular tale of domestic violence revealed to the reader through pieces of clothing the protagonist has worn, is as troubling as anything Raymond

Carver, American master of the terrain, wrote about domestic disturbances. This collection is an excellent introduction to Schoemperlen's works that tracks her development between 1976 (when she fell under the direct influence of Alice Munro without abandoning her own sense of blue-collar life in places like the Lakehead where she was born) and 1996 when she found the form and content that make her first novel so singular. *Red Plaid Shirt* also includes "How to Write a Serious Novel About Love," which is speculative and instructional as it goes about its business: like an Escher drawing, there's endlessly changing focus with more than one perspective always in play — the author is inside and out-side, vulnerable and detached, distant and self-mocking as she works her way through the complexities of everyday urban life. It's the template for *In the Language of Love* and ought to be mandatory reading in Creative Writing 101 wherever it's offered.

~

GAIL SCOTT

Heroine (1987)

My copy of *Heroine* is well-thumbed but one look at the cover with its black, grey, white collage of cityscape, claw-footed bathtub, English and French graf-fiti, vertical and horizontal bars of orange, HEROINE in black on white and A NOVEL BY GAIL SCOTT in white on black sans serif lettering (check it out on the Amazon.ca website) is all it takes to remember what it was to open it for the first time and read without the commentaries that have accumulated over two decades as it turned from a casual read into a "text" that is near-sacred within the kind of Women's Studies programs Zoe Whittall sends up in *Bottle Rocket Hearts*. So it was a delight to discover that its fundamental pleasures are still accessible and memorable to young men: "andrew" of main beach, QLD, Australia writes on the Amazon site:

I read this book eleven years ago in Brisbane. The girl I fell in love with had a friend who'd lived in Canada and been given it. I was blown away by the concentric plot, the language and the flawed dignity and the weary beauty of the narrator's tale. I'd love to read this book again 'cause I was nineteen back then. I don't have a credit card so I'll just keep grazing in old bookshops with the faith in them funny ordinary little miracles. This book is one of the, say, two dozen novels that have truly added magic to my sweet short life and have given me that ecstatic gratitude [that sweet, sweet feel] for art and life. I reckon you should read it ...

A woman takes a bath and masturbates: that's about all that happens externally in *Heroine*. Internally, she writes herself into existence as a work-in-progress in a city that is a soundscape. As her radio broadcasts coverage of the tenth anniversary of the FLQ kidnappings, she plays with the idea that it's possible to make a traditional story (beginning, middle, end) about a couple discussing revolution. If this sounds boringly self-indulgent, it isn't. Scott has a gift for capturing tensions we all feel as our inner operating systems argue and negotiate what traditional commandments we must break and which rules we must impose on ourselves if the pursuit of happiness isn't going to become a sentimental exercise and love will fulfill rather than impoverish us.

~⌒

LARISSA LAI

Salt Fish Girl (2002)

Larissa Lai's *Salt Fish Girl* intertwines stories of Nu Wa, a shape-shifter from Old China in a nineteenth-century incarnation, and a young woman four decades in the future. Its 2044 and Miranda is living in Serendipity, a walled city in the

Pacific Northwest, and has been infected by Dreaming Disease. The future is ruled by biotechnology, cybernetics, corporatism.

Salt Fish Girl is shaped by Latin American conventions of magic realism, so it's dreamlike in its psychology and intensely real in its politics as Lai shifts between sci-fi, social commentary, poetry, women's literature, and some of the peculiarly gay-Chinese-in-Canada sensibilities that Wayson Choy brings tellingly into his memoirs. Lai is herself and the rich stew she concocts reflects her own diversity: she was born in California, grew up in St. John's, Newfoundland, attended UBC for her BA, the University of East Anglia for her MA, and the University of Calgary for her Ph.D.

"This is a story about stink, after all," the narrator (who is fish, snake, girl, and woman) says, "a story about rot, about how life grows out of the most fetid, smelling places." Lai writes with her nose stuck in some things that are less offensive to some readers than others: for instance, Miranda smells of durian fruit (the smell of cat piss) that won't offend cat-fanciers in the same way that it might repel doggier types. But whatever your nasal preferences, there's so much "romantic" interest going on that Miranda's "stink" becomes ambient like a nightclub's washrooms. Miranda and Nu Wa both live shocking violent love stories that bring into play an element lacking in much dystopian fiction — the great migrations of the twentieth century as experienced by the participants. Lai's sensibilities as a novelist are closer to Rawi Hage's than to Margaret Atwood's. Asked in an interview about the complex relations between past and future among the Chinese immigrants in her work, she told an interviewer,

> on the one hand you have this relation to the past which is mythic, so you're constantly trying to imagine it as this romantic thing that you've sorrowfully left behind or as this terrible violent thing that you've escaped from. And on the other hand you've left that place because of the future. You want to go to a better future and you're constantly mortgaging the present to that future. I think a lot of people are coming from those fragmented backgrounds and into these fragmented futures that are actually really really difficult to wrap your head around.

Salt Fish Girl is layered so it repays multiple readings; no surprise then that it has attained the same kind of "sacred" status among Gen-X and -Y women who come from immigrant communities or find lovers within them that Gail Scott's *Heroine* has among Boomers negotiating the French-English divide. If you take the future of Canada seriously, you must read this.

KAREN McLAUGHLIN

From This Distance (2009)

When it comes to this book, I have several years jump on other readers. Karen McLaughlin asked me to read it when it was an out-of-shape, flabby, deliciously funny manuscript that had in it something I'd never encountered in any novel — intimate knowledge of living on-site among the engineering elite at several of the major construction projects that have transformed Canada's energy production and overturned a lot of domestic situations among the builders.

To focus all she knows and feels about this country from Grand Manan where she was raised to Thetis Island where she now lives, McLaughlin puts Robyn Gallagher in a car she has inherited from the mother-in-law she believes misjudged her. In it, she sets out from the town where she buried Muriel, on the banks of the Bay of Fundy, to go on a cross-country road trip back to her home in Calgary. Although there are hazards along the way, Robyn discovers that her journey crosses more than just physical terrain. The long stretches of solitude enable her finally to speak her mind to Muriel, to settle old scores, and to seize the opportunity to reflect on where she stands — both within herself and within the world. At times furious, funny, and deeply compassionate, *From This Distance* is the life-affirming story of one woman's liberation from limited expectations. This is one of our very best road stories.

ANNALS OF OURLIT VIII

HENRY JAMES AND THE HALF-LIFE
OF TOO MANY NOVELS

Contemporary neurology tells us that reasoning isn't based in a single, general-purpose computer with a *homunculus* sitting inside the human head looking out at the world as the true self penetrating obscurities — but is an aggregation of multiple operating systems. Each system is appropriate to one of perhaps fourteen departments of reality — intuitive physics, intuitive natural history, intuitive engineering, intuitive psychology, a sense of space, a sense of number, a sense of probability, intuitive economics, a mental database, and logic, language, and three further components of specific concern to novelists — fear, disgust, and morality (according to Steven Pinker's listing in *The Blank Slate*, 2004).

In 1958, when I was fourteen and first thought about writing books of my own, what I thought about was telling stories where fairly ordinary people found themselves doing extraordinary things in the real world. Reading Joseph Conrad's *Lord Jim* was a revelation — Jim (who is a young man as stuffed with popular sea tales as Don Quixote is with tales of chivalry) dreams of becoming a hero but turns coward when tested and pays the price several times over in misadventures with pirates and other scoundrels. After reading it, I picked Henry James's *The Future of the Novel* off a shelf of paperbacks at Regina's Canada Drug and Book (where I normally just got my school supplies) and bought it because it had something to say about Joseph Conrad. I'd found Conrad's way of telling a story so strange and amazing that I wanted someone to explain it to me and I doubted that my Grade 9 English teacher was interested.

I had only a vague idea who Henry James was (one of my older sisters had brought one of his novels home from university with her) and soon found what he'd written was not intended for the kind of mind I possessed. What I liked best in his book, what I studied most closely, was Leon Edel's "Introduction." "The volume takes its title," Edel began, "from a long-buried essay ... which first appeared in 1900" and was reprinted now "for the first time" in fifty-six years. A buried treasure! A prophecy that had come true! Or failed! For me to open and read! What a spur to curiosity! James was an unusual prophet, a man usually concerned with the immediate and the predictable but a writer, Edel wrote, who "could not forego this occasion to act as oracle for the novel."

"This occasion" was the turning of the nineteenth century into the twentieth and it seemed a remarkable coincidence to me — remember that I was fourteen — that I'd be precisely the age of his essay when the next century came round. What struck Edel most about this essay was James's optimism: "Till the world is an unpeopled void there will be the image in the mirror," James says as he states his conviction that there will be novels as long as there are people and that no other art form will ever be better at working with those images so long as what writers create is "various and vivid." And when that happens, the novel becomes the greatest of anodynes or ultimate painkiller. A novel that seriously attempts to create *the various and vivid* is infinitely elastic: it can go anywhere and observe everything. It can be as intensely poetic as Conrad is in *Nostromo* and yet encompass the life of a whole society. It can be as political and para-doxical in feeling as George Orwell's *1984* and be prescient.

In his essay "Why I Write," Orwell asserts "the opinion that art should have nothing to do with politics is itself a political attitude." Commenting on Orwell in her "Forethoughts" to the essay collection, *Quarrel & Quandary* (2000), Cynthia Ozick (Henry James's most prominent contemporary advocate prior to Colm Tóibín) writes:

> The central question, perhaps, is this: is politics a distraction from art, or is it how we pay attention to the life that gives rise to art? And might not the answer be: both, depending on the issues and the times? ... History is and is not ephemeral: situations and events evaporate, but their moral and intellectual residue does not.... In a post-theological era, a romantic paganism (sometimes labelled "spirituality") freely roams. What Saul Bellow calls "the oceanic proliferating complexity of things" sweeps the mind away from concentration. Concentration on

what? On the non-transient. And it is on that negative ground that I set my purpose.

Henry James was not complacent. He complained that a near-oceanic proliferation of novels lacking variety, vividness, concentration got written and found publishers year after year. Timid editors encouraged mediocre writers to cater to adolescent females as "ideal" readers. Praising James's own courage, Edel wrote that nothing "could be more outrageous than the bare story of *The Wings of the Dove*: a man making love to a dying girl so that he may inherit her money and thus marry the woman to whom he has been pledged and who becomes his mistress as part of the whole diabolical bargain." Then he wrote:

> James would have no cause for complaint today, or rather his complaint would inevitably be of another order.... In our time we can almost imagine him as saying (perhaps to Mr. Norman Mailer): "*Allons donc*, it's all very well to get into the bedroom, and even into bed, if you want to take the novel that distance — but aren't you, young man (and you are so outrageously young!), in going scarcely anywhere else, rather neglecting, shall we say, the daylight side of life?" In some such way he would still plead for variety as against monotony; would go farther, for he would argue that in taking the reader into endless bedrooms the modern novelist is being as immature as the Victorian who tried to pretend there were no such rooms at all.

In search of Norman Mailer's bedrooms and beds, I discovered that the librarian on duty at the Regina Public Library thought a fourteen-year-old wasn't adult enough to check him out. Curious about my interest in him, she asked where I'd heard of Mailer and lessened my embarrassment with her enthusiasm for Leon Edel: Edel wasn't merely a Canadian writer; he'd been raised in Jensen and educated in Yorkton! The first Canadian book I'd ever bought was by someone from Saskatchewan!

After high school, Joseph Leon Edel (1907–1997) moved from Yorkton to

Montreal with his parents so that he could study at McGill. Despite current neglect, Edel was the first Canadian author to become equally well known and respected in London, Paris, and New York. Although he wrote insightfully about James Joyce, Willa Cather, the Bloomsbury Group, and others, he'll be forever identified with his five volume biography of Henry James (1953–1972) and with *Literary Biography* (1957) — a small book of a mere 113 pages that is, arguably, the most influential literary work of the twentieth century by a Canadian. In it, he asserts that biographers must seek out continuity in human lives, struggle as mightily as psychoanalysts to perceive the "overlap between what an individual did and the life that made this possible." *Literary Biography* teaches readers to seek out the writer's project in a work and to judge books in terms of their success or failure in advancing the writer's own projects — not the reader's own. What I learned from Edel (after the librarian stamped *Literary Biography* not Mailer's *The Deer Park* on my card) is to follow natural inclinations and read novels existentially rather than as cultural artifacts to be studied. What I learned from Edel writing on Henry James writing on the novel is that the novel can do anything, go anywhere, be as vernacular as Saul Bellow or as mannered as Nabokov. Novelists who don't push boundaries end up pushing buttons, eliciting stock responses, convincing themselves that there's nothing at all wrong with becoming conventional, bourgeois, suburban, imprisoned by the need to be *likeable* and so alike one another that they fail to rise above ignorance and prejudice and consider anything that might not be a worthless caricature of a real thing. None of our novelists — not even David Adams Richards and Margaret Atwood, as various and vivid and brave as they are — have pushed boundaries as far and shown the novel to be as elastic as Barbara Gowdy. *Helpless* failed commercially because it refused to knuckle under to ignorance and prejudice, refused to cheat the mirror.

～

BARBARA GOWDY

Helpless (2007), *The Romantic* (2003), *The White Bone* (1998),
Mister Sandman (1995)

Helpless (2007)

Sonny Rollins, the tenor saxophone colossus who was awarded the Polar Music Prize by the Royal Swedish Academy as "one of the most powerful and personal voices in jazz for more than fifty years," tells people who ask him what he thinks about when he plays that "you can't think and play at the same time." What Rollins means is that he practises until he internalizes all the elements he needs and then lets the music explicate "in the moment" whatever it dares to do. The result is music that is tightly focussed and casually brilliant, inexorably logical yet unpredictable, remarkably intelligent yet deeply felt. Rollins's music — especially when he plays a Thelonious Monk tune like "Misterioso" — is the sonic equivalent of Barbara Gowdy's storytelling in *Helpless* — disciplined and free, allusive yet dissonant.

Gowdy, who spent years training as a pianist before taking up fiction, is forever moving forward, improving technically, finding better ways to express what in the here and now is truly momentous, really worth questioning. Meeting over lunch at Dooney's Café in mid-February of 2007 to discuss her sixth novel just prior to its publication, she told me:

> What I think I've been questioning all these years in my writing is, Who is it we find worthy, what kind of human being? What are our yardsticks, and how qualified are we to judge? I am unswervingly on the side of giving the individual the benefit of the doubt. I don't extend that same goodwill to nations or cultures (I'm suspicious of large groups of people claiming like-mindedness) but to individuals I do.

In *Helpless* the lives of four adults — Ron, Nancy, Mika, and Celia — intersect through the agency of nine-year-old Rachel, Celia's daughter. It's early summer and Toronto is in a heat wave. Celia, a single parent who clerks four days a week at a small, independent video shop and performs "jazz and blues standards at the Casa Hernandez Motel on Lakeshore Boulevard ... Friday and Saturday evenings," is too broke to buy an air conditioner but principled enough to resist turning her extraordinarily beautiful mixed-race daughter into a child model. "Little girls are a big deal right now," she's told by a photographer-hustler who buys them iced teas in Java Ville and promises "a thousand plus residuals" per session if her daughter is allowed to appear in "certain high-end ads." "You know you're beautiful, right?" he asks and Rachel just shrugs. Celia's response is that nine is a little young to start trading in on looks.

This guy isn't the only man to have noticed Rachel: she's being stalked by someone who isn't as easily deflected. Ron is an overweight appliance repairman with a drinking problem who normally reserves his nurturing instincts for his collection of vintage vacuum cleaners. Seeing Rachel for the first time, "a murky, underwater feeling enveloped him.... Her skin was light ... tawny. Her hair, a miraculous chromium yellow, was pulled into a ponytail of tiny spiral curves, like the springs in old ballpoint pens."

Misinterpreting Rachel's home life while peering into Celia's apartment from behind a dumpster parked in the alleyway, Ron snatches Rachel from outside her Cabbagetown home in the middle of a citywide blackout. Believing he's rescuing her from physical, emotional, and sexual abusers, it's his intention to keep Rachel safe and out of harm's way until he and Nancy (who is unable to have a child of her own) can subvert her affections, escape to Florida, and raise her as their own child. The "safe place" in the basement underneath his appliance shop is a prison cell fit for a princess with mauve-and-white décor, canopy bed, menagerie of stuffed animals, large-screen plasma TV, Disney on DVD, top-of-the-line electronic keyboard, remarkable doll's house, art supplies, and just about everything any child could want — except there's no Internet connection, no access to a phone, and the windows are frosted and barred. Beneath an avuncular surface that persuades Rachel she will be released as soon as the streets are free of "slave drivers" (as she puts it), Ron is constantly "agitated" — at war with an obsession with prepubescent girls that has troubled him since adolescence. Although Ron "wants to rescue and protect," he's too self-deluded to consider the consequences or the shock waves of misery it creates once the police launch round-the-clock, door-to-door investigations.

Helpless is immediately accessible and menacing as a thriller but defies and eviscerates genre-writing even as it simulates with tight sentences, jump cuts, and so real a sense of threat that it'll take more self-restraint than most readers can manage not to skip to the end for reassurance that fear and disgust will not prevail. Gowdy makes no attempt to portray Ron as an irredeemable monster — he's a sad sack with a sorry past and a stupid sense of his own virtues. What Gowdy provides instead are close-ups of three of the most elusive components of human reasoning — danger based on fear, contamination based on disgust, and the moral sense. Gowdy's artistry is essentially theatrical — musical and dramatic — not psychoanalytical: she wants to make people feel, to give lessons in feeling strange, freakish, repellent, utterly different, and overwhelmed by aesthetic and moral choices so that we do not repress, deflect, or submerge emotions that can bring meaning to life and life to the thresholds of beauty, truth, and goodness.

Barbara Gowdy's genius in *Helpless* — and that's not too strong a word for it — is to portray several kinds of goodness and make each of them more interesting than mass culture persuades us their opposites inevitably are. Like Nabokov (who she is unlike in so many other ways), Gowdy refuses to flatter the marketplace and provide half-witted banalities in the guise of evil. Over lunch, she fretted over the reception *Helpless* was likely to receive. Would reviewers recognize it for what it was and not for what they might want it to be? Some did get it right. No one said it better than M. A. C. Farrant in *The Vancouver Sun*:

> The sleight of hand — the magic — that Gowdy achieves at the end of the novel is ... astonishing. We realize that it has been love, and nothing but love — Gowdy's enduring subject — that has been driving this time bomb of a novel, all along. Once again we are rendered helpless before its skewed, though brilliant, face.

"Misterioso" indeed.

The Romantic (2003)

Thomas Mann, the writer who always comes to mind whenever I think about Gowdy's novels, was particularly struck by two sentences while reading Harry Levin's *James Joyce: A Critical Introduction* in 1944 (according to Hermann Kurzke in *Thomas Mann: A Biography*, 2003). Levin wrote of Joyce, "He has enormously increased the difficulties of being a novelist" and of Joyce's generation, "The best writing of our contemporaries is not an act of creation, but an act of evocation, peculiarly saturated with reminiscences." Contemplating Joyce through Levin's words, Mann suddenly saw more similarities than differences. He wrote in his diary, "Stylistically, I now really know only parody. In this close to Joyce." Mann began to see that "under the cover of a conventional use of language, he has been perhaps as adventurous an innovator as Joyce." It was a good thing that he could see it because few of his critics, Levin included, ever did. After the publication of *Dr. Faustus*, Professor Levin dropped Mann from his course on literary modernism at Harvard and replaced him with Kafka.

Brian Fawcett, who has read Gowdy as closely as anybody, thinks that the story collection *We So Seldom Look on Love* is her *self-defining* work as a writer: In these stories, it's clear that she believes our redeeming grace lies in our ability to learn through love to be inclusive in ways that defy social conventions. It's clear, that is, if you read her in a spirit of contemplation and attend to her evocations of lives peculiarly saturated with reminiscences of goods known and paradises fleetingly glimpsed. Glimpsed not gained: the Edens are epistemological not geographical. Gowdy wants her readers to "contemplate" possibilities. She does not advocate anything but she does refuse to offer false or sentimental choices in eight tales of outrageous situations (a marriage dialogue between a woman and her transsexual fiancé, litigation between Siamese twins who share the same two-headed body, the female necrophile whose story gives the collection its title and is the basis of the movie *Kissed*) that investigate the uncomfortably close connection between suffering and comedy.

The novels that predate *Helpless* progress in literary artifice to confound expectations as she illuminates her own understanding. One by one, they up the ante, enormously increase the difficulties of being a novelist in our time, and place by loosening traditional restraints and creating ever-increasing spaces in which to work. On bad days, days that cough up yet another impeccably researched but utterly dated "novel" from one of her near-contemporaries, I wonder if any writer in this country other than Catherine Bush has noticed the ways in which Gowdy is hollowing out literary forms and, following Thomas Mann's lead, radically recreating them from within. In Mann's *Dr. Faustus*, Adrian (a composer) says to the Devil, "One could raise the game (of making music) to a yet higher power by playing with forms from which, as one knows, life has vanished." The Devil replies, "I know, I know. Parody."

For Mann's Devil, parody is a cheap trick and he offers Adrian a radical breakthrough, a new form of artifice beyond parody in exchange for the composer's soul. Adrian is trapped by the offer and succumbs to it. There's no exit for him because he's caught up in a musician's version of Nietzsche's death of God: Art with a capital A (which was once a grand illusion) is now a lie, a denial of reality rather than a transfiguration of it. Unlike Margaret Atwood, who has answered a world that has lost its sense of order with the mythical methods of Northrop Frye, Gowdy discreetly travesties those same methods in ways that are directly analogous to Marshall McLuhan's send-ups of Frye. She attacks a myth through the myth's own virtues.

In *The Romantic*, she reminds us, like Cervantes, that the real hero of romance is always the romanticizing imagination and not the romanticized beloved. Louise Kirk falls in love with her childhood playmate Abel Richter. Louise and Abel (the evocation of Heloise and Abelard is intentional) roam a Toronto-area ravine together, examining flora, fauna, and each other with lust and idealism. Abel, an adopted boy living with German immigrant parents, is the outsider Louise feels herself inwardly to be. He's her perfect soulmate, or so she thinks. Abel has ideas of his own, especially the big idea that one's destiny is achievable only in "complete isolation." From there, she leads us to discover with Louise (and the way she does this is through the accumulation of anti-romantic domestic detail in Abel's world) that the greatest feat of heroism lies always in facing the toughest question life ever offers any of us: How do we fill in the gutted hole left by the death of a lover with something other than unhappiness-ever-after?

As Louise reads the essay on "life as oblivion" that is among the things she inherits from Abel, we realize along with her that the heroic survivor of any true love story is the lover who withstands nihilism by offering the world as kind and as accurate an interpretation as possible of the person who has been lost. This too is in Cervantes but is often lost in translation from his age to ours: if we have difficulty fully understanding Louise but embrace her with at least a little of the magnanimity with which she accepts Abel, it's because she, like Don Quixote, holds up a reflecting mirror that gives us back ourselves in ways we never before imagined.

The White Bone (1998)

Most of us encounter fables earlier even than myths and learn through them that before dealing with the "ever after," we have to deal with the here-and-now in ways that are counterintuitive. Our ways — the ways of self, family, tribe, clan — are not the only ways nor the best ways of acting: we must also behave well with strangers both at home and abroad. Lessons in civility and civic virtue work their way down from clan to individual through "the wise ones" so it's not at all surprising that fables often employ clan totems — animals — as principal characters. Nor is it surprising that the animals are never simply themselves: as teachers, they are invariably shape-shifters. *The White Bone* is all about not-quite-elephants imagining themselves as not-quite-humans in order that humans can imaginatively recreate themselves from a non-human point of view. Why should any of us do this? A better question: what do any of us foolish people have to lose by spending a few hours thinking of ourselves as matriarchal visionaries who sing all the time? As exiles on the road to a Safe Place?

The White Bone opens with five family trees and be forewarned, the first fifty pages demand concentration and give little indication of how rewarding this book will prove to be because the family trees of She-Spurns (a.k.a. Mud), She-Deflates, She-Soothes, Tall Time, and the others are followed by a glossary of elephant language: one example, if you have "trunk," you possess "depth of spirit" — something elephants need to withstand the onslaught of severe drought underfoot and helicopters inhabited by ivory-seeking "hind-leggers" overhead.

The book is a series of quests as they seek "Safe Place," elephant heaven, which can be located only by finding and throwing the White Bone of the title so that it points in the right direction.

The first book that came to mind while reading *The White Bone* was Steinbeck's *The Grapes of Wrath*. Like the Joads, the She-S's find out that you can't escape drought without coming face-to-face with questions of physical and cultural survival. There are some interesting parallels between Steinbeck's characters and Gowdy's (Rosasharn and Mud, Jim Casy and Tall Time and so on) that are fun tracking on a rainy afternoon for anyone interested in seeing how two stories with very different DNA make analogous use of authentically Jungian archetypes. But the parallel really worth drawing attention to is the common bond between writers as seemingly dissimilar as Steinbeck and Gowdy.

The environmentalist Barry Lopez once wrote that "John Steinbeck brings together the human heart and the land" and urged readers to consider carefully the ways in which he links the external landscape of our relations to the world and the internal landscape of our relations to the place where we live. Steinbeck wanted his writing to recapture a child's vision "of colors more clear than they are to adults, of tastes more sharp." He invites readers to look with rapt attention until we see that nature is not a commodity, animals are not for slaughtering, and humans are a species bound intimately to the places where they live, breed, love, suffer, and die. That accomplished, he then demands that readers shift perspective and gaze inward and look past the isolation, loneliness, failure, desolation we all encounter at first glance until we find our way to empathy and solace, to a Tao-like acceptance of what is. Steinbeck reminds us time and again in language that predates the polemics of the late twentieth century that animal rights are our rights, that outer and inner landscapes are continuous and it is only through the acceptance of that continuity that people either discover themselves or are forever broken. This isn't an original insight: Steinbeck read Emerson and Thoreau. To be fully ourselves and free, we must abandon rote living according to outdated precepts and reawaken the child within and remember childlike that consciousness flows through the whole universe. That vision is more fleeting in Gowdy than in Steinbeck but a distinctly Thoreau-Emersonian moment does come in Mud's vision of humans enjoying the freedom of animals.

Gowdy's elephants are neither the pathetic victims of Yankee greed nor are they Englishmen in furry zipper suits. Her elephants are rational, emotional, visionary; they struggle; they fail; they pray and they sing; they love and they mourn. They are neither us nor entirely other than us. They are not in the least formulaic and are both likeable and unlikeable. They are confused and they are confusing. They simply *are* and that is their point. In his essay "Nature-writing" in *The Cambridge Companion to Canadian Literature*, the editor of Audubon's *Writings and Drawings*, Christoph Irmscher notes that "the question inherent in the answers given by Canadian nature-writers from Alexander Mackenzie to Mark Hume is less Frye's puzzled 'Where is here?' than, more typically, a patiently repeated, genuinely amazed '*What* is here?'" The most interesting of these writers are those who "[l]ike Mackenzie ... have felt uncertain about their presence in an environment that so often confuses the human observer, reducing him or her ... to the size of a diatom. And, like him, some of these writers have gone on to question, more specifically, the adequacy of the human point of view as a 'central focalizing device' in representations of nature, doubting that humans should consider themselves exempt from, or superior to, the 'rhythms' of nature." It's not to Atwood nor to Findley that an enquiring mind looks to figure out what underlies *The White Bone*, it's to Brian Fawcett, the author of *The Secret Journal of Alexander Mackenzie*, and to Christopher Dewdney, author of *A Natural History of Southwestern Ontario*.

Mister Sandman (1995)

Gail Caldwell wrote in her 1997 *Boston Globe* review of *Mister Sandman* that "Gowdy is a comic but dead-serious writer of outrageous proportion.... *We So Seldom Look on Love* made me aware of Gowdy's fierce intelligence, her intensity posing as comedy, and her lovely attention to the hidden illumination of the universe." These attributes are also present in *Mister Sandman* but for Caldwell "they're overwhelmed by the novel's uneven point of view and desultory centre." *Mister Sandman*, she writes, is "a work that begins and ends beautifully, but wanders in its vast middle into a stumble between sex and slapstick." Some days, I half-agree. On other days, I'm in more wholehearted agreement with

Margaret Atwood's praise in *The Times Literary Supplement*:

> *Mister Sandman* displays the same quirkiness, the same mordant sense
> of humor, the same ear for the vernacular, the same innocent-eyed
> acceptance of the bizarre, that characterizes her two previous novels....
> Gowdy surprises and delights; she also — which is rare — gives us
> the moments which are at the same time preposterous and strangely
> moving.

It's frank and ribald and, as *The Bloomsbury Review* noted, "It's truly a monu-
mentally entertaining, brilliantly constructed novel."

The Canarys of *Mister Sandman* are an odd lot: Gordon and Doris are the
parents of Marcy and Sonja, who at the age of fifteen gives birth to Joan, an *idiot
savant*. Both parents are bisexual and Marcy has no notion of or need for serial
monogamy. Joan becomes a collective consciousness as she listens mutely to the
others confidences. But the novel asks Joan Canary to carry so much weight and
she ends up more messily grotesque and less compellingly metaphorical than she
ought to be. Readers have to work hard to find the illumination promised by
Gordon Canary's scriptural evocation of Luke: "For the children of this world
are in their generation wiser than the children of light." That said, I part company with Caldwell's assertion that "One of the tacit rules of fiction is that it
inhabits its own moral universe; you don't get to invent characters and then
make fun of them at their expense." Hasn't she read Dickens? Or Thomas
Mann? Not everything Gowdy satirizes is equally well targeted, but that's
another matter and a judgment that likely says as much about my tastes in sex
and slapstick as Gowdy's skills.

Barbara Gowdy is hilarious in ways that Thomas Mann never allowed himself
to be but what I enjoy most in her work are the moments when I smile inwardly
rather than laugh out loud. Those smiles are expressions of uncertainty, of not
understanding why we are smiling when there doesn't seem to be anything to
smile about. What do you call what she is doing when she is undermining storytelling from within? "Parody," is the Devil's answer. Perhaps the best term for
it is "being difficult" in the sense that Mann would have understood it: he, like

most of the major writers of the twentieth century, is drawn to the idea of a difficulty that redeems, that costs more than we can easily afford but includes the possibility of being forgiven for buying all the wrong things because we paid too dearly for them. Difficulty, for Gowdy as for Mann, is a pursuit that renews the passion for life and is inseparable from it. She understands that fiction is a poor tool for settling arguments and defining social contexts. Fiction works best through indirect communication because its primary task in our time is to get readers to retrace the steps that led to the conceptual confusions upon which inadequacies rest. Her fiction can only be properly understood if it is placed within the context in which it functions — as an elucidation, without advocacy, of what it is like to see the world in the way her characters see it. Her mission is to make reality more inclusive, not to correct or constrain it. Her characters all offer readers ways of re-thinking their relation to the world in much the same way that Jack Benny, Thomas Mann's favourite comedian, did by creating artificial environments in which characters make jokes at their own expense, not ours. By forgiving them, we forgive ourselves.

Gowdy was the first Canadian writer since Norman Levine to win a large readership in Germany without recourse to writing about the Rockies, horses, cowboys, and Indians. Gowdy's German readers, not her English, American, or Canadian ones provided the royalties that allowed her to cease work as a temp in law offices and write full time. Her "fame" in Canada rests on being several times a bridesmaid for the Giller, Governor General, and other awards. She's also "notorious" as the author of the *We So Seldom Look on Love* stories that are far from prim and most notable for their compassion towards behaviours that are usually regarded as freakish. As Gail Caldwell says in her 1997 *Boston Globe* review of *Mister Sandman*, "Gowdy is a comic but dead-serious writer of outrageous proportion." She's hilarious while "being difficult" in the sense that Mann would have understood it: difficulty, for Gowdy as for Mann, is a pursuit that renews the passion for life and is inseparable from it.

∼

MARGARET ATWOOD

Cat's Eye (1988), *Alias Grace* (1996), *The Penelopiad* (2005); Duet:
Oryx and Crake (2003) & *The Year of the
Flood* (2009)

When Margaret Atwood's *The Penelopiad* was published in the autumn 2005, I
did something I hadn't done in years with a new Atwood: I bought a hardcover
copy — full price — the week of publication and read it in one shot. As even
Harold Bloom admits:

> pragmatically none of us (whoever we are) ever has time to read abso-
> lutely everything, no matter how great our lust for reading. And for
> most of us, the harried young in particular, inadequate authors will
> consume the energies that would be better invested in stronger writers.

Margaret Atwood is one of our strongest novelists, far less inadequate than just
about anyone else (only Joan Barfoot, Austin Clarke, Barbara Gowdy, Wayne
Johnston, David Adams Richards, and Josef Škvorecký are as consistent).

At least three, possibly four of Atwood's mainstream novels — *Life Before
Man* (1979), *Cat's Eye* (1988), *Alias Grace* (1996), and *The Penelopiad* (2005) —
are among the most intellectually and emotionally engaging novels of ideas written in our time. Expect to see Atwood awarded the Nobel Prize for Literature
sometime around her seventy-fifth birthday in 2014 and expect the Swedish
Academy to say things not unlike the things said about José Saramago, the 1998
Nobel laureate from Portugal: namely, that a bestselling author from a small (in
terms of Canada's literate and literary population) country who has gained an
international readership and critical acclaim is being awarded the Nobel for being
both imaginative and blunt, playful and offensive. And expect Atwood to deliver
an acceptance speech worth hearing because the world needs blunt, offensive,
prick-kicking authors in the public eye with the self-confidence the Nobel Prize
bully pulpit provides to deliver high, hard ones. Atwood does that kind of thing
uncommonly well. Even so, Fearless Fosdicks such as Stephen Marche still write
such tosh as "Margaret Atwood['s] ... career, much like CanLit itself, has entered

a Shavian twilight, where every book she produces takes away from her legacy." As Al Capp liked to say of his inept dick, the world is never short of idiots who shoot people for their own good, are pure beyond imagining, and are fanatically loyal to those who exploit, starve, and discard them: my copies of Marche's novels were deeply discounted at a collapsible table in a subway station.

Atwood has had far more reason than Marche to complain of the difficulties facing young novelists: look at how long it took her to achieve success! She first became a finalist for the Governor General's Literary Award for Fiction with her fourth novel, *Life Before Man*, ten years after *The Edible Woman* (1969), her first novel (which had languished in Jack McClelland's desk drawer for many, many months) and another six years before *The Handmaid's Tale* (1985) won the Arthur C. Clarke Award, the Governor General's Literary Award for Fiction, and was a finalist for the Booker Prize. Since then, *Cat's Eye* (1988) was a finalist for the Governor General's and the Booker Prize; *The Robber Bride* (1993) was a finalist for the 1994 Governor General's; *Alias Grace* (1996) won the Giller Prize, and was a finalist for the Booker Prize and the Governor General's; *The Blind Assassin* (2000) won the Booker Prize and was a finalist for the Governor General's; *Oryx and Crake* (2003) was a finalist for the Booker Prize and the Governor General's; and *The Penelopiad* (2005) was longlisted for the 2007 IMPAC Award.

Like shelf space, our brains are finite, a mere 100 billion nerve cells. "If we accept that knowledge is a finite island in a sea of inexhaustible mystery," writes Chet Raymo in *Skeptics and True Believers* (1998),

> then two corollaries follow: (1) the growth of the island does not diminish the sea's infinitude, and (2) the growth of the island increases the length of the shore along which we encounter mystery.... It is at the shore that the creative work of the mind is done — the work of the artist, poet, philosopher, and scientist.

Atwood's shoreline is never a place to visit purely for the pleasures of her inventions of plot and character. It's bursting with ideas as she turns and returns to poetry and prose and theory, short stories and children's books and anthologies and drawings and television scripts and opera librettos and journalism. But it's Atwood the novelist who has always held the strongest claim to attention.

Cat's Eye (1988)

In middle age, Elaine Risley, an artist, returns to Toronto for a retrospective of her paintings. In a self-portrait she sees three little girls — Carol, Grace, and Cordelia — who appear as Marleyesque ghosts revealing who she has become and failed to become because of bullying by her "best friends" when she was eight and ill-equipped to be one of the girly-girls of that era. What follows is a meditation on Stephen Hawking's question, "Why do we remember the past, and not the future?" Atwood's answer is that time past and time present keep us too occupied creating multiple versions of the self. There is far more at stake here than a "study" of Elaine. In earlier novels, Atwood's thinly fictionalized selves, as Brian Fawcett notes in his essay "Margaret Atwood's Achievement" in *Unusual Circumstances, Interesting Times and Other Impolite Interventions* (1992), "were generally more interesting and smarter than anyone else. Generally they got all the best insights and speeches, and the joke was invariably — and usually painfully — at someone else's expense." Fawcett continues:

> Such excesses are understandable, in retrospect. She was, after all, work-
> ing a field blessed with an overabundance of upper middle class males,
> most of them pretenders and jerks who thought women were either
> sports or walking kitchen utensils.

Until she smashed the mould with *Cat's Eye*, Atwood's novels were thematically unified, tightly programmed, and moralistic in their conclusions as she ground modern life down to mythological substructures in search of a "spirit" in need of one sort of redemption or another. In *Cat's Eye*, she's deeply iconoclastic as she writes against the kind of novel she had previously been identified with: her little girls are power freaks, the feminist meetings in the sixties are hysterical, and her main character finds peace and protection in the arms of a man who isn't pinned beneath her and held to personal account for all the sins of patriarchy.

And instead of Upper Canadian uplift, the novel closes with a sense of Atwood having deeply pondered Nietzsche's *On the Genealogy of Morals*, especially the passage dealing with priests, and found in it the progenitors of certain "sisters."

> As is well known, the priests are the *most evil enemies* — but why? Because they are the most impotent. It is because of their impotence that in them hatred grows to monstrous and uncanny proportions, to the most spiritual and poisonous kind of hatred. The truly great haters in world history have always been priests; likewise the most ingenious haters; other kinds of spirit hardly come into consideration when compared with the spirit of priestly vengefulness.

Alias Grace (1996)

In *The Modern Library: The 200 Best Novels in English since 1950*, Carmen Callil and Colm Tóibín describe the experience of reading *Alias Grace* as "gleeful and exciting" as Atwood retells the real life misadventures of a sixteen-year-old Upper Canadian housemaid named Grace Marks who was found guilty as an accomplice in the murder of her employer and his mistress in 1843. Her death sentence was commuted to life imprisonment in a trial that divided opinion throughout the Empire and America. Marks spent thirty years in jails and asylums and often served as the "star attraction" for those who wanted to study "evil" in women.

Employing the device of Grace telling her story to a sometimes sympathetic, sometimes disbelieving Doctor Jordan (a rudimentary psychologist) provides Atwood with all the scope Callil and Tóibín find she needs to embroider "intricate patterns of mystery, wit, and paradox on the rough fabric" of the journalistic record. In sum, they say,

> *Alias Grace* has the sharp flavour of Margaret Atwood's formidable intelligence; her ability to control form and structure is always remark-able. Within her easy mastery of social realism she accommodates serious matters, crucial ideas. The battle for power represented by enig-

matic sexual encounters shows men manipulating women, *and vice versa*, in all the ways that flourished then *and linger now*. [my italics]

The Penelopiad (2005)

In his review for *The Globe and Mail*, Don Akenson writing as Donald Harman Akenson (a subtle but important distinction that places the full weight of his credentials as world-class historian and literary critic of ancient texts behind his words) notes gleefully and with excitement that he detects *genius*:

> Because we so frequently view the root plot of *The Odyssey* as Atwood reinvents it — this is the base text of *Desperate Housewives*, about women who kill time waiting for hubby to come home after a bad day at the office — it is easy to miss the measure of skill it takes to make us take the plot seriously and to see it as mythic in nature. Somehow (it is a measure of her genius that one cannot quite say how), she makes us hear the voice of Penelope, reflecting in Hades on her life, as if it were the voice of the most interesting gossip you have ever had coffee with; and these two modes, mythic and conversational, do not conflict, but resonate with each other.

Atwood realizes that *The Odyssey* exerts much of its power in recitation and intercuts her prose with choral poetry that works in the Greek as well as the Gilbert and Sullivan manner. One of several wonders in a book Akenson finds "wonderful" is a verse interval where "Atwood manages the almost impossible task of replicating in English the dactylic hexameters of ancient Greek metrical form. And without showing off: The poem pushes the story along."

The Penelopiad was commissioned by Jamie Byng of Canongate Books (who claims Yann Martel as his prize discovery) as part of his *Myth* series of 100 small volumes of 25,000–30,000 words in which "international literary superstars" revise the world's ancient tales. Rumour has it that Atwood soon regretted signing on because of the very tight completion date imposed on her but wouldn't renege on a contractual obligation. This "cheapens" the result in some people's eyes but shouldn't: Atwood often writes best when she writes very quickly and briefly, leaving much understated and more implied. For Akenson, Atwood's *Penelopiad* "suggests not just one, but two, three or maybe four possible reinventions of *The Odyssey*, that's all bonus" and expresses the hope that "*The Penelopiad* is a précis for/of the real thing: a full-scale version by Atwood of *The Odyssey* that would stand properly on the shelves besides the Homeric and the Joycean versions. May the gods make it so." Atwood alongside Joyce and Homer? Preposterous? A foundling playing at the feet of giants? Only in the blind eyes and deaf ears of Saint Stephen Marche. Atwood's mastery of tales-within-tales in *Cat's Eye* and *Alias Grace* demonstrates the technical credentials necessary to measure her against them. And she's as steely in her reflections as either. But leave Joyce out of the picture — there's more gained in reflecting on Atwood's Homeric qualities, especially in a millennium when Stephen Hawking's question, "Why do we remember the past, and not the future?" becomes daily more pressing and has come to dominate her latest works.

Duet: *Oryx and Crake* (2003) & *The Year of the Flood* (2009)

Homer was more visionary than realist: the worlds of the *Iliad* and the *Odyssey* are inventions he shared with other poets who found much of their present and all of the preceding three centuries so unspeakable (patricide, matricide, infanticide, cannibalism) that he and his fellow poets reached back five hundred years to a less bestial age for verses to first reverse and then check and balance the excesses of their time. To begin to comprehend Homer's art, imagine a Solzhenitsyn without pen and paper so deeply mired in Stalin's gulag that the only art open to him is song and the only plots and characters that would not earn him instant execution were *Hamlet* and *Don Quixote* and that he was safe with them only if he sang according to the prescriptions of socialist realism. This is an inexact analogy but not an overstatement of the condition of story-telling in the Homeric age. Homer sang of Mycenae, a civilization Shakespeare rightly understood as proto-Elizabethan (*Troilus and Cressida*), which had been so annihilated by invasion, disease, and despoliation that so deep a darkness descended over the Peloponnesus and eastern end of the Mediterranean that it is still impenetrable. Homer's poems are inseparable from a state of constant warfare in which the thoroughly degenerate rule according to dictates of blood vengeance and only the persevering can survive if they are clever. Against this, Homer sings of the possibilities open to those heroic enough to tear consciousness free from instinctual response and domesticated enough to open heart and hearth to hospitality. In doing this, he was remembering the future. And Atwood?

G. K. Chesterton's quip that a "thousand romances ... lie secreted in *The Origin of Species*" contains a truth he might not have intended: *Oryx and Crake* and *The Year of the Flood* are speculative in the way Homer is and in the way Darwin *sometimes* intended to be: always write in the sure knowledge that probable outcomes can be trumped by alternative possibilities, that the exception can become the rule because nature is deeply, archly, architecturally humorous.

Atwood's *Penelopiad* was a portent that *The Year of the Flood* would so surpass *Oryx and Crake* that what she may have intended as merely one instalment in what her American publisher calls "the MaddAddam trilogy" is so outstanding as to stand alone. In a nice bit of literary game playing, she's said that *Flood* is "not a sequel and it's not a prequel. It's a 'simultaneouel' in that it takes place during the same time span and with a number of people in it who are peripheral in *Oryx and Crake* but are central in *The Year of the Flood*."

Both novels deal with the end of the known world around 2050 when environmental degradation, climate change, and extreme weather are mere background to pandemics and the death of civilization at the hands of "numbers people." Atwood describes the carnage and its survivors in ways that display her great strengths (especially her knowledge and love for the natural world) and verbal dexterity to transfix young people who don't normally read literary fiction. *The Year of the Flood* should boost her ranking with the Nobel committee: it is a work of utter fearlessness as she looks straightforward at what most of us spend most of our time and energy trying hard not to see — the absurdity of the worlds we've built upon acts of ruthless destruction, the bad behaviours those worlds instil in our young, and, more importantly, surprisingly, stunningly the path to hope and forgiveness. *The Year of the Flood* parodies the Church of England hymnal in much the same way as Barbara Gowdy's *White Bone* caricatures the Presbyterian but it takes on the larger task of conjuring the only kind of "Great Code" that can survive the future it portends. Timothy Findley and Nino Ricci cross-dress the Bible: Atwood strips it to its barest essentials

BRIAN FAWCETT'S

Gender Wars (1994)

In the *Art of the Novel* (1986), Milan Kundera asks what human possibilities remain after the end of four hundred years of disintegration of values in the West? Inspired by his reading of Broch's trilogy *The Sleepwalkers*, he enumerates the following:

- The uniform, a sentimental attachment to inherited value which we do not choose but is assigned to us as so many buttons on a coat.
- The fanaticism of the era, a division of the world into kingdoms of Good and Evil that are equally impossible to identify.
- Cheerful, guilt-free, irrationality.
- General rebelliousness.

Later in the same essay, Kundera writes: "All great works (precisely because they are great) contain something unachieved. Broch is an inspiration to us not only because of what he brought off but also because of what he aimed for and missed. The unachieved in his work can show us the need for ... *a new art of the specifically novelistic essay* (which does not claim to bear an apodictic message but remains hypothetical, playful, or ironic."

Brian Fawcett's *Gender Wars: A Novel and Some Conversation about Sex and Gender* (1994) faced an unusual (for Canada) difficulty getting printed. Typesetters at Friesens, the Mennonite employee-held corporation in Altona, Manitoba that prints the majority of books published in Canada, recoiled from setting a rebellious text. *Gender Wars* isn't merely graphic in its sexual descriptions (the issue that caused similar problems with Leonard Cohen's *Beautiful Losers*) — it's also designed to mimic and might be seen to mock the typographical conventions of commentaries on the Bible: some of Fawcett's text is printed in red on white, other passages in black on white, and still others in black on grey on pages where one coloured text is above the other or surrounds it or annotates it as Fawcett tracks and comments upon the quests and conquests of Fred Ferris, heterosexual WASP, from the Sexual Revolution of the sixties and seventies through the onset of AIDS and other STDs in the eighties to the collapse of sexual civilities in the gender politics of the early nineties.

Given the complexities it poses and the *poseur* complicities it exposes, *The Globe and Mail* took the extraordinary step of giving it two reviews on facing pages in its "Books" section: Don Gillmor was given the left page, Patricia Pearson the right — neither, it seems, grasped Fawcett's indebtedness to Kundera or his desire to contribute to *a new art of the specifically novelistic essay*. Odd, that (given Fawcett's great stride in that direction six years earlier in *Cambodia: A Book for People Who Find Television Too Slow*).

Here's what Gillmor thinks the book is about:

> The premise that Fawcett begins with is that the gender war has esca-
> lated to frightening and confusing heights. It has become our sexual
> Vietnam, where the topography is unfamiliar, the local resentment has
> an unfathomable history and many of us don't know why we're here
> in the first place. I wonder though if the war between the sexes has
> escalated or is simply more forcefully stated and relentlessly reported....
> What has evolved is the amount of culpability that we men claim. For
> a long time (several thousand years), we admitted to nothing. We didn't
> do it, whatever it was.... Fawcett takes an approach many of us have
> settled on: I'm okay but the rest of my gender is barbaric, oafish and
> couldn't find a clitoris with a map and a flashlight.... At one point in
> *Gender Wars*, a lover chides Ferris for being a mechanic, more concerned
> with technique than communion. The same criticism could be levelled
> at the author. The technical feats are impressive, but we are often
> excluded from the act.

Here's what Pearson thinks the book is about:

Ostensibly, Fawcett's book is a deconstruction of white male sexual attitudes from the utopian spring of the sexual revolution to the grim, dystopic winter of our current discontent. Somewhere between the poles is a civilized equilibrium of gender in which *eros* can flourish. But where is it? What is its shape? This seems to be Fawcett's central question, which he frames by employing two texts that run atop one another, the first a fictional narrative about the exploits of a man named Fred Ferris, the second a series of non-fiction essays on such subjects as cunnilingus, sexual hygiene, the meaning of patriarchy and the philosophy of Albert Camus. As you might imagine, this is not an easy book to read.... I can tell you what I agree with. Men have kept themselves misinformed about women for far too long. The rise of a selfish society ... has encouraged men to perpetuate the irresponsibility of ignorance while inciting women to join in the fun.... Where I disagree with Fawcett is in his assumption that men are the ones who must end this. Where does this conventional wisdom come from, that men rape, rampage and philander as a result of the stuff in their balls? ... In other words, I don't believe that endorsing the false dichotomy between predatory men and nurturing women will usher us out of the mess. What I do believe is that we must reinvest intimacy with social and moral purpose. Love, receive love in turn, and introduce sex into the union of consummation.... Ultimately, the reduction of intimacy to issues of power and flesh transforms Fawcett's conversation into a lengthy lie of omission. He alludes to the fact of love in his own life, but his fictional character merely undresses and dresses again.

Me? I'd say it's a definitely and defiantly a Kundera-esque novelistic essay on possibility for lovers in a dangerous time. And I remind readers lucky enough to find a copy to undo a few buttons, loosen your ideological ties, put a smile on your face, and let out a rebel yell before reading. Oh, and please remember Kundera does say, "The spirit of an age cannot be judged exclusively by its ideas, its theoretical concepts, without considering its art, and particularly the novel."

ANNALS OF OURLIT X

CROSS-DRESSING THE BIBLE:
NINO RICCI'S

Testament (2002)

TIMOTHY FINDLEY'S

Not Wanted on the Voyage (1984)

Crucially, the key characteristic of the Hebrew and Christian scriptures is that they are ridiculous. That's how God's voice sounds when filtered through really brilliant scribes. The divine voice demands that the faithful believe all sorts of wild things. So, when one tries to write a novel with the scriptures as back-text, it's necessary either to find joy in the ridiculousness of the divine voice and, if possible, spin it faster and faster ... Or, one can ... accept everything with the flatness and low emotional affect of a Believer who questions nothing. In that mode, one just slightly rearranges things; yet it is a path of emotional compression that requires immense talent if it is not to bore the reader. It should not be assayed by anyone still requiring training wheels.

Don Akenson, in his review of Nino Ricci's *Testament* for *Books in Canada*, goes on to say that the writers who have done this best in recent times include Joseph Heller (*God Knows*, 1984), Gore Vidal (*Live from Golgotha*, 1992), Norman Mailer (*The Gospel According to the Son*, 1997) and Spike Milligan (*The Bible: The Old Testament According to Spike Milligan*, 1991). *Testament* isn't "in their league by a long shot, but neither is the book an abject failure. It's not a potato pancake, just lying there, but it is a soufflé that doesn't rise very high." For Akenson, the problem "is that Ricci takes a middle course ... tells us the kind of story that we get from ex-priests who still want to stay in touch with the church. They constantly affirm that Jesus was definitely a Great Guy, but not the Son of God." On the plus side, he noted "Ricci has done his homework well."

> He has read almost all of the main work on the Historical Jesus that has been done in the last twenty years and he samples and adapts that material responsibly. For example, my instructions that one should use the original Hebrew and Aramaic names of Jesus and his followers, in order to avoid making them Christians long before Christianity was invented, is adopted. As is my argument that the scriptures fairly clearly indicate Jesus' illegitimacy, and Gwen Nowak's suggestion of his Roman male parentage; and the work of the Jesus seminar, of John Dominic Crossan, of Joseph Meiers, of E. P. Sanders, and dozens of others are employed with skill and propriety.

Some things that enfeeble Ricci's work in Akenson's eyes are strengths in mine. Ricci composes his novel as four new gospels — those according to "Yihuda of Qiryat" (Judas Iscariot), "Miryam of Migdal" (Mary Magdalene), "Miryam his Mother" (the Blessed Virgin Mary) and "Simon of Gergesa" (who is a fictional amalgam of pagan shepherd, Simon Magus, and the Good Thief) — narrated in the first person singular. While Ricci isn't as successful as he might be in differentiating all their voices, the two women do come off as women and not as a ventriloquist's dummies. That's the verdict of several dozen young women who read it for seminars I directed, some of whom preferred *Testament* to any other novel they've ever been assigned.

Books about Jesus outnumber those about Shakespeare, Napoleon, Lincoln, or Hitler. There are at least two dozen diverse and sometimes wildly fanciful novels about Jesus and ten dozen biographies available in English or English translation. This is a modern phenomenon. As Akenson demonstrates in *Saint Saul: A Skeleton Key to the Historical Jesus* (2002) only a few facts about Jesus were essential to Paul and his followers: Paul simply will not have it said that Jesus was born of a virgin — such a superstition was incompatible with seeing him as Son of the Lord God. It's not revolutionary to say that Jesus is not divine by virtue of a miraculous birth; that idea goes straight back to Paul. The canonical gospels of Matthew, Mark, Luke, and John provide only a few highly selective "facts" but many powerful sayings attributed to Jesus within barebones narratives that serve mainly as vehicles for a proclamation of Jesus as Christ and Christ as the key to the Kingdom of God. That's what has counted most for most Christian believers. But there have always been believers who wanted to fill in the empty spaces the official accounts leave in the life of Jesus or discover the things he said that have been left unrecorded. One legend holds that each of the original apostles (including Judas in some accounts, and Mary Magdalene in others) created gospels of their own. Other legends affirm that the post-crucifixion Jesus travelled throughout India or that he settled down to married life in the south of France with Mary Magdalene to raise a family whose sons fathered a royal bloodline in France and a bestseller for Dan Brown. In 1846, a then-unknown English writer calling herself George Eliot translated the German philosopher David Frederick Strauss's *Life of Jesus*. Strauss attempted to explain why even educated Christians believed in events that did not have any historical basis, were contrary to common sense, and violated the natural order. His book, a *cause célèbre*, fostered a new focus on Christ's life as a mythical construct that neither supernaturalist believers nor rationalist doubters could adequately interpret or ever understand. Charles Dickens reacted to Eliot's translation of Strauss by reaffirming his own comfortably orthodox beliefs and writing the thoroughly conventional *The Life of Our Lord*, his only bestseller nobody now reads.

When Ernst Renan, a French historian, published his *Life of Jesus* in 1863, he rejected Straussian skepticism and read the gospels in terms of his travels in Syria and Palestine and against whatever he could discover in the archaeological record. For Renan, Jesus was an uneducated but wise Jewish prophet from a green and shady rural Galilee. Renan's Jesus (who independently became Emerson's) preached that the individual conscience was in direct connection with God and that there was no need whatsoever for any institutional religion.

By the beginning of the twentieth century, controversies between mythologists and historians over who Jesus actually was and what he might have actually said and done led the German theologian and Bach scholar Albert Schweitzer to publish *The Quest for the Historical Jesus* in 1906. Concluding that "all post-Gospel lives of Jesus say much more about their authors than about their subject,"

Schweitzer declared the quest to find Jesus in the gospels or anywhere else futile. He abandoned theology and music, took up medicine, set off for Africa as a medical missionary, and inspired many to follow the unhistorical, unmythological Christianity preached by St. Paul. Thus began the modern tradition in which novelists imaginatively recreate Jesus in response to their own spiritual crises: a lineage that includes D. H. Lawrence's *The Man Who Died*, Robert Graves's *King Jesus*, Nikos Kazantzakis's *The Last Temptation of Christ*, José Saramago's *The Gospel According to Jesus Christ* as well as an odd lot of novels that flesh out Jesus from unorthodox viewpoints by authors as diverse as Morley Callaghan, Anthony Burgess, Guy Davenport, John Updike, Reynolds Price, Jim Crace, and Simon Mawer.

Ricci's *Testament* failed to stir up much debate among Canadian readers. It seems that few Canadians wanted to argue about a Jesus called Yeshua who would have been, quite literally, a Roman soldier's bastard if a marriage of convenience hadn't been hastily arranged by the young woman's family. Few writers have more sympathy and understanding for those who bear the mark of "illegitimate" birth than Ricci whose *Lives of the Saints* (1990) deservedly gets rediscovered every time he publishes a new book. *Testament* doesn't merely accept Yeshua's irregular parentage as a possibility; it proclaims it early, explores it from several vantages, and makes it a key in the sequence of events that lead to arrest and crucifixion. Ricci's Yeshua is an Everyman, riddled by the contradictions and internal conflicts that dominate *Lives* and its successors: estrangement from the ascendant society, conflict between generations, family strife, opposing worldviews, search for selfhood, and how women might address these questions in historical situations where they had very little public voice.

Yeshua of Notzereh is so radical an egalitarian that he treats women in a resolutely modern way, and they respond to him with myth-shaking naturalness. Viewing him through the eyes of *Testament*'s two Miryams is extraordinary. Mary Magdalene has come down to us as a redeemed prostitute, although there's no scriptural evidence for this characterization. Ricci rejects the stereotype and makes Miryam of Migdal less melodramatic and easily understood as a young woman in search of a future that won't free her from being a dutiful daughter only to entrap her as somebody's wife. One of the traditional titles given to

Jesus's mother is Our Lady of Sorrows and that's the essence of Miryam the wife of Yehoceph — a mother who struggles to comprehend the peculiar, difficult, sometimes impenetrable stranger who is always her son but never her husband's child. Ricci, who has achieved the status of quasi-feminist through acute sensitivity to the minds and hearts of vulnerable, uneducated women, said in an interview, "The women's points of view [in *Testament*] are a natural for me, in that they are certainly missing from the traditional accounts. We never really get to hear from the women, and yet they are there, which is one of the surprising things about the Jesus tradition. The inclusion of women does seem a revolutionary aspect of his ministry."

TIMOTHY FINDLEY

Not Wanted on the Voyage (1984)

Timothy Findley's *Not Wanted on the Voyage* (1984) is his best novel but among the less read. Why? Because it makes many readers cry buckets! Just the thing for a retelling of Noah and the Great Flood recounted in Genesis. Findley's God is ridiculous and spins downwards in just the way Akenson prescribes: God is tired, doddering, gets no respect (bystanders pelt his carriage with eggs, vegetables, stones as he passes by; assassination attempts are made on his life), decides to die and take almost everything with him: he exempts Dr. Noyes and his family. Noyes has been described as a "flaming asshole" but he's married to a heroic alcoholic who understands animals so well that she can lead sheep in chorale singing.

Findley employs multiple narratives — Dr. Noyes, Mrs. Noyes, their offspring (Shem and his wife Hannah, Ham, Japeth and his virgin wife Emma) take turns. More takes place inside the head of Mottyl, Mrs. Noyes's almost blind, twenty-year-old cat who is unforgettable as she puzzles out the politics that rend the family during the voyage as they come to terms with some stowaways, including Lucifer who has boarded ship as Lucy, a seven-foot drag queen with a thing for Ham.

Findley's imagination soars as he gets inside so many odd characters and puts a brake on his language. *Not Wanted* is storytelling in the Grimm tradition — factual, unspectacular, horrifying as it probes the mystery of salvation: Saved for what? Pull up a box of Kleenex and read your way into the heart of Saturday night — the sixth and messiest twilight of creation — and rediscover the things that made fairy tales matter to you as a child.

∼

NINO RICCI

Lives of the Saints (1990)

Ricci's first novel spent seventy-five weeks on the bestseller list and was discovered by more readers when two subsequent novels featuring Vittorio Innocente were published in a trilogy that's less than the sum of its first part, which is tightly plotted, rich in character, and superbly edited. *The New York Times Book Review* characterized it as "an extraordinary story — brooding and ironic, suffused with yearning, tender and lucid and gritty."

In the village of Valle De Sole, a small corner of the Italian Apennines that's almost unchanged by the larger events of the first half of the twentieth century, villagers ostracize Christina, Vittorio's mother, when she's impregnated after her husband, Mario, has emigrated to America. When she's unable to abide shunning, she and Vittorio sail to Canada and far more difficult circumstances than she foresees. One of the triumphs of the book is to show how distinct, different, and disorienting the experience of New World immigration has been for Italians who came to much smaller and tighter-knit communities in Canada than in the United States.

~

KEITH MAILLARD

Gloria (1999)

Gloria Merriman Cotter is spending her last summer at home in Raysburg, West Virginia, between college and graduate school at Columbia University where she intends to study with the noted critic, Lionel Trilling. It's 1957, the Eisenhower era is in full swing, and Gloria — the daughter of a steel company executive and a socialite — paints her toenails, works on a tan, swims, drinks, and fends off advances at the country club whenever her creator isn't flashing back to critical moments in her life-to-date.

To come of age in that milieu means Inner Conflict: Gloria's parents want her to be outstanding at fitting-in and expect her to marry daddy's sort of man — a "good earner." She's been there, done that at boarding school (where she transformed herself from bookworm to butterfly — cheerleader first, ultimately prom queen) and at college where the good sorority sister in her began to metamorphose into a beauty with brains — May Queen, Phi Beta Kappa.

Keith Maillard came to Canada in 1970, a Vietnam War evader. In 1976, he published his first novel, *Two Strand River*, which has cult status among both the transgendered and devotees of Canadian magic realism. Since 1980, he's published a series of naturalistic novels set mostly in a fictional Raysburg, West Virginia, and become a mainstay of UBC's Creative Writing Department. In 2004, he returned to the raw material first published in *The Knife in My Hands* (1981) and *Cutting Through* (1982) and reshaped it into the *Difficulty at the Beginning* quartet (2005–2006), which some admirers contend ranks among the best multi-volume novels of the twentieth century. But *Gloria* is the novel for which he's known by the largest number of readers, including twenty-something women who devour its hundreds of pages over a weekend in the same way younger selves or sisters devour Harry Potter. Maillard is meticulous in recreating Gloria's world of eyelash curlers, crinolines, girdles, and kid gloves — nailing Gloria's fashion dilemmas right down to the Revlon shades to stick on her lips and nails. Depending on taste, this is all utterly hypnotic or deadly boring but Maillard being Maillard, this isn't all there is. In the subplots, he explores loves, friendships, status-seeking, and social constraints that are in the foreground of *Difficulty at the Beginning*, which begins with *Running* about two buddies bonding in Gloria's world, a book with a sizeable cult following all its own among runners.

"MIDNIGHT AT THE OASIS"

Reading Novels of Joy
and Redemption

ANNALS OF OURLIT XI

PICO IYER, ALBERTO MANGUEL, NEIL BISSOONDATH
and Three Global Villages on Two Legs

In the June 2002 issue of *Harper's Magazine*, Pico Iyer (a self-described "global village on two legs" who was born in England to Indian parents, immigrated to California, was educated at Eton and Oxford, and now lives in Japan) reviewed Dennis Bock's *The Ash Garden*, Yann Martel's *Life of Pi*, Madeleine Thien's *Simple Recipes*, and Catherine Bush's *The Rules of Engagement* in an essay headed "The Last Refuge: On the Promise of the New Canadian fiction." What he found most exhilarating about what he termed the "New Canadian novel" is that it offers a kind of multiculturalism that can be "known only at the individual level, where people understand that it is only in the imagination that we can begin to penetrate the Other (or to allow the Other to penetrate us)" — multiculturalism based on shared beliefs not shared roots and, especially, on the most universal of all shared beliefs, the belief that art transcends ideology and political identity.

Reading Bock's *The Ash Garden* ("an assured and compassionate debut ... that ... aims to come to terms with the great blot of the American Century — America's central shame — in a quiet village outside Toronto."), Iyer found himself thinking about Michael Ondaatje's *The English Patient* (1992) — a book that "ends where Bock's begins — with the dropping of the bomb on Hiroshima — and whose central character is also a person without a face." Iyer identifies *The English Patient* as "the defining work of modern Canadian fiction, not only because it won so many readers worldwide but because it presents us with a stirring vision of what Canada might offer to a world in which more and more people are on the move and motion itself has become a kind of nation." What made *The English Patient* "most resonant," Iyer wrote,

> was its meticulous and highly self-conscious attempt to chart a new kind of identity outside the categories of the Old World's order. "We were

German, English, Hungarian, African — all of us insignificant to them," says the title character, as he thinks back to an "oasis society" before the war in which people from everywhere assembled to map the North African desert. "Gradually we became nationless. I came to hate nations." ... And as he reminisces about the tribal flow of post-national souls coming together in the desert, he — and we — cannot fail to notice that the people around him in the villa are "international bastards" in his phrase, moving around one another too, as the novel repeatedly puts it, like separate planets, "planetary strangers."

"To meet Canada on the page (of its new writers) is to come to the conclusion that multiculturalism is far better handled by writers of fiction than by writers of laws. Decency cannot be legislated from above nor fairness administered in the abstract," Iyer continued. The fiction writers he celebrates start from below and take readers individually to the heart of dislocation and nostalgia, place us inside the restless and homeless in ways that make multiculturalism a challenge to be met imaginatively rather than a chore to be shouldered grudgingly. Works of fiction worth talking about are something more than the products of individuated imagination (they do give voice to something larger than the romanticized self) and measure something more than a writer's personal ambition.

Iyer remarked, in passing, that it was only after he'd finished reading *The English Patient* that he found his way back to Ondaatje's previous novel, *In the Skin of a Lion* (1987), and realized that *The English Patient* was a sequel that draws upon a deeper energy — "the rare blessing that Canada has long enjoyed as a New World sanctuary of sorts, the place that escaped American slaves sought out in the nineteenth century, at the end of their Underground Railway, the neutral zone where India's national cricket team traditionally took on Pakistan's in a safety unimaginable in either India or Pakistan."

Canada is grappling with Act III of a global drama that is elsewhere only in its prologue.... Canada ... was thinking about globalism and pluralism, the possibilities of multiculturalism, long before the rest of us knew the terms existed. Tricultural at birth and bilingual to this day, Canada has had to imagine identities protean enough to stretch across five and a half time zones and to accommodate a province constantly agitating for secession. In that context, it seems only apt that Canada is (through Marshall McLuhan) the literal birthplace of the global village.

And,

Writers from other countries, especially those of mixed backgrounds, are creating a new kind of fiction based on mingled homes and migrancy: Salman Rushdie has laid down the cartography of this new floating space, and writers like Caryl Phillips and Zadie Smith and Anita Desai have begun to fill it in from different perspectives. Yet in America and Europe, by and large, multiculturalism is seen as merely a fact of life; in Canada it is often seen, and treated, as an opportunity. Toronto, after all, is by official U.N. statistics the single most multicultural city in the world; it is also, statistically, the safest city in North America and, by the reckoning of many, the one with the richest literary culture.

The only surprise about Iyer's analysis is that it was — at the time — more and readily accepted outside this country than within, especially his unassailable (to my mind) assertion of Toronto's richness of literary culture. That richness has much more to do with another "global village on two legs," Alberto Manguel, settling in Toronto in 1982 than people now talk about.

Born in 1948, Manguel grew up in Israel, a son of the Argentinean ambassador. As a teenager working in the Pygmalion Anglo-German bookshop in Buenos Aires, he met Jorge Luis Borges. Borges was blind and Manguel read to him several times a week from 1964 to 1968. In 1969, Manguel travelled to Europe and worked for various publishing companies: Denoël, Gallimard, and Les Lettres Nouvelles in Paris, and Calder & Boyars in London before returning to Buenos Aires as a reporter for *La Nación*. In 1974, he became foreign editor at the Franco Maria Ricci publishing company in Milan. Then he moved to Tahiti where he worked as editor for Les Éditions du Pacifique. In 1978, Manguel went to

England and set up a short-lived publishing company before returning to Tahiti until 1982. A year later, he moved to Toronto, became a Canadian citizen, and lived here for eighteen years before settling in the Poitou-Charentes region of France where he has built the library that holds his 30,000 books.

In his Toronto years, Manguel was an indefatigable freelancer — book reviewer, radio broadcaster, anthologist, translator, novelist, and regular contributor to *The Globe and Mail*, *The Times Literary Supplement* (London), *The Village Voice* (New York), *The Washington Post*, *The Sydney Morning Herald*, *The Australian Review of Books*, *The New York Times*, and *Svenska Dagbladet* (Stockholm). The underlying story of his life here was his Canadian *citizenship*, his sense on arrival that "in Canada, for the first time I felt I was living in a place where I could participate actively as a writer in the running of the state." His activism brought about a sea change in how the rest of the world came to view Canadian writers and how an ever-enlarging group of Canadian writers have come to view themselves through inclusion in his anthologies and his placing of their works in world literature through reviews, articles, and radio commentaries. Manguel's first review of a Canadian writer appeared in the June–July 1983 issue of *Books in Canada*. He wrote that he'd discovered "a brilliant, moving depiction of the world as seen by a child drifting into manhood" in a first novel from Oberon Press, concluding that "*The Education of J. J. Pass* brings to mind that other quest for the past, Flaubert's *L'Éducation sentimentale*:

> Of course, Rigelhof is not Flaubert — and yet, as in Flaubert's novel, the writing recaptures the senses of the years gone by, rebuilding with words a world of smells and sights and sounds.
>
> J. J. Pass is a younger brother to Frédéric Moreau.... *The Education of J. J. Pass* is a remarkable achievement. A lesser writer might turn his own experiences into the equivalent of family films on a rainy afternoon, produced strictly for personal consumption. Rigelhof instead has taken his experience apart and rebuilt it into a fiction true to life, both moving and revealing. By imagining these memories, he has made our own wiser and richer.

Lucky me! The praise did not seem excessive nor the comparison unjustified to my publisher in England but it wasn't persuasive to the folks at Peter Gzowski's *This Country in the Morning*. I'd written about two step-brothers — one a Polish refugee, the other Canadian born — who turn their backs on Canada for England and Spain, one for gentrified wealth and the other for a medieval hermitage in the mountains and a contemplative life. The problem was, a *This Country* researcher told me, that I wasn't Polish and Peter was interested in me only as a Polish-Canadian writer who he'd seen compared somewhere to Robertson Davies. In those days, that was considered a major compliment!

The cover of that June–July 1983 issue of *Books in Canada* featured Michael Ondaatje, who was the subject of a profile by John Oughton, which begins:

> The stranger rode in from the East with his typewriter blazing, and carved a permanent notch in Canadian literature. Like his native Sri Lanka, which gave the Western world its first taste of cinnamon, Michael Ondaatje has brought a special flavour to Canadian writing with his startling and often violent images, exotic settings, and elegant language.

You don't have to read much of this kind of thing to feel some empathy if not instant rapport with Neil Bissoondath's contentious *Selling Illusions* (1994), a book Iyer was given by a friend who knew he was musing on Canada as a land of grown-ups capable of "mosaic thinking."

∽

MICHAEL ONDAATJE

In the Skin of a Lion (1987)

In the Skin of a Lion (1987) is "one of the best novels written about *work* in the twentieth century" (as Carmen Callil and Colm Tóibín write in *The Modern Library*) and, obviously, one of the essential Canadian novels of the past twenty-five years. Dramatizing the construction of Toronto in the Great Depression, it focuses on the designing, planning, and building of a bridge as seen through the eyes of Patrick Lewis. Lewis looks at things as through the lenses of cameras — portrait and cine — of the period and the tale unfolds as group photographs and newsreel footage. Callil and Tóibín insist that this is "also one of the best novels about dreams and disappearances and magic" and again they are right.

Any writer prone to envy who looks at Ondaatje's achievements between 1967 and 1982 is gob-smacked and possibly unhinged by the volume and strength of his literary achievements within the twenty years that precede *In the Skin of a Lion*. These are the years in which he emerged from the University of Western Ontario's Graduate School in English as an Imagist poet with *The Dainty Monsters* (followed in 1969 by *The Man with Seven Toes* and *The Collected Works of Billy the Kid: Left-handed Poems* in 1970 *et alia*), then turned novelist with *Coming Through Slaughter* in 1976, and then semi-fictional memoirist of his Sri Lankan childhood with *Running in the Family*. Less self-regarding writers are educated by the experience and find his voice helpful in finding their own. These works are Ondaatje's triumph and literary legacy.

~⌒

NEIL BISSOONDATH

The Soul of All Great Designs (2008)

In 1985, when Neil Bissoondath published his first book (*Digging Up the Mountains*, collected stories), much was made of the fact that he's V. S. Naipaul's nephew: more should have been made of his connection to the late Shiva Naipaul, V. S.'s younger brother. After Shiva died on August 13, 1985, Martin Amis wrote, "Shiva Naipaul was one of those people who caused your heart to lift when he entered the room. [I]in losing him, we have lost thirty years of untranscribed, unvarnished genius." Those who know Bissoondath say, as one interviewer did, that he's "fiendishly charming, with an infectious laugh and a winning smile, and he can speak engagingly on anything from the nature of insurgency to the perfect recipe for a gin and tonic" — a heart-lifter. Resemblances go deeper: Uncle Shiva and his nephew are equally scathing in their attacks on the banality and diffidence of Western liberalism. Bissoondath's book-length polemic, *Selling Illusions: The Cult of Multiculturalism in Canada* (1994, rev. 2002), is more indebted philosophically and stylistically to his uncle Shiva's analysis of the rise and fall of Jim Jones and Jonestown, *Journey to Nowhere* (1980), than to anything readily found in V. S. Naipaul's writings. Bissoondath argues that Canada's well-intentioned multicultural policies and grants encourage isolation and stereotyping of cultural groups by supporting banal and mediocre "traditional arts" and by refusing to challenge domestic misogyny, racial prejudices and crassness of political and religious hierarchies thereby creating a macrocosm as potentially self-annihilating as Jonestown.

Bissoondath escaped his uncles' immediate influences by choosing Canada over England, York University over Oxford, and French over English as a university major, and by assimilating socially into Québécois society. Since 1995, Bissoondath has lived in Quebec City with his Québécoise wife and teaches at Université Laval. His novels are *A Casual Brutality* (1988), set in a fictional Caribbean republic; *The Innocence of Age* (1993), set in a racist Toronto; *The World Within Her* (1998), a return to the Caribbean; *Doing the Heart Good* (2002), set in anglophone Montreal; *The Unyielding Clamour of the Night* (2005), set in a fictionalized Sri Lanka; and *The Soul of All Great Designs* (2008) set in an unnamed Toronto.

There are at least two things to admire in any of his fictions: the humorous depiction of character and the deftness of social observation (which actually work together in a one-two combination that makes the first less benign and the second more ambiguous). Bissoondath's novels never move in the direction they seem headed: characters become unglued from the commonplace by the politics of the situations they fall into and by the Platonism their author shares with many other Trinidadian writers who go after graven images not shadows when they find themselves in philosophical caverns (Shiva Naipaul's *Journey to Nowhere* is known as *Black and White* everywhere except North America).

The Soul of All Great Designs requires preamble because it's designed to piss off a sizeable part of its potential readership and befuddle many who might want to befriend a book as angry as Rawi Hage's *Cockroach*. Alec is an interior decorator who registers false positive on his clients' "Gaydar": men are attracted, women unthreatened by his unexpressed sexuality. That's fine; he's a young businessman selling style not substance, giving clients what they want not what they need. Sex? Alec buys it from female escorts. Love? He lavishes it on the classic car he's rebuilding — a four-door, six-cylinder '28 Chevrolet Sedan. Then Sue enters his life.

Sue is Sumintra, a recent graduate (English major) who helps with her father's catering business. The dutiful daughter of hard-working Hindu-Canadian immigrant parents scarred by the Air India bombing, she's passively aggressive in her resistance to arranged-marriage proposals and sexually stirred by Alec's soft-spoken self-confidence and refinement, never guessing his blue-collar roots. Passion aroused, she begins a clandestine relationship that starts merging the halves of her divided self — much too much to Alec's discomfort. And what begins as an offbeat love story segues into a character-driven thriller. It's another of those books an attentive reader doesn't get the first time through: when it ends, you circle back to the beginning to pick up missed clues and then reread the whole thing dazzled by, as Elizabeth Grove-White noted in her review in *The Globe and Mail*, "Bissoondath's unobtrusive command of plot, of style, of voice, of incident." Grove-White concludes,

> In its reckoning of the costs of throwaway identity, *The Soul of All Great Designs* belongs in bookstores and on award lists around the world. Even more, it belongs on the bedside tables of fiction-lovers everywhere, particularly those who've wondered if the contemporary novel hasn't finally run out of steam. Lucid, compassionate and genuinely compelling, *The Soul of All Great Designs* breathes new life into an old genre, testifying to the novel's lasting power to prod us into sudden awareness of unfathomable strangeness in everyday life.

It's witty and erotic, elegant, and fluid in the way Gowdy is and as shocking. Like her (and unlike his uncles), Bissoondath can stare stupidity straight in the face and not grimace with contempt.

~

ALBERTO MANGUEL

News from a Foreign Country Came (1991)

When he arrived in Canada, Alberto Manguel claimed that he wasn't "a real writer." What he meant was that he was a reader of books who made his living as a man of letters — anthologist, translator, editor, erstwhile publisher, columnist, reviewer, radio personality. Twenty-five years and more than three dozen books later, has he revised his opinion? Readers have.

News from a Foreign Country Came is the first of his five fictions and was published before many Canadian readers were ready for its setting, backstories, and the mannerisms of Antoine Berence. A former French army officer who has retired to Quebec City with his wife and daughter, Berence served in Algeria until it gained independence. Then he took his family to Buenos Aires to serve Argentina as an advisor in the post-Peron crackdown. The story of who he really is and what he actually did is told from two perspectives — his own and his wife's. In his own mind, Berence is impeccable in every possible way — a poet without a public audience, a monologist with only a mirror to admire him. The more he reflects himself back to himself, the more impossible a self-creation he becomes — precious, ponderous, self-serving, overwrought. When his wife becomes the victim of an attack meant for him, she meditates upon her marriage to a monumental, self-serving bore who served his political masters all too well.

In 1991, there was an awkward political silence in this country (and especially in Quebec) about the monsters who have come to live among us from elsewhere in the world. Protest was left to our poets. And to Manguel. Master of the apt quote, he begins with an epigraph from Richard Outram's "Aftermath of a Conversation." Outram, arguably (and Manguel has argued the case effectively), was Canada's finest poet — reason enough to quote it in full:

Aftermath of a Conversation
Red blood from the red gills of lumpen fishes
dries on the parched dock. And this is true: one can imagine having
  anything one wishes.
Most men don't torture children. But some do.

Admittedly, one can imagine even being wise
  in the intolerable ways of man, should he so dare.
The gull, you said, settled to peck out the living eyes
Of stranded salmon; my Dear, you do not care

to answer anyone in kind, and not from pride.
To be inhuman sometimes fits us like God's glove.
Who may imagine us as creatures who deride
Their being God, and being very terrible to love.

~

LIAM DURCAN

García's Heart (2007)

Given all our author tours and the literary festivals, it's easy to meet just about any Canadian author you want. The oddest, most unexpected meeting I've had is from a bed at the Montreal Neurological Hospital when Dr. Liam Durcan came in to witness the after-effects of a stroke I'd had two days earlier. For some, the medical relationship that exists between us might raise questions about my judgment of Liam Durcan's literary abilities: so, here's the plot synopsis from *Publishers Weekly*:

> Durcan ... dissects the ethics involved when politics, medicine and vio-lence collide in this finely wrought novel about a neurologist turned biotech entrepreneur who travels to The Hague to witness his mentor's war crimes trial. Patrick Lazerenko is a punk teen in Montreal when he first meets Hernan García, the Spanish immigrant owner of a neigh-borhood grocery store. Caught trying to vandalize Hernan's store, Patrick is roped into working off the damages and soon finds himself attached to the García family. When Patrick sees Hernan's backroom medical consultations with local immigrants, he is inspired to become a doctor himself. Years later, a journalist exposes Hernan — dubbed the Angel of Lepaterique — as having been mixed up in the CIA-backed torture of subversive citizens in Honduras in the 1980s. Parallels to Abu Ghraib and Guantanamo are acute (and even overtly identified) as Hernan is accused of witnessing and aiding in detainee torture. Subplots ... provide a rich backdrop to the trial, but the centerpiece is the mélange of complex feelings that arise within Patrick, who finds himself simultaneously condemning and rooting for Hernan.

How well does he do this? Well enough that *García's Heart* won the 2008 Arthur Ellis Award for Best First Novel sponsored by the Crime Writers of Canada. And well enough that Kevin Patterson (a fellow physician/novelist) wrote in his review for *The Globe and Mail*:

> Durcan takes us right into the nub of the neuroscientific conception of the self. How tenable, after all, are our ideas of free will and individual responsibility, when genes for risk aversion and alcoholism and almost every element of what we understand as personality have been identified? And as interesting a debate as this might be in *Scientific American* essays, Durcan's skill as a novelist takes us deeper yet, into the entirely unabstracted essence of the problem.... Durcan's first book of short stories, *A Short Journey by Car* (2004), presaged this slippery, engrossing effort, and was a Globe 100 Book. His writing has only solidified since then.... [A] sense of rupture and dislocation and of new possibility at the end of *García's Heart* becomes Durcan's principal and most compelling point: The novelist trumps the neurologist, and what matters is what stirs us, and the fact of that stirring.... You must read this book.

If a novel fails to excite a reader's nosiness about its characters, its time and place and plot, then it's worthless to that reader — just then. Not all novels — not even the greatest of them — are meant for all readers at all times. Up at the Neuro, not all stroke patients nor all their relatives find the activities of a traumatized brain fascinating. For them, *García's Heart* is inappropriate. You must read this book *if you can*. I devoured it on its own merits.

~

DENNIS BOCK

The Ash Garden (2001)

Senior editors at Knopf in the USA, Bloomsbury in the UK, and Rowohlt in Germany only had to focus their minds on one place, one day, and read no more than the opening scene of Dennis Bock's first novel, *The Ash Garden*, before they put pens to chequebooks and handed over the sort of advances that usually go to the creepy people who write novels in which psychotic monsters/gangsters/ robots maim, disfigure, torture and torment numerous victims before they gratuitously kill them in new and revolting ways.

That one place? Hiroshima, Japan.

That one day? August 6, 1945.

That opening scene?

> One morning toward the end of the summer they burned away my face, my little brother and I were playing on the bank of the river that flowed past the eastern edge of our old neighbourhood, on the grassy floodplain that had been my people's home and misery for centuries.

When Fat Boy was dropped on Hiroshima, 175,000 civilians were disfigured in ways that no one in the world had ever seen before. The lucky ones died instantly. The unlucky ones are all of us, everywhere in the world, who survived that day and all born afterwards under the shadows of that bomb and the bombs that have been tested, made more powerful, and stockpiled by the thousands.

Bock's Professor Anton Böll is a physicist who participated in the Manhattan Project that enabled the first atomic bombs to be built. He's also one of the technical observers sent to Hiroshima days after the bombing to assess effects. On its fiftieth anniversary, he's still explaining it. When Emiko, a documentary filmmaker, travels to Port Elizabeth, Ontario, where Böll lives after retiring from the Pickering nuclear power station, and asks him to state his views, he says,

> There are still some among us who can admit to themselves that we needed to do what needed to be done. I am one of those people. Although there was a price to be paid, and we knew it, we were able to complete our work. I'm not saying it was for the betterment of human-ity.... It was to finish the war, to finish the work others had started. That was our aim, and we achieved that aim.... With the bomb, ideas of right and wrong ceased to exist.... I do not have scars on my face. I do not deny the pain caused that day, and every day after that. For

the rest of your life. Everyone's life who was there. I am not an animal. No one in their right mind would say any different. But this is what I know. I know the world requires a certain payment from us all, pain and suffering, hunger, destitution, solitude, for the freedoms we enjoy.

Böll's interviewer is the grown-up little girl whose face was burned away and whose voice is heard in the first scene. Shifting voices and times, *The Ash Garden* moves between the dropping of the bomb and their meeting; Böll switched sides from the German to the American and married a Jewish refugee he met in a Canadian internment camp, Emiko spent her adolescence treated by American reconstructive surgeons. Böll doesn't just talk — he has reels and reels of raw footage of the carnage in Hiroshima to give her.

Bock manages to honour the generation that made war without betraying the young who suffered at their hands. His characters are as strange as the people down the street and as familiar as us as they remember what must never be forgotten of the diseased peace that flows forward from the wars of the twentieth century.

~

KEVIN PATTERSON

Consumption (2006)

Some first novels tower over their contemporaries by the scope of their ambition and the power of their vision. In 2005, it was Joseph Boyden's *Three Day Road*; among the 2006 spring releases, it was Rawi Hage's *DeNiro's Game*, Madeleine Thien's *Certainty* and, *annus mirabilis*, Kevin Patterson's *Consumption*. If you're a fan of Steven Heighton's, you'll embrace *Consumption*: Heighton, an author who weighs words like grains of gold, writes that Patterson "brings wisdom to life in ... a sweeping parable, which starts in the past and then builds into a moving critique of a modern world that both fattens and consumes its young."

Originally from Manitoba, Patterson went to medical school by joining the Canadian army. A specialist in internal medicine, he now divides his practice between the Arctic, war zones, and the coast of British Columbia. As *The Water in Between* (1999), his sailing memoir, and *Country of Gold* (2003), his story collection, made clear, Patterson loves to operate as doctor and writer where multiple worldviews intersect. It makes him a well-informed and insightful guide to conflicts within the coastal community of Rankin Inlet that's the setting of *Consumption*, a tale that also carries its readers to Winnipeg, New York, New Jersey, and the South Seas.

Consumption is deceptively simple and gripping to read. It's the story of one woman and her family. What a woman! What a family! Victoria is the daughter of Emo and Winnie, and sister of Tagak. Born in 1952, she's reared in the nomadic hunter ways of her forefathers until her parents are driven from the tundra to the largest hamlet on the west coast of Hudson Bay by the failure of the caribou hunt, then kept there by government policy and easier living conditions. At ten, Victoria develops tuberculosis and is sent to a Winnipeg sanatorium for treatment of a severe case that requires surgery and six years of therapy.

Educated by Kablunauks (southerners) and semi-adopted by a Cree family, the teenager masters both their languages and becomes acclimatized to books, radio, store-bought food, and living with emotional intensity. When she returns to her parents, she drifts further from the traditions of her people by marrying Robertson, the British manager of the Hudson's Bay Company store, who becomes the father of her daughters, Marie and Justine, and Pauloosie, her son, the eldest and most Inuit of her children.

Victoria's home is stretched and stressed by forces that can beset any late-twentieth-century North American family — her son disdains the traps of middle-class life and strives to be a man like his grandfather; her daughters embrace pop culture and dream of a Toronto apartment, jobs at MuchMusic, and partying on Queen Street West; her husband is distracted by lucrative opportunities falling into his lap; and her lover wants to draw her back to their shared childhood. Home life is whacked further by diseases and disorders endemic in the North and by the epidemic of greed unleashed by diamond mining. And by Arctic weather:

Storms are sex. They exist alongside and are indifferent to words and description and dissection. It had been blizzarding for five days and Victoria had no words to describe her restlessness. Motion everywhere, even the floors vibrated, and such motion as was impossible to ignore, just as it was impossible not to notice the squeaking walls, the relentless shuddering of the wind. Robertson was in Yellowknife, and she and the kids had been stuck in this rattling house for almost a week, the tundra trying to get inside, snow drifting higher than the windows, and everyone in the house longing to be outside.

What makes *Consumption* more than a domestic account of a highly-sensitive-wife-and-mother's struggle to heal herself while nurturing her family through upheavals is the author's ability to track Victoria's life from several angles. The eyes of every family member are on her but they are observed by Kablunauk outsiders — a schoolteacher, an Oblate priest, and the local doctor, Keith Balthazar. Shifting points of view reveal perplexities among decent people trying to do right while living among what the American poet Wendell Berry calls "punishments and ruins" in his essay "A Few Words in Favour of Edward Abbey."

What Berry says of Abbey (best known as the author of *The Monkey Wrench Gang*) applies to Patterson, who must be absorbing him in much the way that Abbey absorbed Joseph Conrad. Like Abbey, Patterson understands that we shouldn't lay the blame on such abstractions as "global warming" or even "bad politics" for what is happening. We are destroying ourselves by a bad way of life that *enslaves* us — to quote Abbey — "in the sense that we depend for our daily survival upon an expand-or-expire agro-industrial empire — a crackpot machine — that the specialists cannot comprehend and the managers cannot manage.... We are, most of us, dependent employees." Patterson's work is written in defence of the natural order and human nature. He is a traditionalist, a conservative advocate of aesthetic realism, for whom *character* is still the defining quality. "Such writers" as Dickens, Conrad, D. H. Lawrence, and their moral successors, Berry notes, "submit to standards raised, though not necessarily made, by themselves."

Kevin Patterson writes clean, serviceable prose that is cinematically accurate, digitally precise. When you close the book, you feel you've been watching a movie, albeit one without much of a soundtrack. With the major exception of Dr. Balthazar and the minor one of Father Bernard, most of the characters are more or less inarticulate. Balthazar has so much to say that he can never find enough listeners and saves many of his sharpest insights for "The Diseases of Affluence," a fifty-page manuscript that forms an epilogue to the novel that seeks to "bring wisdom to life" and succeeds.

∿

YANN MARTEL

Life of Pi (2001),
The Facts Behind the Helsinki Roccamatios (1993)

Life of Pi (2001)

Am I the only person in the world who doesn't love *Life of Pi*? Sometimes, it feels that way. Simply put, I prefer fables more opaque and animal-free. Blame Walt Disney! If the non-human must be animated, give me a household appliance (a brave little toaster or reading lamp) or a robot that's a neatness freak (Wall-E)!

Life of Pi, for the few people reading this who don't know, is narrated by Piscine Monitor Patel, the son of a Pondicherry zookeeper. Bored by the jokiness of his name, he finds refuge in Pi, the "elusive, irrational number with which scientists try to understand the universe." Born a Hindu but fascinated by Christianity and Islam, he is a follower of all three and finds awe and magic in their complementariness. When the Patels migrate to Canada, taking a menagerie of animals with them, their Japanese cargo ship meets disaster on the Pacific. Pi and a group of animals — a hyena, a zebra, an orangutan, and Richard Parker, a Royal Bengal Tiger — survive. Reduced in number and circumstances, they reach the coast of Mexico. Rescued by the authorities, Pi meets with representatives of the Japanese government who want to know what happened to their ship. He tells them two stories. The one readers have just read and another much more conventional version. The reader is left to decide which is likelier. My favourite description of *Pi* is Garan Holcombe's: "Marquez's story of a castaway rewritten by Salman Rushdie on hallucinogenic drugs."

The Facts Behind the Helsinki Roccamatios (1993)

In 1993, Martel's first book, *The Facts Behind the Helsinki Roccamatios and Other Stories*, knocked my socks off. All four stories are fresh, exuberant, and risk-taking but none more so than the title tale, a "novella" that can bear the weight of separate publication as a novel despite its brevity. Paul is a college freshman infected with AIDS via a blood transfusion. He and his student mentor invent one hundred stories, each linked to an actual twentieth-century event, that construct the history of the Roccamatio family of Helsinki. It's out-of-the-ordinary in its subtlety and fluidity.

∽

NANCY HUSTON

Plainsong (1993)

In 1993, Nancy Huston was at the centre of a sandbox spat when she received the Governor General's Literary Award for Fiction in French for *Cantique des Plaines*. The author was not a French-Canadian and her book had been written first in English and that version, *Plainsong*, didn't make the shortlist for the same award for English-language fiction. In 1998, Huston further complicated things for those who like to keep authors in language boxes by reversing the process and issuing *L'Empreinte de l'ange* first in French and then in English as *The Mark of the Angel*. This time both were shortlisted.

Huston was born in Calgary and moved to New Hampshire fifteen years later. After graduating from Sarah Lawrence College, she relocated to Paris, obtained a post-graduate degree from the École des Hautes Études en Sciences Sociales by writing a thesis on swear words under the supervision of Roland Barthes, and married the cultural critic Tzvetan Todorov.

Plainsong (the fifth of what has become a steady stream of books over the past three decades) examines four generations of a Canadian family from the 1890s to the 1970s. In childhood, Paula promised her grandfather that she'd complete the book on the philosophy of time he was writing. But when she takes up her task, she begins writing him into an imagined family history as if to tell him the redemptive rather than real story of his lifetime.

Paula's grandfather is an intellectual whose philosophical bent and dream of a studious life is defeated by early marriage to an unimaginative woman, the fathering of many children, hard times, and a temperament that has too much mercury in it. Nancy Huston has a deeper historical consciousness than many writers who tackle prairie life and a sharper intellect as she conjures up gold miners, farmers, teachers, alcoholics, philanderers, and domestic abusers within Paula's story. The granddaughter's love for a failed dreamer raises Huston's novel above evocation and into the realm of religious lamentation, an act of love that sustains imagination.

ANNALS OF OURLIT XII

WHAT IS CANADIAN IN OUR LITERATURE AND WHO QUALIFIES AS A CANADIAN AUTHOR?

1984

How dare they!

How dare they award Josef Škvorecký the Governor General's Literary Award for Fiction in English for *The Engineer of Human Souls*, a novel written in Czech and translated by Paul Wilson?

1993

How dare they!

How dare they award the Governor General's Literary Award for Fiction in French to Nancy Huston for *Cantique des Plaines*? The author isn't French-Canadian and she wrote the book in English — and that version, *Plainsong*, didn't make the shortlist for the same award for English-language fiction — and then rewrote it in French.

1998

How dare they!

How dare they shortlist Nancy Huston for the Governor General's Literary Award for Fiction in English for *The Mark of the Angel* and then again for the French-Language award for *L'Empreinte de l'ange* which she wrote in French and then rewrote in English?

2002

How dare they!

How dare they award Austin Clarke the Giller Prize for *The Polished Hoe*? It's set on the fictional West Indian island of Bimshire. It's written in Island English.

Do you smell the sick sweet stink of lambshit?

I smell lambshit here, here, here, here and in too many other places in our recent literary history.

Lambshit?

In 1887, Friedrich Nietzsche wrote in *On the Genealogy of Morality*:

> It is not surprising that the lambs should bear a grudge against the great birds of prey, but that is no reason for blaming the great birds of prey for taking the little lambs. And when the lambs say among themselves, "These birds of prey are evil, and he who least resembles a bird of prey, who is rather its opposite, a lamb, — should he not be good?" then there is nothing to carp with in this ideal's establishment, though the birds of prey may regard it a little mockingly, and maybe say to themselves, "We bear no grudge against them, these good lambs, we even love them: nothing is tastier than a tender lamb."

Nietzsche is describing the good man, the "good" little writer, as a person of *ressentiment*, giving wings and wool to a psychological, philosophical, and literary concept introduced by Kierkegaard a generation earlier in *Two Ages: A Literary Review*:

> The *ressentiment* which is establishing itself is the process of levelling, and while a passionate age storms ahead setting up new things and tearing down old, raising and demolishing as it goes, a reflective and passionless age does exactly the contrary: it hinders and stifles all action; it levels. Levelling is a silent, mathematical, and abstract occupation which shuns upheavals.

Margaret Atwood prefers to speak of Tall Poppy Syndrome — the levelling social attitude that cuts down the meritorious as presumptuous, attention seeking, or without genuine achievement. But her metaphor is too botanical, too bloodless even if it was first used by Aristotle (who chose sweet corn to the flowering source of opium). Benjamin Franklin Fairless, president of United

States Steel Corporation, was more Grimm-ish, closer and odder in fellowship with Matt Cohen's *Typing: A Life in 26 Keys* in 1950 when he said "[Y]ou cannot add to the stature of a dwarf by cutting off the leg of a giant."

Ressentiment is not simply resentment. It is a rejection of the value of another and the other's values as a justification of oneself. Sartre called it "bad faith." There's a stinking heap of it in the continuing argument about multiculturalism in this country. As *Quill & Quire* reported in May 2003 in an interview of Austin Clarke by Donna Bailey Nurse, a "funny thing happened" after Clarke won the Giller: "a number of influential critics went on record naming Guy Vanderhaeghe's novel *The Last Crossing* as the best book of the year." Clarke was bothered by the implication that he had won "because he was black." He told his interviewer,

> I was disappointed by some of the remarks made by some of the so-called literary gurus of this city and country.... I felt their comments were bordering on an unspeakable attitude. It was alarming. But then, of course, it was not alarming, because I have lived here too long to be alarmed.... I have felt for a long time that there was a reservation so far as what I would call the natural acceptance of literature that could not be determined to be Canadian, although naturally nowadays, it is Canadian. How do you define a Canadian writer? Is a Canadian writer a person who is born here, and whose family goes back two or three generations, and whose sensibilities are so Canadian that he has got to write about Canadians? And if he writes about Canadians, are we subliminally saying that his characters have got to be white? *The Polished Hoe* is a Canadian novel. It is not a book about Barbados so much as it is a book about people in this country who are from Barbados and who are reflecting back two or three generations. It is true we don't have sugarcane plantations or slave plantations today in Canada. But when slavery was raging throughout the world, it was not absent from the Canadian psyche.

Our attitude to slavery shifted. Values always do, even so-called "core values" — the ones someone or other is always wanting to designate "essential" to "national identity." Fifty years ago, Tommy Douglas — Father of Medicare — was "unCanadian" and the virulently anti-democratic RCMP (do consult Terrence Heath's *Casualties*) was ever so *Us* (as long as *we* weren't socialists or Native or Métis).

Literary culture when it is pursued in good faith is about the processes through which the implicit is made explicit — ugliness is exposed to beauty, falsity is undermined by truth, bad is thwarted by the good. Literary culture — the processes by which books get written and read — is a dialogue, a co-operation between writers and readers who are working towards common purposes in good faith with mutual respect. Literary culture is, before all else, an exercise in civics.

"I suppose that a Canadian is someone who has a logical reason to think he is one," Mavis Gallant writes in her "Introduction" to *Home Truths: Selected Canadian Stories* (1982). Stating her own "logical reasons":

> My logical reason is that I have never been anything else, nor has it occurred to me that I might be. I do not mean that traits that make me different from other people in places where I have lived and traveled are recognizably Canadian.... I have sometimes felt myself more at odds in Canada than anywhere else, but I never supposed I was any the less Canadian. Feeling at odds is to be expected; no writer calls a truce. If he did, he would probably stop writing.

In a symposium on "What is Canadian Literature?" that ran in the pages of *The Globe and Mail* (August 8 and 15, 2009) Professor Andrew Lesk quotes Gallant and remarks on her profundity, "as it affirms 'being Canadian' as an act of civic identification, not one bound by ethnic, racial, religious and geographical restrictions."

It is a creative, open decision, as broad as the country itself. It invites people from all over the world to share in the history of the nation and join ... in contributing to a magnanimous citizenry, simply through the act of saying Yes.

When Canada welcomed the world to Expo '67, a majority of Canadians weren't prepared for what came next — a great chorus of "Yes" from a stream of eager-to-be-citizens, New-Not-Hyphenized-Canadians who spoke our official languages and were both more visible (by dress, customs, and skin pigmentation) and less passive recipients of the slurs, slights, and setbacks inflicted on Eastern Europeans before WWII and the immediate post-WWII arrivals who were so displaced, so traumatized by ethnic, sexual, social, political, and economic "cleansings" that their children were urged to "pass" in order to succeed and to subvert rather than confront and conquer racism from sea to sea to sea.

Bharati Mukherjee arrived in Montreal in 1966, the year before Expo, and left Canada for the United States in 1980 (after two years in Toronto) where she realized her dream of becoming a celebrated American writer in 1989 by winning the National Book Critics Circle award for *The Middleman and Other Stories*. In the introduction to *Darkness*, her 1985 short story collection, she'd written:

> In Canada, I was frequently taken for a prostitute or shoplifter, frequently assumed to be a domestic.... The society itself, or important elements in that society, routinely made crippling assumptions about me and my "kind."

Toronto, in particular (where her husband Clark Blaise had taken up a position at York University in 1978), was not her kind of town: racial hostility (she told Joel Yanofsky in a 1990 interview for *Books in Canada*) caused her "such distress that I could only think of ways of becoming a human rights activist instead of sitting down and writing." When she did write, what she wrote was aloof expatriate fiction until life in the USA taught her to stop seeing "Indianness as a fragile identity to be preserved (or worse, a 'visible' disfigurement to be hidden)" and "see it now as a set of fluid identities to be celebrated." Her novels after she settled at Berkeley are mainstream Americana and diligently plotted to probe the tensions between violent behaviour and utopian thinking integral to American experience.

Writers are volunteers, not conscripts, free to choose where and when they fight which battles. That said, one still wonders what would have happened had Mukherjee and Blaise not fled down the 401 with tens of thousands of others in the lead-up to the first Quebec referendum on sovereignty. By 1977, Mukherjee was well-established within McGill's English Department and Blaise was the foremost member of the Creative Writing program at Concordia University. Mordecai Richler aside, they were the best known and most highly respected members of English Montreal's literary community. When they departed, all the heavy lifting in the cultural debate fell on Richler's shoulders. If the economic security and social instability of Montreal was really too much for them, one can't help wondering what would have happened within Toronto's writing community had they toughed it out and blazed paths for writers such as M. G. Vassanji and stayed on long enough to see writers such as Priscila Uppal establish herself. The speculations aren't idle: in 1987, Mukherjee and Blaise co-authored *The Sorrow and the Terror*, a critical analysis of the 1985 Air India bombing that illustrates the remarkable powers these writers can bring to public debate. But Mukherjee's "No" logically places her outside Canadian literature.

Janette Turner Hospital's situation is more complicated. She arrived in Kingston at the end of the sixties from Queensland, Australia via Harvard where her husband was a Fellow and she'd worked as a university librarian. After taking an MA in medieval literature at Queen's, her writing career blossomed following a sabbatical in southern India when her first story "Waiting" was published in *The Atlantic Monthly*, then expanded into *The Ivory Swing* which won the Seal Books First Novel Award in 1982. (How dare they!)

In 1986, *The Globe and Mail* listed her as one of Canada's Ten Best Young Fiction Writers. By then, she'd published the first three of nine novels and the first of four short story collections. Since 1999, she's been James Dickey's successor as Carolina Distinguished Professor of English at the University of South Carolina.

Much like D. H. Lawrence (the affinities go deep), Turner Hospital's writing is nourished not thwarted by the geographical dislocations of her life. She was raised in a strict Christian environment where her family, as she's said, "had a Biblical metaphor for every occasion" and the Bible is the great chronicler of the sort of displacements that can transform a reader of its Prophets into the kind of acute observer of political and social systems she has become. As in the case of Lawrence, dislocation and the Song of Songs (abetted by her Queensland childhood) has created such a passion for erotically and metaphysically charged landscape that her prose can become as humid and florid as rainforest. Again, like Lawrence, she writes with her whole body engaged.

Turner Hospital describes the driving force behind her novels as tragic humanism:

> I despair, therefore I insist on hope.... I do believe in redemptive moments. I no longer have a safe structure in any traditional sense, but I do believe that redemptive moments exist and that deeply flawed human beings are capable of great and redemptive moments toward other human beings. And that's what I celebrate. For me, that's what the books are about.

Like Austin Clarke, Neil Bissoondath, David Adams Richards, Barbara Gowdy, and Margaret Atwood, Turner Hospital is distantly but distinctly related to Euripides. Humans flourish freely only by confronting the hard fact — this is what King Pentheus refuses to learn from Dionysius in *The Bacchae* — that our rationality must come to terms with forces that are not reasonable by striking some sort of truce that is always provisional and deeply personal. The alternative is to be torn to pieces, terrorized into un-freedom. Her characters are as complex, confounded, and conflicted as the situations in which they find themselves. There's probably no writer in North America this side of Philip Roth more willing to place characters in the front lines of the civic battlegrounds of latter-day capitalism and its neo-colonial intentions. She's said of her work,

> I've always been intensely interested in examining ordinary human beings, people without political agendas, who are suddenly caught up in the fist of history and crisis. If someone happens to be in the wrong place at the wrong time, what happens to their lives from that point onwards? How do they negotiate life, history, politics thereafter?

Her latest novel, *Orpheus Lost* (2007), explores the worlds that collide when Leela-May Magnolia Moore encounters Mishka Bartok accompanying himself on a violin as he sings "Che farò senza Euridice?" from Gluck's *Orfeo*. At that moment, he's in the subway station beneath Harvard Square in an America so altered by urban terrorist attacks that the abduction, interrogation, rendition, torture, and ultimate disappearance of suspects can pass almost unnoticed even in the intellectual centre of Boston. After a fellow graduate student turns suicide bomber, these oddly matched lovers begin their descent into a post-9/11 under-world. In the effort it takes to rediscover one another amid the madness, the lovers learn much about spiritual redemption through the pain of being faithful to one another in a world where religious fanaticism is brutally destructive and political power is inevitably in the hands of the inept and irresponsible.

The political immediacy of Turner Hospital's settings — the terrorists and weapons of mass destruction of *Due Preparations for the Plague* (2003), the Waco-like cult of *Oyster* (1996) are the ones that get the most things right in worlds gone seriously wrong — and the ideological innocence of her characters are the principal reasons why her works should be discussed in the same breath as Brian Moore's (and Graham Greene's and Joseph Conrad's) despite her stylistic differences and distinctly feminist twists. Like these exemplars, Janette Turner Hospital has turned to the thriller genre as a way of exploring issues of conscience within the context of contemporary events. Unlike them, she's steered clear of stylistic transparency and economy of expression is favour of their opposites. *Orpheus Lost* is a "literary" thriller narrated from multiple points of view that entwine with dreams, nightmares, and flashbacks.

Janette Turner Hospital established her *Canadian* credentials in 1985 with *Borderline*. A meat truck carrying illegal immigrants is intercepted at the Canadian-American border. An unconscious woman is overlooked by the authorities and impulsively smuggled into our midst where she finds herself unexpectedly but believably welcome. As Pete Seeger said on his ninetieth birthday, the greatest positive change is that communities now welcome diversity rather than shun it. Our literature has powerful reasons for wanting to claim her as one of our own. Does she still claim us?

"Feeling at odds is to be expected; no writer calls a truce. If he did, he would probably stop writing," Mavis Gallant says. Whenever I'm nauseated with the stink of levellers' lambshit, I think what fun it is to test them against William Shakespeare and his works! Shakespeare was much at odds with his society. If he was even half as sympathetic to the Roman Catholic cause as recent scholarship suggests, many of his countrymen would have rejected his right to call himself an Englishman. And the Englishness of his works? Consider how few of his plays are set on English soil in settings contemporaneous to his own. And the Englishness of his language? Until his characters spoke it, had such English ever before been spoken?

TRAVELLERS AND FELLOW TRAVELLERS

During the current recession, India seems to be the place to live and work if you're a young writer who can't make the rent in Toronto, or even Montreal's Mile End, and still have time and energy and inclination to spend three years on a novel that might not find a publisher: call centres need trainers for a plainer spoken English than is the custom and Internet business sites need proficient editors. What you earn in a year in Delhi can give you a long enough stretch on a beach in Goa to produce something an agent might look at with interest. During the earlier recession of the eighties, Japan was the place to be. A decade later, it was China or Latin America. Charles Foran is one of a group of writers — Peter Oliva, Steven Heighton, Dennis Bock come immediately to mind — who went abroad looking for teaching jobs to support their writing after the oil crisis of 1979 gave way to the recession of the early eighties. All returned to Canada with altered aesthetics. In Foran's case, the four novels he wrote weren't what readers here were interested in reading just then and didn't succeed like Oliva's, Heighton's, and Bock's. Whatever frustrations that caused, they didn't turn Foran humourless nor prevent him from becoming a literary journalist of the skill and insight that Knopf, Mordecai Richler's publisher, was looking for when it selected him to write *Mordecai: The Life* with the co-operation of the Richler family. At the press conference announcing the project in 2006, Foran said:

> Growing up in a suburb of Toronto, I longed to experience imagina-
> tively a corner of urban Canada that had been rendered in the manner
> of Joyce's Dublin or the London of Dickens — reconfigured through
> character and language until it existed, permanently, as a "real" literary
> place. Richler provided the whole country with that "corner": Montreal's

palimpsest of often competing histories and narratives. Not for nothing, when I moved to Montreal, was my first address 5765 Esplanade, a few blocks up from the home of Richler's grandfather and two streets west of St. Urbain.

Foran's route from suburban Toronto to Montreal (and currently to Peterborough with his family) is full of side trips and extended journeys, especially to Ireland (where he studied) and Asia (where he taught in mainland China and Hong Kong). A collection of his essays and travel writings, *Join the Revolution, Comrade* (2008) gives a good sense of the restlessness and originality of his non-fiction writing. It's worth noting that Foran was teaching in Beijing in June 1989 when the protestors were massacred in Tiananmen Square. The events of those days and their after-effects are the subject of the title essay in his collection and fuel his novel *Butterfly Lovers* (1996). The Richler book might just awaken interest in it and the other three novels that deserve better fates than they've found.

Among the four, *Kitchen Music* (1994) takes first place. Pat Keane and his Vietnamese lover, Hia Thi Loi, travel from Toronto to a remote fishing village in Ireland, the place where Keane's father, a notable local fiddler, lived and died. As the narrative arcs between 1950s Ireland, Vietnam after the fall of Saigon, and contemporary Toronto, the dilemmas faced by those whose roots are severed as they seek to make homes for themselves in a world without inhabitable "homelands" are truthfully stated and honestly resolved without sacrificing tender and beautiful moments. What I mean about bad timing is that a decade later, David Bergen wins awards and strong sales tackling similar themes with less in the way of lived experience and inferior technique.

~∽

PETER OLIVA

The City of Yes (1999), *Drowning in Darkness* (1993)

The City of Yes (1999)

"In the winter of 1993 — while employed by a local gym to erase squash-ball marks from the corners of four square walls, day after day — I decided to put my English degree to better use and find some kind of work abroad. I told myself that I'd grown tired of editing squash players with big white erasers. The yen was riding high and Japan seemed like a logical place to look for a job, perhaps teaching English." This is how the narrator of *The City of Yes* introduces himself as he relates a year in his life as a young Albertan in Japan. He chooses to live and work "in a nondescript suburb of Kumagaya city, completely surrounded by rice fields." Tokyo is a day away. He plunges into language lessons. As he teaches blunt and serviceable English, he learns the intricacies of Japanese language and customs, especially its modes of storytelling. Enzo, a bachelor colleague who lives in the apartment next door, shares his free evenings and together they take short trips to Hiroshima, to Sapporo, and to "Electric Town" in Tokyo — the world's foremost emporium of electronica. It's Enzo who introduces him to the story of Ranald MacDonald, an authentic nineteenth-century Canadian adventurer who deliberately shipwrecked on the shores of Japan when it was officially closed to the West.

MacDonald, the child of a Hudson's Bay Company trader and a Chinook princess, was convinced that the Japanese were near relatives of his maternal ancestors. Japanese authorities weren't amused by MacDonald's "accidental" arrival or open-minded to his theory of ancient Japanese settlement of the Pacific coast. Subjected to solitary confinement in Nagasaki, MacDonald was not allowed access to Japan — except through conversation with his guards as they tried to puzzle out each other's languages — until he was shipped back home 1849.

The City of Yes is a fictionalized memoir but rings with such deeply felt truths that readers might want to believe that the teachers and students and fellow travellers are more real than imagined. Oliva cheerfully admits that both he and his narrator have done any number of identical things — such as visiting all the schools in an entire province of Japan dressed as Santa Claus. A more important point in common is that they enter into the spirit-filled stories and visual metaphors embedded in Japanese calligraphy and convey them to Western eyes with wry humour:

> When crows become too old, or too fat and lazy to fly away from soybean fields, they are fashioned into lacquer brushes. The lucky ones are ground into charcoal cakes, mixed with water, then brushed into written words. The ink is silent, low in static, and distilled to resemble a pool of black cormorant feathers. But if these birds are to glimpse immortality, they will become dark streams of calligraphy, tributaries of words that pour down paper scrolls, opaque screens and mulberry walls. They are happiest when they splash through windowpanes, for the glass in this place is also made of paper.

Drowning in Darkness (1993)

Oliva's first novel, *Drowning in Darkness* (1993) has recently found renewed life in France where it was published by Gallimard (2005), following successful translation into Spanish. Oliva's great-grandfather, grandfather, and father worked as coalminers in Alberta's Crowsnest Pass and *Drowning in Darkness* draws upon the stark reality of those lives and rococo fantasies fuelled by the methane in the mine as a trapped Italian miner dreams the story of a woman who becomes her own dream. Aritha van Herk writes, "Trapped within story within darkness within a mine within a mountain, this novel outstrips its own space and design. Full of tremendous power, *Drowning in Darkness* submerges the reader in the magical interruptions of darkness and disappearance." Here's that power at work:

> In Scilla, Sera's town, the houses were more like bridges than buildings, built next to the sea. Every house along the water's edge had a tunnel

built through its walls, just large enough to drag a row-boat under the kitchen floor. There were small stretches of rocky beach near the ends of the town but they were seldom used. The tunnels were more convenient and the land pushed the houses too close to the Mediterranean for the *cittadina* not to love it a little. Some claimed to live their entire lives with one foot in the sea. At high tide, waves lashed at their walls, washed into their side streets and spread blue from their windows across the strait to Sicily. Sera could hear it lapping under her bed as she slept.

Drowning in Darkness is listed in *The Oxford Companion to Canadian Literature* as one of the four "most technically and imaginatively accomplished novels produced between 1983 and 1996."

~~

STEVEN HEIGHTON

The Shadow Boxer (2000), *Afterlands* (2005)

The Shadow Boxer (2000)

Steven Heighton — poet, essayist, short story writer, and novelist — is as protean and accomplished a writer in his generation as Margaret Atwood is in hers, albeit not nearly as prolific. His nine fine books (to the uneven twenty-something Atwood had produced by a similar stage in her career) have been translated into Italian, French, Japanese, German, Turkish, Hungarian, Spanish, Russian, and Lithuanian and are (in my limited experience) the books by a Canadian most likely to be found in the hands of overseas travellers awaiting connecting flights at Heathrow's Terminal Three. Although nominated for any number of literary prizes in Canada, he's almost as much of a perpetual bridesmaid as Barbara Gowdy. Part of this is his doing:

At the turn of the millennium being a true rebel means, by postmodern standards, unabashedly uncool — an aesthete, devoted to the old pursuit of truth and beauty in artistic form.

This "rebelliousness" (he speaks of in the interview published in *Writers Talking*, 2003), has made him an unrelenting reviser, his toughest editor, a fact worth keeping in mind when approaching *The Shadow Boxer*, a book mistaken by some as excessive. *The Independent on Sunday* nailed the underlying strategy:

> Steven Heighton's first novel comes out of its corner with both fists swinging.... Essentially the story of one man's troubled love affair with literature, *The Shadow Boxer* fizzes with life and energy, its prose a heated mix of lyricism and muscularity. A bravura performance ... a post-beat *Bildungsroman* of the sort that isn't written much any more ... its adhesion to the old vanities of authenticity and the primacy of experience [make it] nothing less than a full-blooded argument with postmodern trickery. Intense and poetic ... has a swaggering, larger-than-life quality.

Sevigne (the odd first name is Swiss) Torrins, is impulsive, an idealist who wants "to make himself a writer, swagger, shine and recite on the ivory stages, find love — all the old dreams." He metamorphoses from an earnest adolescent with a pocket full of poems into a passionate young man whose careless innocence leaves more experienced women in emotional turmoil until he emerges as an adult.

When his parents separate and break up a suburban home under the flight paths of Pearson International, Sevigne chooses Sault Ste. Marie and his father rather than Cairo with his older brother, their mother and her lover, a Canadian diplomat. Sam Torrins is in a spiral of self-destruction. A former cook on Great Lakes freighters, he's a sailor who jumped ship to crawl inside a bottle, a drunk with a nebulous plan to supporting himself and his son in his old hometown by manning the grill of a greasy spoon, He doesn't have much to offer but he does give his son a passion for stories and the words in which to tell them, a taste for boxing and the moves to do it well, a connectedness to the Great Lakes water-shed and a kind of parental love that's rarer in books than in life.

Heighton writes in ways that any fan of the late Brian Moore will appreciate. Resemblances between them go beyond the ability to render air, earth, water, sweat, blood, and tears with precision. Both claim James Joyce's emotional ter-ritories as their own and border-hop continents in ways that make the foreign familiar and the familiar foreign. *The Shadow Boxer* is in the tradition of *Portrait of the Artist as a Young Man* but it's the end of the twentieth century not the dawn, and Sevigne's ability to fly cheaply, albeit uneasily, between his father in Ontario and his mother in Egypt propels his imagination both outward and homeward in ways that were inaccessible to Stephen Dedalus.

The old gods have blessed Heighton in ways no postmodern critic ever will: there's not another writer in this country more shockingly *real* while being so mannered. Or so musical — *The Shadow Boxer* is symphonic, Mahler-like in shifting intensities as it segues between the sensory and the psychological: sentences sing, there's tension and release, motifs, variations of theme from movement to movement as Sevigne leaves "the Soo," reconnects with mother and brother in Cairo, attempts to "make it" in Toronto's literary *demimonde*, and turns to an island in Lake Superior where he survives a winter of solitude in an old lighthouse. As he rewrites the book he began in Egypt, he finds the focus and freedom to return to the city as an adult.

Afterlands (2005)

The back cover copy proclaims that "*Afterlands* is a sprawling adventure story, part epic of Arctic endurance, part Mex-western, a *Lost in the Barrens* meets *The Magnificent Seven* kind of book, with an unrequited love affair between a German seaman and an Inuit matron to add passion to an already passionate book."

The historical incident upon which Heighton improvises is the 1871–1872 voyage of the *USS Polaris* to plant the American flag at the North Pole. Half of the expeditionary party — nineteen men, women, and children of various ethnicities — were cast adrift on an ice floe off Ellesmere Island where they were marooned for over six months as the floe wound its way hundreds of kilometres down the Labrador coast. Lieutenant George Tyson, the ranking officer, published an account as *Arctic Experiences* in 1874 (republished in 2002) and then toured America as a lecturer. Heighton uses Tyson's published words and surviving field notes, often in tandem, to reveal exaggerations common to nineteenth-century explorers and truths too raw for the proprieties of the era. The drifters steal food from one another, plot murders, consider cannibalism, suffer delusions, go mad, and turn into mutineers.

In Tyson's book, Roland Kruger, his Prussian second mate, is blamed for what goes wrong. Rendered infamous and unemployable by Tyson's portrait of him as "a prime troublemaker and mutineer," Kruger fled to Mexico where he longed for Tukulito, the "Esquimau" woman with whom he and Tyson both fell in love. Because little is known of Kruger beyond the fact that he was coura-geous at the moments of greatest danger, his "afterstory" — unlike Tyson's and Tukulito's — "springs purely" from Heighton's sense of what a German sailor without fortune might endure and endeavour among the indigenous Sina as they are encroached upon and killed off in the nation-building of Mexico.

Kruger's longing for Tukulito is as unforgettable as the woman herself. Full of vitality when others are not, Tukulito kept the floe from turning into a charnel house. Her abilities to fill up other lives as her own empties away makes what she comes to mean for Kruger (and those who read of his wanderings) much more central to *Afterlands* than the cover suggests with its offhand "add[s] passion to an already passionate book."

～⌇

WAYSON CHOY

Duet: *The Jade Peony* (1995) & *All That Matters* (2004)

The Jade Peony's three narrators grow up with a single household in Vancouver's Chinatown during the Depression, WWII, and the Japanese invasion of China:

Jook-Liang is a "useless" female whose life revolves around imitating Shirley Temple, tap dancing, the movies; Jung-Sum is an adoptee who discovers he's homosexual; and Sek-Lung is the only Canadian-born member of the family. Their personal stories are of struggle against their community's expectations and Canadian racism.

All That Matters covers similar territory from the point of view of Kiam-Kim, the "First Son" who is a silent presence in *The Jade Peony*. In 1927, Kiam-Kim arrives in Vancouver at the age of three with his widowed father and strong-willed grandmother from "Old China" as the "paper family" of a businessman who lacks heirs. Through this child's eyes, Choy reveals the alternative reality of the Chinatown within the port of Vancouver — an ancient culture struggling to find a foothold within a New World harbour that is far from safe.

What matters most for Choy is detailing the ways (especially in kitchen scenes) in which traditional values alter (even when upheld) in transmission between generations. What draws readers is his skill in resurrecting a vanished world, populating it with youngsters whose refusals to transgress boundaries short circuit the blossoming of their desires and with the formidable presence of Grandmother Poh-Poh — a former slave whose folkways are a storehouse of ghost stories, herbal remedies, curses, blessings, and charms, and whose social skills include mah-jong get-togethers.

Choy is the same age as Margaret Atwood and *The Jade Peony* shared Ontario's 1996 Trillium Prize with her novel, *Alias Grace*, but Choy started writing relatively late because his first love has been teaching. His books — which include the memoirs *Paper Shadows: A Chinatown Childhood* (2001) and *Not Yet: A Memoir of Living and Almost Dying* (2009) — educate (not by didacticism except when he lingers too long in kitchens) by drawing readers out of a rougher, more callous Canada into the refinements of the Chinese in Vancouver kept alive during their worst decades among us.

~ↄ

DARCY TAMAYOSE

Odori (2007)

When Joy Kogawa's *Obasan* was published in 1981, it was an immediate commercial success and then gained *unusual* political success — *Obasan*'s protagonist Naomi Nakane became the best known "voice" in the Japanese-Canadian community's campaign for an official apology and redress for injustices suffered during and after WWII. Since the official apology of 1988 made by Brian Mulroney, Kogawa's tale has been so widely taught that it's the Canadian novel most readily recognized by high school students in English Canada and in Japan where it's often encountered in junior grades as *Naomi's Road* (1986), Kogawa's version for children.

Darcy Tamayose is young enough to be Kogawa's niece. She's a journalist in Lethbridge, a graphic designer and artist with a teaching agenda like Kogawa's: her exhibition "Riding Back and the Sacred Circle" travelled the Alberta school system and she's written *Katie Be Quiet* (2008) for young adults. But her aesthetic is different — she works on a larger scale and at wider angles and is, in the middle of it all, as powerful a war artist as Joseph Boyden, Rawi Hage, Madeleine Thien, or anyone else her generation has produced.

A car accident kills her husband and puts Mai Yoshimoto-Lanier in a coma. In her suspended state of consciousness in an Alberta hospital, her great-grandmother from Okinawa, a *kataribe* — a traditional storyteller — tells Mai stories of several generations of her family. There's history, myth, traditional lore, and folklore in her telling. As Tamayose has said in interviews, many of the elements in *Odori* replicate events in her own family's wartime experiences. Like the twin sisters of the novel, Tamayose's mother was sent from Canada to Okinawa as a two-year-old to receive a traditional upbringing that was interrupted by the War in the Pacific and turned upside down by the battle that forced the civilian population to retreat into ancient caves on the island. After too much isolation and too much carnage at too young an age, her protagonist (like her mother) returns to Canada and another kind of isolation in the Rainmaker Hills. In both journeys, Tamayose leads readers sense by sense by sense into worlds we've never tasted, seen, or felt in quite this way before.

Odori is lyrical but its lyricism enhances and never detracts from deeper purposes: a quiet welcome to a *zendo* built of ink on paper, a work of depth and beauty that somehow slipped under nearly everybody's radar. Tamayose employs the same device of a person in a coma hearing voices that Boyden employs in *Through Black Spruce* but she does it better, mining a vein as rich as Boyden's superior *Three Day Road* as she reaches back into the caves of Okinawa and extracts stories from the War in the Pacific that startle, horrify, and heal.

~~~

LAWRENCE HILL

The Book of Negroes (2007), *Any Known Blood* (1999), *Some Great Thing* (1992)

The Book of Negroes (2007)

In the second half of 2008 and continuing through 2009, just about every Canadian who buys Canadian novels bought (and presumably read) Lawrence Hill's *The Book of Negroes* and *Any Known Blood*. The publisher claims sales of more than 300,000 copies within that non-calendar year. The explanation isn't purely literary since it ties into the election of Barack Obama.

Like Obama, Hill is the son of a bi-racial American couple — a black father and a white mother. Hill's father (the activist Dan Hill Sr.) and mother left the USA in the fifties to settle in Toronto and raise their children (the eldest, Dan Hill Jr., is the singer-songwriter best known for "Sometimes When We Touch") to be overachievers. Larry Hill (who holds a BA in economics from Laval University in Quebec City and an MA in writing from Johns Hopkins University in Baltimore) speaks French and Spanish, has lived and worked in Spain and France and travelled extensively in Niger, Cameroon, and Mali, is a forerunner in the emergence of Canadian novelists who are multilingual world travellers capable of functioning at high levels of professionalism in the world at large. Formerly a reporter with *The Globe and Mail*, a parliamentary correspondent for *The Winnipeg Free Press*, and a volunteer with Canadian Crossroads International, Hill has written non-fiction between novels — *Black Berry, Sweet Juice: On Being Black and White in Canada* (2001) is a memoir that complements Obama's own in tracking the story of how Hill's father (a son and grandson of university-educated, ordained ministers of the African Methodist Episcopal Church) came to meet, woo, and wed his mother (the daughter of a Republican family in Oak Park, Illinois, who graduated from Oberlin College and joined the civil rights movement) and give birth to children whose very existence redefines race, class, and community.

What's surprising about Hill's literary life is not its current success but how long it's taken for his novels to catch on. In 2007, *The Book of Negroes* seemed a shoo-in for the Giller Prize; it didn't make the shortlist. When it did win the Commonwealth Writers' Prize for Best Book and the Rogers Writers' Trust Fiction Prize, the spike in sales was just a thumbtack. In 2009, it got another boost by coming out on top of CBC Radio's Canada Reads competition.

The Black Loyalists by Canadian historian James Walker in 1980 led Hill to the story that in 1792 twelve hundred Black Loyalists embarked from Halifax, Nova Scotia, in fifteen ships bound for Freetown, Sierra Leone. Some on board were not just travelling to Africa — they were returning to their land of birth in a back-to-Africa exodus more than a century before Marcus Garvey's and decades before freed slaves founded Liberia. These raw facts gestated for two decades before Hill let his storytelling invent the life and times of Aminata Diallo, who is kidnapped in Africa, enslaved in South Carolina, escapes to serve the British in the Revolutionary War, escapes again to British North America, and returns to Africa.

Written more in the manner of Dickens's tales of the exploitation of children than as a Toni Morrison-like "slave narrative," Aminata's story begins in a literally gilded past — her father is a Muslim goldsmith in a prosperous village in what is now known as Mali — and follows a picaresque trajectory filled with as unlikely a set of coincidences as those animating *Oliver Twist*. Because Aminata is literate and a midwife, she not only witnesses historical turning points, she influences outcomes and keeps records.

Readers first encounter Aminata as an old woman who has "trouble dying." It's 1802 in London, England: "By all rights, I should not have lived this long. But I can still smell trouble riding on any wind, just as surely as I could tell you whether it is a stew of chicken necks or pig's feet bubbling in the iron pot on the fire." The trouble riding her way is William Wilberforce and his cohort seeking her testimony in their crusade for the abolition of the slave trade. But she has a larger story to tell and will not be marginalized: she has acquired multiple languages, reads Swift and Voltaire, and has ghosts to lay to rest: "all those who never made it through the bullets and the sharks and the nightmares, all those who never found a group of listeners, and all those who never touched a quill and an inkpot."

Aminata Diallo's "private ghost story" is more daring and convincing than most historical novels. It's a rattling good yarn that tells many unpalatable truths about the ways in which British North America created and inculcated its own peculiar and persistent systemic racism.

Any Known Blood (1999)

Any Known Blood sucks readers in and keeps them reading with less of Dickens's flim-flam than *The Book of Negroes*. Langston Cane V is 38, divorced, a government speechwriter until axed for undermining official policy. With time on his hands, Cane (the eldest son of a white mother and black father) seeks out his family's past through five generations that begin in the Virginia slave trade and end in Oakville.

History lessons take a back seat to boisterousness, wit, and eroticism. In Baltimore, Cane survives a drive-by shooting and learns street smarts from an illegal Cameroonian immigrant. Straightforward, good-humoured storytelling is all the more potent for seeming so effortless, particularly in erotic scenes that are passionate and playful.

Some Great Thing (1992)

His son was born in 1957 at the Misericordia Hospital in Winnipeg, before men had to start watching their wives give birth. Asked about it years later, Ben Grafton replied, "What's a man to do in a place like that, except grow all bug-eyed and wobbly and make a shining fool of himself?" ... Ben Grafton didn't enter the delivery room.... He was a forty-three-year-old railroad porter who had coped with all sorts of nonsense in the past and had long stopped wondering what people thought of his being this or that.

Ben bestows a hero's name on the boy — Mahatma. When Mahatma Grafton returns to Winnipeg after university and becomes a crime reporter on a local paper, he spends a hilarious year among welfare crusaders, burned-out journalists, French-language-rights activists, and a visitor from Cameroon who sets up a loose connection to *Any Known Blood*. This is social comedy and commentary as rich and dark and brilliant as Richler's in his London years. Its prescience about race, language, and government policies is only now being recognized.

∼૭

ANN CHARNEY

Rousseau's Garden (2001), *Distantly Related to Freud* (2008)

Rousseau's Garden (2001)

Rousseau's Garden, Ann Charney's second novel, is unusually good in ways that are rare: it's caustic, intelligent, mature, and oddly endearing. Like André Alexis's *Asylum*, it's not what many Canadian readers expect a novel to be.

Charney is interested in character and ideas. With a backwards nod to the narrative traditions of Flaubert and Henry James, a sideways glance to voiceover conventions of European cinema, and a bold step forward to a time when the face of fiction might be less troubled by Hollywood "values," *Rousseau's Garden* tells its readers a great deal about the complexities of character and the subtleties of ideas that arise when marriage, parenthood, friendship, and love are at odds.

Claire Symons travels from Montreal to be with her husband Adrian Arensberg, an art historian, while he researches a book on gardens in France. Claire is Adrian's second wife of three years and stepmother to his teenage daughter. She's a professional photographer with her own connection to France: Dolly, Claire's mother, was a sculptor who had regularly visited Paris. On her last visit before dying in a street accident, something happened to change Dolly. The age now her mother was then, Claire retraces Dolly's last journey, visiting her mother's friends and favourite places and while rereading her mother's favourite writer — the eighteenth-century philosopher, Jean Jacques Rousseau:

> Rousseau's exaltation of nature provided her with the esthetic impulse to redefine her work as a sculptor. Claire could almost recite Dolly's explanations by heart: she had grown dissatisfied with her early representational figures. Rousseau's work had inspired her treks into the countryside where she sketched natural forms, translating them later into her studio into abstract geometric solids.... "With Rousseau as my guide I perceived the energy and movement inherent in each form of nature."

As Claire photographs the grounds of a crumbling chateau that are "said to be the work of André Le Nôtre, the greatest of French gardeners, who designed the gardens at Versailles," she is "shadowed by invisible presences" that seem to help her create photographs in which "Everything appears as it is, quite ordinary at first glance. Yet each scene is pervaded by a feeling of loss, a reminder of the perishable nature of all gardens. It's as if she had read my heart."

Ann Charney creates a similar effect with words. Like Claire, Charney is a sorcerer who enables her readers to find our own reflection in her pages if we're willing to meet the demands of her aesthetic. What is most admirable about her work here and in *Defiance in Their Eyes: True Stories from the Margins* (an unac-knowledged Canadian classic of creative non-fiction) is an uncanny ability to connect the inner lives of people with their outward realities.

Distantly Related to Freud (2008)

In art, music, and literature, Freud was conservatively bourgeois. Peter Gay sums his tastes up in *Modernism* (2008). Freud, he relates,

> admired Ibsen but was silent about Strindberg; he liked among living novelists the skillful craftsman and socially sensitive but scarcely avant-garde John Galsworthy, and seems not to have known the novels of Virginia Woolf, even though she and her husband Leonard were his English publishers; the pictures on his walls reveal no sign of response to Austrian modernists like Klimt or Schiele, and his furniture shows that the experimental designs of Viennese modernists had made no inroads on him. His principled opposition to the received social and cultural attitudes of his class lay elsewhere.... His view of human nature, to summarize it tersely, features placing mind into its natural world, which means that it is susceptible to causal laws, whether phys-iological or psychological.... The psychoanalytic technique of free association in his patients was the equivalent of the Impressionist painter taking his easel out of doors or the modernist composer aban-doning traditional key signatures. Freud, the self-declared scientist of the mind, was in sizable company in making contradictory feelings — ambivalence — central to his picture of the world.

"Only a good-for-nothing is not interested in his past," Freud claimed. Without such an interest, the tragic dimension of life is overlooked and undervalued. In 1952 Montreal, Ellen (who is eight, the only child of a widowed mother) "was at the window, waiting for the refugees to arrive." She is a child "given to dreaminess and invention, reluctant to see things for what they were." She and her mother are nomads whose migrations began in Europe and continued flat to flat in Montreal until that window in a house "set high on the Northern flank of Mount Royal" that's grander than anything she's known. It comes at the cost of taking in lodgers from the same part of the world where her mother grew up and where she was born — a place of which she knows tantalizing little: it was "a superior civilization that had mysteriously vanished without a trace" except for odd artifacts — including a portrait of Freud, a distant relative on her maternal grandmother's side.

Ellen's story isn't what a reader might anticipate — a survivor's tale that follows the conventions of post-Shoah storytelling. Once the refugees arrive, Ellen hears loud voices in the night speaking languages foreign to her. She wants to learn more but the adults want to spare her. She soon succumbs to creating adventures of sorts in the ordinariness of teenagers discovering themselves as a tribe of their own in postwar America. Ellen comes of age naturally not cataclysmically, surrounded by people who are deeply ambivalent towards her engaging, quirky, and funny misadventures because of all that vanished from their own youth. Ann Charney's novel is so profound in its small ellipses and larger silences that it ranks with the best of Norman Levine's Toronto stories — "Because of the War."

~

KATE TAYLOR

Mme. Proust and the Kosher Kitchen (2003)

How do you make a Jewish mother out of a young woman who is childless and Christian? This isn't the lead-in to a comedy routine or a question for a rabbi: it's the unspoken conundrum that works itself through the protagonist's psyche in *Mme. Proust and the Kosher Kitchen*.

Marie Prévost was born in 1966 in Paris to a mother who was then an English nanny and a Québécois father who is now an antique dealer on Montreal's Crescent Street. In her mid-thirties, Marie is one of those bright, highly competent, unattached, professional women who show up everywhere that's anywhere where they outnumber male counterparts two to one. Marie finds some satisfaction in her work providing simultaneous interpretation at conferences but she's overwhelmed by feelings of dislocation. Max, the only man who makes her feel at home with herself, is a doctor in Toronto. Marcel Proust, the only author who fully grips her imagination, is long dead and buried in Paris, the city of her childhood. Finding Proust more available than Max, Marie spends accumulated holiday time in the Proust archive in France's Bibliothèque Nationale looking for parts of him that she hasn't already read. There she uncovers the unpublished (and entirely imaginary) diaries of his mother and begins to translate them.

Please don't be afraid to take this splendid book to bed with you simply because Proust's much-loved mother lurks between the covers. Madame Jeanne Proust and her turn-of-the-century bourgeois Paris is the counterweight that provides perspective and a parallel to the story of Max's mother, Sarah Bensimon, and the refuge she creates in her North Toronto kitchen cooking kosher versions of classic French cuisine. This is a book that demands to be read in bed or wherever is the most quiet and private place in your life. In order for it to speak to a reader as personally and confidentially as the author intends, these women can no more be rushed than Mary Mathilda in Austin Clarke's *The Polished Hoe*.

Mme. Proust and the Kosher Kitchen is all about movements in the human heart that can't be reduced to newspaper headlines or stories with clearly defined beginnings, middles, and ends. Life for these women is far more muddled: Jeanne Proust, a Jew, maintains her personal dignity and holds her Roman Catholic family together throughout the Dreyfus Affair despite her husband's opposition to her pro-Dreyfus sentiments and those of Marcel and his brother; Sarah Bensimon escapes the Shoah, survives the blandness and blinkeredness of Toronto's postwar years (which are particularly well described) and brings the flavours of her childhood back to life within strict religious requirements. By uncovering their lives and the love they shower upon difficult sons, Marie Prévost gets to know more than she'd ever imagined about the gaps between French and English, Montrealers and Torontonians, Europeans and North

Americans, Jews and gentiles, gays and straights, and the final decades of two distinct centuries.

Mme. Proust and the Kosher Kitchen is a hymn, a blessing of the domestic creativity, ferocious love of family, and outspokenness of Jewish women in peculiar circumstances. Kate Taylor is a novelist who writes with obvious affection and little pretentiousness about wine, food, talk, books in language rooted in lived experiences rather than creative writing workshops. She has a wonderful ear for the differences between the English spoken in Montreal and that in Toronto: Marie Prévost is convincing not only as a bilingual Montrealer of the generation that came of age when AIDS was little understood, much feared, and sex seemed radically unsafe, but also as a non-literary translator of Jeanne Proust who comprehends the difficulties in recapturing a long-silent voice for a readership separated from it by wars and death camps.

Taylor's company is so interesting that this is one of those rare first novels that feels short at four hundred pages. *Mme. Proust and the Kosher Kitchen* has found its own readership with the same kind of word-of-mouth recommendation that turned Mary Lawson's *Crow Lake* into a bestseller: they're very different vehicles but their protagonists are driven by similar needs to overcome differences with men they can't forget. Those who know Proust have the additional delight of spending time with an aficionado who had fun inventing diary entries that provide a commentary on key events in *À la recherche du temps perdu*. Readers who have not yet had much success reading Proust will encounter fewer obstacles and might just find themselves compelled to take up *Swann's Way*.

～

PRISCILA UPPAL

To Whom It May Concern (2008)

Hardev Dange used to be the Water King of CIDA. Employed by the Canadian International Development Agency, he supervised hydroelectric projects world-wide. As the result of a work-related accident, he's using a wheelchair, housebound in an Ottawa neighbourhood that's become a target for gentrifiers and redevelopers. He shares the house and little else with his son Emile, holidays with his two daughters (their French-Canadian mother, his ex-wife, is long gone) Birendra and Dorothy. His physical needs are met by homecare but emotionally, he's starved: Birendra's energies are occupied finding a husband in External Affairs who'll take her elsewhere; deaf since early childhood, Dorothy works at a tattoo and body piercing parlour in a world of her own; Emile is a Master's student in Anthropology seeking a Ph.D. fellowship and resolution of his sexual identity in San Francisco.

To Whom It May Concern works in ways that a reader won't anticipate from these bare bones because Hardev's financial predicament is topical (an impending mortgage foreclosure); kinship creates a more powerful dialectic than the participants admit; and, most of all, because Uppal finds an exhilarating way to retell an ancient folktale (the one Shakespeare fashioned into *King Lear*) as domestic tragicomedy rather than court tragedy.

Uppal established herself as a leading poet (and academic at York University) before she turned to fiction. *To Whom It May Concern* was preceded in 2002 by a first novel, *The Divine Economy of Salvation*, set in a Catholic boarding school and convent as it explores female religious life in ways that are rare in novels of our time.

∼

ANITA RAU BADAMI

The Hero's Walk (2000),
Can You Hear the Nightbird Call? (2006)

The Hero's Walk (2000)

It's a July morning on Brahmin Street in Toturpuram, a seaside town on the Bay of Bengal. The southern monsoons have yet to arrive:

> In a few hours the heat would hang over the town in long, wet sheets,
> puddle behind people's knees, in their armpits and in the hollows of
> their necks, and drip down their foreheads. Sweaty thighs would stick
> to chairs and make rude sucking sounds when contact was broken.

The telephone is ringing in Big House on Brahmin Street. It goes unanswered because Sripathi Rao, the owner of the house and head of the extended family it engulfs, waits for someone else to lift the receiver.

Overwhelmed by obligations and debts, Rao is ineffectual. A copywriter at a tiny advertising agency who invents silly slogans for inane products, he's busiest and most alive when he's "Pro Bono Publico" — the author of letters to newspaper editors who writes every day on anything "from garbage strewn on the roads to corruption in the government, from lighthearted commentary on the latest blockbuster film to a tribute to some famous musician whose voice had filled his soul with pleasure." When he eventually answers the phone, he learns that his long-estranged daughter Maya and her American husband Alan Baker have been killed in a traffic accident in British Columbia and that their surviving seven-year-old daughter Nandana is to become her grandfather's ward.

The Hero's Walk isn't the story that its opening seems to suggest, a tale of a worn-down older man establishing solidarity with a young child and then making vigorous common cause against a troubled and troubling world. Anita Rau Badami is more ambitious with Sripathi Rao, his dutiful wife, his overbearing mother, his unmarried sister, his environmentally conscious unemployed son, and their neighbours: *The Hero's Walk* is a parable about the failure of the Brahmin caste to come to terms spiritually or materially with the creative surges and destructive curves in contemporary India.

Anita Rau Badami made a splashy debut in 1996 with *Tamarind Mem*, which wowed with its depiction of a mother and daughter and their different perceptions of a shared past and its frequently comic exploration of the changing possibilities for women from the Indian subcontinent. Except for scattered moments in the inner lives of the grandmother and granddaughter, Badami spurns technical cleverness in *The Hero's Walk* in favour of an almost-folkloric style: Brahmin Street is less an address than a political metaphor. As July's heat gives way to December's torrential rains, Sripathi Rao doesn't become the hero of a classic Sanskrit epic or even a Bollywood film but rather a man capable of leading family and neighbours through the unanticipated catastrophes of daily life.

Can You Hear the Nightbird Call? (2006)

When we met at WordFest in Banff, Anita Rau Badami was less than pleased by the review I'd given *The Hero's Walk*: I'd insisted on a political dimension in her writing that she said she hadn't intended — she was a storyteller. The politics of *Can You Hear the Nightbird Call?* are undeniable: three women are linked by political turmoil in the Punjab during the partition of India and Pakistan in 1947, and then in the 1980s when the demand for an independent Sikh state of Khalistan brings its violence to Canada. Sharanjeet Kaur is the ambitious wife of a prosperous Sikh businessman in Vancouver. She's accustomed to using beauty and wealth to get her way in everything. Leela Bhat, her closest friend, is a woman much like herself — driven by dreams of success but frustrated in her ambitions. Nimmo, Sharanjeet's niece, lives a modest middle-class life in Delhi, certain that disaster lies in wait around the corner of every single day. To preserve her son Pappu from as much of it as possible, she sends him to Vancouver to be raised by his auntie.

When the quarrel between Khalistani separatists and the Indian government comes to a head in June 1984, Indira Gandhi sends the army into the sacred

Golden Temple in Amritsar, shocking Sikhs everywhere. When Gandhi is assassinated by her Sikh bodyguards, violence against Sikhs is unleashed, the relationships between the women are destroyed, and tragedy ensues. An omniscient but inconspicuous narrator smoothes the reader's path through the stories of three generations of characters as the plot moves toward the Air India bombing in 1985. But before getting there, Sharanjeet Kaur's Delhi Junction Café, an informal parliament for South Asian migrants in Vancouver is well observed as a new generation of less-hyphenated Canadians "marry out" to the consternation of their parents. This is a book that we need to read, not as gossip but for its intellectually vibrant grasp of our language and politics flexing and stretching to accommodate a new internationalism.

~⌒

SHANI MOOTOO

Cereus Blooms at Night (1996)

Somewhere in the Caribbean on the imaginary island of Lantanacamara in the city of Paradise, Mala Ramchandin's reveals her family's secrets to Tyler, a cross-dressing youthful gay male nurse at the poorhouse in which she's incarcerated by court order. Comic tittle-tattle grows darker as a murder is revealed.

Mala's storytelling brings Tyler an unexpected lover and readers a broadening of mind and a deepening of affection for men and women who are mis-fitted for the lives forced upon them by societies incapable of reimagining themselves de-Europeanized and freethinking. *Cereus Blooms at Night* is a plea for tolerance wrapped inside the writing debut of an accomplished visual artist. Mootoo — who was born in Dublin, raised in Trinidad, came to Canada as a nineteen-year-old art student, and has exhibited internationally (including at MOMA in New York) — de-hyphenates contemporary experience: she's said that the last thing she wants to be known as is "an Indo-Trinidadian-Irish-Canadian-lesbian writer."

The plot of *Cereus* is intricate as several love and crime stories twist and turn back upon themselves. Being a bit lost in such a fully imagined world is a small price to pay in time and energy to begin to understand the complex racial, gender, class, and sexual interactions at work on the dark side of a tourist's Paradise.

~

SHAUNA SINGH BALDWIN

The Tiger Claw (2004)

Does the codename "Madeleine" ring a bell? Or the *nom de guerre* Jeanne-Marie Regnier? They were aliases of Noor Inayat Khan, the Baker Street "sparrow" in Churchill's Special Operations Executive (SOE) who parachuted into Occupied France as radio operator for the Prosper Network, was captured by the SS, tortured, executed at Dachau, and posthumously awarded the George Cross, an MBE, and the Croix de Guerre.

The Tiger Claw is inspired by Noor Khan and factually based but (according to its author) "departs quickly into imagination, bending time, creating characters ... rearranging or inventing some events to explore as if through her eyes, to feel what may have been in her heart." That's understandable: the "facts" about "Madeleine" raise questions such as these: Why did a committed Indian nationalist serve the British? Why was her mission doomed? What gave her such a ferocious spirit to escape that she was kept naked, shackled, and manacled throughout months of captivity?

Bits of Noor Khan's life were publicized immediately after her death and more were documented in Jean Overton Fuller's postwar biography *Madeleine* (1952) but it was William Stevenson's lopsided account in *A Man Called Intrepid* (1976) that made her widely known and too narrowly appreciated. For Stevenson, she was "typical of those individual acts of self-sacrifice that could never be publicized then, but now help to explain what motivated the directors of secret intelligence, compelled to watch with equal eye the ruin of cities and of a single life."

In Noor's ruins, Singh Baldwin finds a woman surpassing Stevenson's understanding and a Muslim woman who has much to teach many in our time. A great-great-granddaughter of Tipu Sultan, the eighteenth-century Muslim ruler who died in the struggle to stem the British conquest of Southern India, Noor ("light of womanhood") Khan was born in the Kremlin on New Year's Day 1914 to a Sufi father who was a spiritual advisor to the Russian Imperial Court and an American mother related to Mary Baker Eddy, the founder of Christian Science. Raised in London and Paris where she studied composition and wrote for harp and piano, Noor studied child psychology at the Sorbonne, became a journalist, and authored a book of children's fairy tales. In the early months of the Second World War, the Khans escaped to England. Her brother enlisted in the RAF and Noor was recruited by SOE. In order to explore how Noor's politics and mysticism were shaped by the men in her life, *The Tiger Claw* interleaves the story of her training and mission in France with a prison journal written to the daughter she never had within the framing device of her brother's search for her at the end of the war. Multi-layering of narrative makes for a slow-moving spy story but Singh Baldwin is turning a genre inside out and giving it a good shake in order to explore the interplay of racism, sexism, and imperialism among family, allies, and enemies.

Shauna Singh Baldwin is more overtly political than most of younger novelists and becomes more ambitious with every book. Here, she wants to recreate Noor Khan so "that she might live on in the world's memory" stripped clean of fifty years of ideologically driven myth-making. Her Noor is neither a colonial spy fighting for Mother England nor a Joan of Arc seeking a crown for General de Gaulle nor a female Jesus nor an idealistic naïf. Years of research on three continents as well as extensive contact with Noor's relatives result in a portrait that explains her actions in compelling and convincing ways — a noble undertaking.

~

MADELEINE THIEN

Certainty (2006)

Certainty gives a distinctive voice to death and grieving through close observation of the premature passing of a deeply loved young woman on her father and her partner in ways that illustrate an unselfishness that has particular relevance. *Certainty* is, in a sense, a neo-feminist *Gilgamesh*: it affirms the fundamental values of altruism and selflessness just as neural networks, environments, pandemics, geopolitics, and weather systems increase anxiety and go viral.

In contemporary Vancouver, Dr. Ansel Ressing, deep in sleep, curves his body around Gail Lim's and is driven by her phantom limbs into the reality of her absence from their bed. Gail died suddenly six months earlier of a stroke triggered by bacterial infection. For ten years Gail and Ansel had lived in an unremarkable, restored Queen Anne house in Strathcona, Vancouver's oldest neighbourhood, a block away from her parents and within walking distance of Chinatown. While Ansel worked in BC's TB clinic among refugees and AIDS sufferers, Gail produced radio features and documentaries all over the world. Ansel never considered a career outside medicine (his mother and father are both doctors) or an adult life unconnected to Gail's but she had been less at ease in her life, obsessively troubled by her parents' past and the ways it persisted with each other, with her, and with the world at large.

Gail's mother Clara Leung grew up working alongside four younger sisters in their father's restaurant in Kowloon, Hong Kong, "a city heated by the press of bodies." Living above the restaurant "one on top of the other, sharing clothes, hairbrushes, and slippers," they also shared restaurant chores before and after school. Through "too many books ... too many idle dreams," Clara escaped to the University of Melbourne, literary studies, and the hope "one day to be a schoolteacher." In Melbourne, she met Matthew Lim, a fellow student who had abandoned civil engineering for a degree in history. Matthew is without family, country, bereft and wandering since 1945 and his mother's hasty remarriage to a widower in Tawau after his father's murder in Japanese-occupied Sandakan,

North Borneo (the site of notorious POW death marches). Matthew and Clara marry and emigrate to Canada in 1960 where neither can find a teaching job. Clara starts her own business as a seamstress and Matthew apprentices as a cook in a Chinatown restaurant.

As Ansel provides what comfort he can to Clara and Matthew, he listens to tapes Gail recorded for the documentary she was making about the world of her father's childhood. With her death, Gail's story and her father's come together in deeply satisfying and mostly satisfactory ways. *Certainty* is a first novel not a flawless one — secondary characters and subplots are left underdeveloped, for instance — but Thien's prose, as Alice Munro says, leaves one "astonished by the clarity and ease of the writing, and a kind of emotional purity." Even though she's in her early thirties, she's already as adept as mid-career Munro at devising tales-within-tales in which the problems of individual lives reflect the true character of the times. The epigraph for *Certainty* comes from a letter of condolence written by Albert Einstein to the family of one of his closest friends: "For we convinced physicists the distinction between past, present, and future is only an illusion, however persistent." With intelligence and insight, *Certainty* explores the emotional conditions under which time bends and a parent's past can enter into a child's future without poisoning it.

Certainty beat out both Heather O'Neill's *Lullabies for Little Criminals* and Peter Behrens's *The Law of Dreams* for the 2006 Amazon.ca/*Books in Canada* First Novel Award. In choosing it (*Books in Canada*, October 2007) above those two and three others, Sean Virgo, one of the judges wrote:

> *Certainty* does not so much dramatise time and place, as offer vignettes of each — so distilled and evocative that they achieve in a few lines what lesser books might attempt in several cumulative pages. Madeleine Thien's novel is structurally daring, shuttling between times, tenses, and viewpoints, yet it is so quietly assured that the reader senses no strain or self-consciousness. And the characters breathe, and stay with us.

Another like-minded judge, John Moss, wrote:

> *Certainty* shatters the normal correlations between time and conscious-
> ness to collapse decades into moments, explode moments across
> decades, in ways that break the rules of physics, the conventions of
> story, and wondrously illuminates the human heart. Thien writes
> with intelligence and resonant sensitivity; she writes with an educated
> imagination and sophisticated confidence, as her novel realigns the
> literary firmament. Anyone who can leap with lyrical passion among
> generations, across diverse ethnicities, and so relentlessly expose the
> desperate complexities of love, knows about the art of words. Anyone
> who can build an intricate narrative mosaic around a protagonist who
> is both alive through the text and dead when the novel opens, who can
> shift among lives, across continents, soaring through time from North
> Borneo before the Japanese occupation to present-day Vancouver,
> combines the intimate and the epic with the sure touch of a master.
> *Certainty* is distressing and exhilarating, hauntingly familiar and exotic,
> a brilliant achievement.

It's possible that the late Val Ross, one of the dissenting judges, who much preferred Peter Behrens's over-the-top (in terms of credibility of plot and aphoristic
prose) up-market historical romance, put her finger on *Certainty*'s lack of domestic
appeal when she wrote:

> Thien opts to tell her story with complex chronology and multiple
> narrators. There's great intelligence at work her, and great delicacy, but
> for me it is too delicate, too complex, too intricate.

Happily, Madeleine Thien has found a multitude of more attentive readers in
Europe and Asia.

～

M. G. VASSANJI

No New Land (1991)

Moyez Gulamhussein Vassanji had been living in Canada for sixteen years (the first 11 as a nuclear physicist specializing in algebraic models), building a solid reputation in literary circles as co-founder (with his wife Nurjehan Aziz) and editor of the *Toronto South Asian Review* and TSAR Publications and as the author of two previous novels and a short story collection when he became an overnight success by winning the inaugural Giller Prize (with the blessings of Alice Munro, Mordecai Richler, and David Staines) for *The Book of Secrets* in 1994. He became a two-time Giller winner in 2003 for *The In-Between World of Vikram Lall* (which jurors preferred to Margaret Atwood's *Oryx and Crake*). Since then, he's published another collection of stories, another novel, a brief life of Mordecai Richler (2008), and an award-winning travel book, *A Place Within: Rediscovering India* (2008).

Richler called *No New Land* (1991) "A novel of considerable charm and intelligence, informed by a delightful sense of irony" and so it is. The writing is tight as Vassanji chronicles Nurdin Lalani's life with his family within a Don Mills apartment building filled with Shamsis from Tanzania before and after he is wrongly accused of sexual assault. Vassanji handles his materials with consummate understatement and delight in irony, persuading readers that "We are but creatures of our origins, and however stalwartly we march forward, paving new roads, seeking new worlds, the ghosts from our pasts stand not far behind and are not easily shaken off."

His later works seem to me too instructive, too insistent, overstated but there's at least one glorious, stunning exception — "Elvis, Raja," the longest (and oddest) story in *When She Was Queen*. Diamond from Nairobi and Rusty from Bombay meet as shy freshmen in New York when "the world was on fire and soon there they were in long hair and new jeans, screaming 'Off the pigs!' with all the other students protesting against the Vietnam War." Diamond becomes an antique bookseller in Toronto and Rusty a professor of cultural studies in Greenfield, a college town three hours out of Chicago, where his speciality is "Elvis first as agent then as icon of subversion, from 'JH Rock' to the present." What happens between the old friends and Elvis when Diamond drops back into Rusty's world on his way to Las Vegas, the Klu Klux Klan is encountered and a Ouija board is consulted is as wonderfully weird, fresh, exciting as anything I've read in recent years. Diamond and Rusty are full of unrealized possibilities, fit for the sweeping, multi-layered, turbulent narrative of near-hallucinatory power that characterizes *No New Land*.

~

ROHINTON MISTRY

A Fine Balance (1995)

It's India during the emergency of June 25, 1975 to March 21, 1977 when Prime Minister Indira Gandhi has suspended civil liberties. Civil disobedience provokes mass arrests, abuse and torture of detainees, labour camps, censorship, forced vasectomy of thousands of men, arbitrary destruction of slums and low-income housing, thuggery, and propaganda from the national television network. In a flat in Bombay, two Hindu Untouchables work as tailors for a Parsi seamstress who has a fellow Parsi, a student of refrigeration and air conditioning, as her lodger.

Mistry writes under the firm guidance of Zola, Balzac, and Dickens. He is a political writer but not a plodder — as exuberant as Dickens in manic mode as he captures the laughter, weeping, and raillery of the underclass within a turn of a page. There's no exaggeration in what Colm Tóibín and Carmen Callil write of Mistry in selecting *A Fine Balance* as one of their 200 best novels in English since 1950:

The vastness of India and the condition of its people are his subjects, but his genius lies in his exact observation, which brings to life every atom of his characters' experience, so that we live and breathe with them, laugh when they laugh, suffer as they do.

Mistry has lived in Canada since 1975 but he chooses to write not of the diaspora but rather of political and social forces in India that have created the Indo-Canadian communities in our midst. When I asked the casually brilliant twenty-something daughter of friends of mine (a young woman who grew up in a house filled with more Canadian poetry, short stories, novels than most of us have seen outside public libraries) to name her two favourite Canadian novels, she answered unhesitatingly, "Barbara Gowdy's *The White Bone* and Rohinton Mistry's *A Fine Balance*." Sometimes it's necessary to travel long way from home (even to places where *our ways* of speaking and writing English are regarded as distinctly odd) to see what's happening on the streets where we live.

∼

RABINDRANATH MAHARAJ

Homer in Flight (1997)

Homerwad Santokie, the Ulysses of this thoroughly Trinidadian, thoroughly Canadian, mock heroic *Odyssey* is a tidy, neat, and orderly file clerk who flees the messiness of Trinidad for Toronto — a beacon of cleanliness, gentility, and safety — and a promise of an important job, a fine house, a loving wife, splendid children. Relatives have told him so. At 33, he's still naïve. Outwearing the welcome of his cousin in Ajax, Homer finds himself living in a high-rise and working at the Nutrapure juice plant in Dixie before moving to a basement apartment in Burlington. It takes him less than a year to realize that "Canada was just a nice, neatly packaged version of dirty little places like Trinidad." It takes some deceptions (being tricked into marriage, tricking a Catholic school to hire him as a librarian) and the greater self-deception of writing the kind of "settling scores" novel that a vanity press "publishes" at the author's own expense before he begins to glimpse what his namesake the great poet of antiquity wants us to see in the travels and travails of Odysseus: we learn less about ourselves from the strangers encountered in even stranger lands than from dismantling assumptions we make about ourselves. Along the way, if we're fortunate (which might mean only being unlucky in the right times and places), the world at large might teach us that the greatest gifts life offer have more to do with triumphs over delusion than any other success.

This novel is far better than any reviewer has written. That has much to do with the literary complexity that undergirds seemingly straightforward social realism. Maharaj has mastered more of V. S. Naipaul's literary sleight-of-hand than either Neil Bissoondath or André Alexis, fellow Trinidadians who are better known: beneath Maharaj's surface realism, there's comedy of manners; beneath the comedy of manners, there's satire; beneath the satire, there's farce; beneath farce, there's a visionary who has found his own pathway from Joyce to Kafka to Ovid to Homer.

~

RAWI HAGE

Cockroach (2008), *DeNiro's Game* (2006)

Cockroach (2008)

When he accepted the $160,000 International IMPAC Dublin Literary Award for his first novel, *DeNiro's Game*, on June 12, 2008, Rawi Hage said:

> The history of mankind is full of wars, divisions, the flow of blood, the flight of refugees, and misery. I long for the day when an African child will be able to roam the world as if it is rightly his; I long for the day when Palestinian, Guatemalan, Iraqi, and Afghani children will have homes to keep and build upon. I long for the day when we humans realize that we are all gatherers and wanderers, ever bound to cross each

other's paths, and that these paths belong to us all.

And then quoted Amin Maalouf, a fellow novelist born in Beirut and exiled by the civil war but one who chose Paris rather than Montreal as his new home, French rather than English as his literary language:

De ma bouche tu entendras l'arabe, le turc, le castillan, le berbère et l'hébreu, le latin et l'italien vulgaire, car toutes les langues, toutes les prières m'appartiennent. Mais je n'appartiens à aucune. Je suis qu'a Dieu et à la terre, et c'est à eux qu'un jour prochain je reviendrai.

Or, as Hage translated it:

You will hear Arabic, Turkish, Castilian, Berber, Hebrew, Latin, and common Italian from my mouth because all languages and prayers belong to me. But I do not belong to any. I belong to God and to the earth, and one day, I will go back to them.

Cockroach, amply confirms that, as the IMPAC jury said in its citation, "Luck was not a factor in his winning the [award] but the brilliance of ... a powerful, stark yet lyrical and compassionate book." The things that make Rawi Hage a major literary talent and *Cockroach* as essential reading as its predecessor include gut-wrenching lyricism, boldness, emotional restraint, intellectual depth, historical sense, political subversiveness, and uncompromising compassion.

Cockroach's clarity of prose and purpose (and ferocity of judgment) might remind older readers of the books Mordecai Richler wrote before he turned to satire. Like the early Richler (and the Richler of *Barney's Version*), Hage's writing is hyper-energized by the smaller and larger indignities of immigrant experience, existential anxieties of the second half of the twentieth century, righteous indig-nation as old as the prophets, and an up-to-the-minute ink-black humour that's unwilling to turn a blind eye and a deaf ear to the troubled and dispossessed but also insists on calling their deeds and words to account.

Cockroach spans one month of bone-numbing winter among restaurant workers, taxi drivers, and welfare-fed intellectuals-in-exile in Montreal's Lebanese and Iranian communities as achingly experienced from beneath the belly of these underdogs. The narrator is a petty thief with a large imagination who has tried to commit suicide by hanging himself from a tree in Mount Royal Park:

> ... my suicide attempt was only my way of trying to escape the permanence of the sun.... I had attempted suicide out of a kind of curiosity, or maybe as a challenge to nature, to the cosmos itself, to the recurring light. I felt oppressed by it all. The question of existence consumed me.

Rescued by policemen on horseback, he's ordered to meet regularly with a court-appointed therapist, Genevieve, who insists casually on a first name relationship and firmly on probing the childhood sources of his "hidden anger." His response to her naiveté (she knows nothing of the world of *DeNiro's Game* where boys like him become men in war zones without boundaries and women are pawns in the games militiamen play) is to tell her intricate but compelling tales of his youth as an insect, a cockroach, a contemptible thing with no power except the power of personal survival in unwinnable skirmishes to protect his beloved sister from her brutish husband, a militiaman whose viciousness is beyond whatever laws are enforceable in their war-torn country.

> Tell me about your childhood, the shrink asked me.
> In my youth I was an insect.
> What kind of insect? She asked.
> A cockroach, I said.
> Why?
> Because my sister made me one.
> What did your sister do?
> Come, my sister said to me. Let's play. And she lifted her skirt, laid the back of my head between her legs, raised her heels in the air, and swayed her legs over me slowly. Look, open your eyes, she said, and she touched me. This is your face, those are your teeth, and my legs are your long, long whiskers. We laughed and crawled below the sheets,

and nibbled on each other's faces. Let's block the light, she said.... Let's play underground.

What this Kafkaesque bug tells the reader and hides from his therapist is his love for Shohreh, a victim of less domestic conflicts — the religio-political ones in Iran.

Unable to trust his emotions, "repulsed — not embarrassed, but repulsed — by slimy feelings of cunning and need," feeling all too often "like a hunchback in the presence of young schoolgirls," he develops an insatiable appetite to discover everything he can about Shohreh and everyone else (especially the restaurateur who employs him as a busboy) who plays any part at all in the collision of worlds his love for her makes inevitable. Whatever he discovers, he reacts against with the unpredictability of a bred-in-the-bone anarchist. Stories set in motion on the first page keep readers transfixed to the very last. Hage owes something to Camus and more to Kafka (and possibly even more to poets, singers, and story-tellers most of us know nothing about) but what he makes of all of them belongs distinctly to himself.

There was a bar there called Greeny, one of the few rundown bars that had not been given a facelift in my slowly gentrifying neighbourhood. I entered it. Perfect! Dark, just as I liked it. I entered like a panther, and I could hear the wooden floor creaking under my paws. I ordered a mug of beer, some fries, and a large, fat hamburger that came in a basket (brought to me by the granddaughter of Québécois villagers who, one hundred years ago, were ordered by the priest to get pregnant and to kneel beside church benches every Sunday). I gave the waitress the wrong change, and asked for her forgiveness, and to reassure her that I was not trying to stiff her out of the money, I threw her a big fat tip. This made her change her tone, and she called me *Monsieur* as I bit through the bun and the meat.... I like the waitresses. I like how strong and assertive they are. They are immune to all pick-up lines, and their asses, with time, have developed shields, like those of cartoon heroes.... I know ... how to disarm those shields.... It is done with politeness, and also, even more important, gratitude.... I am grateful for everything and it shows.... And at the first sip of beer, the first fries, I forget and forgive humanity for all its stupidity, its foulness, its pride, its avarice and greed, envy, lust, gluttony, sloth, wrath and anger ... its rivers of piss, its bombs, all its bad dancing. I forgive it for not taking off its shoes before entering homes.

Cockroach is an angry and agnostic book that will seriously annoy those unmoved and unshaken Bushites to the south, Harperites in the Canadian West, and Péquistes in Hage's hometown who have yet to "realize that we are all gatherers and wanderers, ever bound to cross each other's paths, and that these paths belong to us all." And whom will it delight? The July 2008 issue of *New Scientist* has statistics and tables to show that readers of narrative fiction score higher on tests of empathy and social acumen than those who don't. That's an old idea, one that runs from Homer through Dickens and beyond, but it's far too generally stated by these contemporary researchers who conduct tests and assemble data and scrutinize things statistically. For Rawi Hage, the writers and artists who matter and make important differences, the ones he singles out in his acceptance speech in Dublin are "all those women and men of letters, and all artists who have gone beyond the aesthetics of the singular to represent the multiple and diverse, to all those men and women who have chosen the painful and costly portrayal of truth over tribal self-righteousness." They are the ones to whom he is grateful and to whom we should all be grateful. *Cockroach* is precisely what its publisher claims it to be: "necessary ... and astonishing."

DeNiro's Game (2006)

Once a reader buys into the opening paragraph of *Cockroach*, everything that follows is relentless, inevitable, and irresistible. That's not the case with *DeNiro's Game*. Structurally, it's very much a first novel — so ambitious that it can't quite stick to its primary impulse, the coming-of-age of young men in a war zone:

We were aimless, beggars and thieves, horny Arabs with curly hair and open shirts and Marlboro packs rolled in our sleeves, dropouts, ruthless nihilists with guns, bad breath and long American jeans.

Bassam and George are rebels in the middle of a cause — actually too many causes.

It's the eighties and Beirut is torn into shards by the Lebanese Civil War of 1975–1990. Much of the city lies in ruins, alliances are shifting rapidly and unpredictably as nearly every party to the conflict allies with and subsequently betrays every other party at least once. Bassam, who narrates and undercuts utter nihilism by summoning up ancient Arabic poetry to counterweight American action figures, sneers and snarls, dreams of leaving his shell-shocked neighbourhood where "ten thousand bombs had landed" and escaping to Rome. While he schemes and daydreams, George joins the Christian militia and rises in its ranks, allowing both orphaned teenagers to motorcycle the streets of West Beirut "with guns under our bellies, and stolen gas in our tanks, and no particular place to go."

If that was all there is to this novel, it would be enough for most readers but it isn't nearly enough for Hage. When friendship with George is tested by the larger political situation, Bassam has to hop a boat to France not Italy. In Paris, it's not just Bassam's storyline but his style that shifts radically as his edginess adjusts to the pace of peacetime and his mood grows more broadly philosophical in this larger, more cosmopolitan setting. Readers are called on to make as rapid an adjustment in expectations as Bassam: some find it mystifying and gratuitously upsetting; others existentially enlightening. The final word, though, goes to the IMPAC judges:

> In recounting Bassam's struggle to escape Hage offers an explosive plot that is also effective as a meditation on war and its psychological cost. There is no easy resolution, no redemptive ending in this visceral account. There is, however, an uplifting and original lyricism to the writing, one where Hage's imaginative flair fuses the present horror into

passages of poetic intensity. The cadences of the Old Testament are there, as are angry Ginsbergian litanies as well as strong European echoes, especially of Camus' *The Outsider*. Remarkably, a dark but rich sense of humour also surfaces in the narrator's self-deprecating reflections.

This is a magnificent achievement for a writer writing in a third language. Luck has nothing to do with this novel's selection. Its originality, its power, its lyricism, as well as its humane appeal all mark *DeNiro's Game* as the work of a major literary talent and make Rawi Hage a truly deserving winner.

~

CHÈRE KARINE

A LETTER TO A QUÉBÉCOISE FRIEND IN SEARCH OF THE CANADA SHE KNOWS SHE DOESN'T KNOW

"Disappointed and dispirited" — how succinct, how sad a reaction to your Introduction to Canadian Literature in English.

You ask, "Was I asking for too much?"

You're not the beggar on his crutch in Leonard Cohen's "Bird on a Wire"; you're the pretty woman leaning in a darkened door, so, no, "you should have asked for more." You challenged me at college and I hope you'll go on challenging your teachers throughout university — not just because you're eager to learn the stories of *les Anglais* but because of what you bring to the classroom in enthusiasm and curiosity as an older student, a self-supporting full-time wage earner, a rural Québécoise studying in an unfamiliar urban environment, reading and writing in a second language.

The first thing you've learned is that we don't embrace our authors as you do yours. It shouldn't be asking too much of your fellow students that they know at least the names and major works of at least *some* of theirs as you do of *so many* of your own and *want* to share the excitement of favourites with you. But there's nothing in English Canada to compare to *les Salons des livres* in Quebec City and Montreal where the spirit of the Enlightenment lives on, thrusts all authors, editors, publishers together in one giant exhibition space with all new books and all backlists and welcomes thousands upon thousands of *les citoyens* to browse, be entertained with storytellers, characters in costume, wine tastings, food samplings, to meet, to greet, to celebrate literacy from cradle to grave in a climate of liberty, fraternity, and equality. You were fortunate but not exceptional in having parents who gave you pocket money to buy one book and have it autographed every Salon and teachers who brought you each year from pre-K to Secondary Five and looked on as you built your very own first library of signed first editions.

The second thing you've learned is that an authentic spirit of egalitarianism is as rare in English classrooms as in French ones. No matter how large the class size, no matter how shy and inexperienced the lecturers or how hurried and harried they are in pursuit of more permanent employment, there must be something more going on than professors practising their *métiers* and students taking notes if the experience of university accomplishes more than artificial add-ons to the vivid experience of various lives lived well or badly. As Cynthia Ozick says, "The encyclopedic triumphs of communications technology — is an act equal in practicality to a wooden leg; it will support your standing in the world, but there is no blood in it." You have only to walk into a massive Calculus 101 class to grasp the difference. The mathematician facing you is doing math — not talking about having done it — and he or she is doing it with the students clustered in the front rows: together they are exploring unknown quantities underlying the known through "dialogue" — a process that has been pursued without serious interruption among mathematicians for three millennia.

"What would I and what wouldn't I teach in an introductory course?" The short answer to your question is more books than you were asked to read and none of the ones you actually read.

Is it reasonable to ask students to read two novels a week? Why not? You've all read your way through Harry Potter. Will you resent five hundred to seven hundred pages a week? Not if you're absorbed by the plots, the characters, the payoffs. And isn't a quick surface reading better than total ignorance? Since this is an imaginary rather than a credited course, it doesn't matter if the readings take the twelve weeks specified or twenty-five or fifty. The point is that these twenty-six books (three are crowded into two of the weeks) read in pairs and read in sequence provide the best overview of the Canadian novel in English that I know how to construct.

Week 1: Zoe Whittall, *Bottle Rocket Hearts* (2007); Rawi Hage, *DeNiro's Game* (2006)

Like Zoe Whittall, we've all sat in classrooms with young women who are at odds with the world — sexually confused, uncertain in friendships, making the rent in crap jobs, sorting out living arrangements with flatmates in their first home away from home, trying to make sense of a non-monogamous lover. If I were teaching this course in Western Canada, I'd substitute Miriam Toews, *A Complicated Kindness* (2004); in Ontario, Catherine Bush, *Minus Time* (1993); on the west coast, Eden Robinson, *Monkey Beach* (2000); in the Maritimes, Lisa Moore, *Alligator* (2005) because I believe in starting as close to the immediately familiar as I can.

Bassam in *DeNiro's Game* is at odds with a much odder world — Beirut during the Lebanese Civil War of 1975–1990. This isn't simply a highly effective meditation on the psychological costs of war: there's an original lyricism in the writing, poetic intensity of a very high order.

One element common to both books is dark humour heightened by narrative self-deprecation.

Week 2: Mordecai Richler, *Barney's Version* (1997); Joan Barfoot, *Exit Lines* (2008)

From Paris 1990, flash back to Paris 1950 with Richler's *Barney's Version* and move from Bassam who could be your Lebanese friend's father to Barney Panofsky who could be another friend's grandfather. When Barney in the early stages of Alzheimer's says, "I've never known a writer or painter anywhere who wasn't a self-promoter, a braggart, and a paid liar of a coward, driven by avarice and desperate for fame" he raises important questions about the reliability of storytellers. When Barney dissects his three marriages, he raises important questions about self-regard, self-destructiveness, and compassion in relationships.

Like *Barney's Version*, Joan Barfoot's *Exit Lines* is so effortless to read that it's easy to fall into the trap of thinking it's simpler than it is. Subtitled *A Darkly Comic Novel about Everything that Matters, from Sex to Death*, this tale encompasses companionship, compatibility, trust, empathy, challenge, warmth, goodwill, consolation, and sustenance in ways that unsettle, haunt, and disturb with black humour that's utterly subversive. She's the least-discussed first-rate novelist in the country.

Week 3: Alice Munro, *The View from Castle Rock* (2006); Don Akenson, *At Face Value* (1990)

Joan Barfoot describes a writer's life as "Thinks, feels, types; re-thinks, re-feels, re-types" — a description that Alice Munro could have coined as her own job description. *The View from Castle Rock* is an excellent novel even if the author insists on calling it "Stories." It indirectly propounds a view of a life lived within and without a historical continuity that's new, surprising, clarifying — unlike any historical fiction or autobiographical fiction that you've ever encountered.

If you have encountered Don Akenson's *An Irish History of Civilization*, you might feel inclined to view Munro's *Castle* as "A Scottish History of an Odd Corner of North America." It's larger than that in much the same way as Akenson's *At Face Value* is culturally richer, politically deeper, and more delightful than the "hoax" it cloaks in order to spoof the silliness of gender prejudice.

Week 4: Joseph Boyden, *Three Day Road* (2005); Tomson Highway, *Kiss of the Fur Queen* (1998)

Native people and their puzzled experience of the non-Native world make a minor but compelling appearance in *At Face Value*. What's utterly novel about the treatment of the Great War (and specifically the contributions of Canada's Native fighting men) in *Three Day Road* is its point of view. Like the young Homer of *The Iliad*, Boyden is precise and unflinching in his descriptions of the ways in which soldiers fall in battle. There is no comforting vision of life beyond the grave, no blessedness, no great promises fulfilled. Darkness engulfs them and their bloodied, scarcely recognizable remains haunt the survivors.

Kiss of the Fur Queen (1998) dances, sings, breaks your heart, and renews your gratitude to be alive and capable of reading it with its utterly distinctive fusion of European tragedy and Cree humour.

Week 5: Lawrence Hill, *Any Known Blood* (1999); Austin Clarke, *The Polished Hoe* (2002)

Any Known Blood sucks readers in and keeps them reading. Black History lessons take a back seat to boisterousness, wit, and erotic scenes that are passionate and playful.

The Polished Hoe is a conversation in something very like real time and needs to be read at roughly the speed of actual speech. Mary Mathilda is part Molly Bloom and part Penelope but she's mostly in a direct line of descent from Aeschylus and the women of his *Oresteia* — Clytemnestra, Cassandra, Electra, and the Furies.

Week 6: David Adams Richards, *The Friends of Meager Fortune* (2006); Michael Ondaatje, *In the Skin of a Lion* (1987)

David Adams Richards and Michael Ondaatje once shared a Giller Prize but are rarely read by the same readers. A shame since they've authored two of the best books written on the subject of work and they've written them with two kinds of poetic sensibility: Richards is visionary; Ondaatje is lyrical.

Week 7: Trevor Cole, *Norman Bray in the Performance of His Life* (2004); Carole Corbeil, *In the Wings* (1997); Margaret Atwood, *The Penelopiad* (2005)

Cole's comedy of an actor as Don Quixote is a wonderful companion piece to Corbeil's actor as Hamlet. Cervantes meets Shakespeare in contemporary Canada.

What could be better? Atwood reinventing Homer as scriptwriter for *Desperate Housewives*?

It's sometimes said that there are only two basic story-lines: a stranger comes to town or a homebody is forced to travel into uncharted worlds. It's also sometimes said that Shakespeare is the master of the one and Cervantes of the other and that the novel in English is rooted in one or the other. But that leaves Homer and the Bible out of the equation since the Odyssey and the Moses/Jesus narratives blaze both trails this perception of leads back to Gilgamesh as prototype for all subsequent storytelling.

Week 8: Barbara Gowdy, *The White Bone* (1998); Yann Martel, *Life of Pi* (2002)

Most of us encounter fables earlier even than travel stories and learn through them that we have to deal with the here-and-now. Lessons in civility and civic virtue work their way down from clan to individual through "the wise ones" so it's not at all surprising that fables often employ clan totems — animals — as principal characters. Nor is it surprising that the animals are never simply themselves: as teachers, they are invariably shape-shifters. Gowdy's elephants are rational, emotional, visionary; they struggle; they fail; they pray and they sing; they love and they mourn. They are neither us nor entirely other than us. They simply *are* and that is their point.

Life of Pi both is and is not a tale of a Bengal Tiger as philosopher who is and isn't. And that is its point.

Week 9: Margaret Atwood, *Cat's Eye* (1988); Catherine Bush, *Claire's Head* (2005)

Difficult women and the difficulties women face in dealing with one another as sisters or friends have always fascinated me: in addition to an older brother, I have five older sisters and one younger one and my mother has been a widow since I turned thirteen. That might be one explanation. Another is that roughly seven thousand of the ten thousand or so students I've taught have been young women, many of whom wished themselves as clever as Atwood's earlier heroines who were invariably interesting, clever, and insightful. Atwood shatters expectations as she writes a counter-novel about the rage of seventies pseudo-sisterhood. This is her richest-textured, most densely layered novel, wise and compassionate.

Catherine Bush has learned from Atwood and from Gowdy but stands very much within fictional worlds of her own making. *Claire's Head* is emotionally compelling, intellectually enthralling, and as much of our world as MRIs and as timeless as the Buddha.

Week 10: Douglas Coupland, *JPod* (2006); Eden Robinson, *Blood Sports* (2006)

What is Vancouver really like? An Olympian village for plutocrats or a murderous butcher shop where street-walkers are routinely "disappeared"? Brian Fawcett says that "the best writing about Vancouver ever committed to paper" is to found in an obscure collection of essays, *Colin's Big Thing* (2003) written by Bruce Serafin, a writer who published too little and died too young. Fawcett's probably right because Serafin thought and wrote with his whole body engaged. Read "Chinatown" from Serafin's second collection, *Stardust* (2007), and measure these two novelists by it.

JPod, "a sequel in spirit" to *Microserfs*, is a seriously funny book as it skewers the shameless and reckless amorality in the business world that defined the past decade and collapsed so many houses of cards. Along the way, he creates a portrait of West Vancouver's showplace side of unreal real estate development ("a rain-forest bull-dozed to make way for jumbo houses that resembled microwave ovens covered with cedar shake roofing") and Hollywood North pretentiousness.

Blood Sports is much darker; it explores East Vancouver as Eden Robinson channels her inner "Stephen King."

Week 11: Guy Vanderhaeghe, *The Last Crossing* (2002); Michael Winter, *The Architects Are Here* (2007)

If you love road novels and have done so ever since first reading *Kidnapped*,

Huckleberry Finn, and *Don Quixote* as a child before graduating to Kerouac's *On the Road,* our literature doesn't offer nearly enough and that's surprising, really, given the mobility of the population. But of the ones we do have, these two are the real deal.

Week 12: Josef Škvorecký, *The Engineer of Human Souls* (1984) Madeleine Thien, *Certainty* (2006)

Škvorecký subtitles his masterpiece, *An entertainment on the Old Themes of Life, Women, Fate, Dreams, The Working Class, Secret Agents, Love, and Death.* Beneath the tragicomedy of romantic loves pursued in a time of petty tyrants, there's the enduring sense of artistry as an offence to stupidity and brutality and the only certain defence against brutality and hopelessness.

Madeleine Thien's *Certainty* works with time and memory much as Škvorecký does in his later works, collapsing decades into moments and exploding moments across decades. She's a less conventional storyteller than Škvorecký (or almost anyone else), moulded by the sciences and math, but every bit as rewarding in her elaborations of the complexities of love in dangerous times in ways that leap across ethnic divides.

Chère Karine, that's what I'd include. *What would I leave out?* Four books too large and difficult for any survey course:

- Don Akenson, *An Irish History of Civilization* (2005)
- Margaret Atwood, *The Year of the Flood* (2009)
- Trevor Ferguson, *Onyx John* (1985)
- Keath Fraser, *Popular Anatomy* (1995)

A pair of easily misunderstood novels by Barbara Gowdy that unlock their true natures only under the kind of ruminative reading best done on one's own:

- *The Romantic* (2003)
- *Helpless* (2007)

I'd also omit all short stories. The Canadian short story requires a course all to itself. It was the first kind of fiction at which Canadian writers — Mavis Gallant, Alice Munro, Norman Levine — excelled and in which they achieved international recognition. It's also the most voluminous genre — and its advocates the most voluble. In *Shut Up, He Explained* (2007), John Metcalf constructed "The Century List" — his selection of the best Canadian stories of the twentieth century. A year later, the editors of *The New Quarterly* and *Canadian Notes & Queries* produced companion issues under the common title of *The Salon des Refusés* in which they offered "correctives" to Jane Urquhart's editorial selections for *The Penguin Book of Canadian Short Stories* (2008). It wasn't so long ago that only poets grew so indignant with one another. And art critics.

In the latter years of the Victorian Age, proponents of Modern Literature followed the lead of proponents of Modern Art and divided viewers and readers in three: the mass of mankind was barbarian — lowbrows — simian in taste, attracted to gaudy trinkets and trivialities at best, brute violence at worst; a smaller but still substantial bourgeoisie who felt superior to the masses but were reluctant to spend time and effort acquiring tastes and values of their own when everything else could be bought and sold — middlebrows; an elite — small in number and aristocratic in temperament who were captivated by innovation and experimentation — highbrows. Those who counted themselves among the elite understood that they had more to fear from the purchasing power of middlebrows than from barbarian guffaws and saved their greatest disdain and reserved their most vicious diatribes for those from whose own ranks they'd generally just risen and without whose support their works would come to nothing. I didn't accept this vision of reality when I was younger and I'm even more opposed to it nowadays. Chère Karine, would you and I have ever met outside the world of books? If we had, would our deepest interests have ever connected? The world of books is a republic, the strongest democracy we've created, and our best defence against humankind's greatest enemies — oligarchs not barbarians. Barbarianism is always limited, always allows for its opposite, cannot conquer all; oligarchy presents only false choices, plunges humankind into absurdities, crushes all freedoms, destroys all hopes, entertains us to death. What I hope from this letter and the book to which it is attached is that you use it in whatever ways you're inclined that enable the books you read to follow you forward into the life that's yours to live.

Cheers.

ACKNOWLEDGEMENTS

Much in this book began life as reviews commissioned by the editors of many small magazines and a few large newspapers. I thank all of them for pushing my reading in new directions, challenging muddles in my thinking, and untangling knots in my prose. I also wish to thank the readers and writers, temperate and intemperate, who have responded over the years for firming up sound thinking and overturning facile responses.

This book as a book (and not a collection of pieces) owes something to a couple of friends against whose pricks I kicked and a great deal more to Marc Côté, its ultimate editor and publisher, who kept me talking, thinking, working even when the writing wasn't going well.

I want to thank Drs. Liam Durcan, David Sinclair, Donatella Tampieri, and all the others in the teams of specialists, residents, nurses and helpers, technicians, therapists up at the Montreal Neurological Institute and Hospital who not only altered my brain but convinced me that neurosystems are much more elastic than I'd ever imagined. And I thank Yvonne Clark, MSW, who taught me a whole new set of cognitive strategies after old ones collapsed.

Another book, as substantial as this, would have to be written to record the ways in which four decades of conversations about public matters with Ann, my constant companion, have formed the foundations for this one. Briefly put, her reading is much broader and more penetrating than mine, especially in English literature of every era and genre, and in contemporary American and Commonwealth novels. Her musical knowledge is richer, more refined and more deeply embedded, and her understanding of history more detailed and profound. One of Ann's great pleasures in life is sharing what she knows and finding the right books for the right readers at just the right time. I am a most grateful beneficiary of all this and much more that is, and will ever remain, private.

BIBLIOGRAPHY

Adderson, Caroline. *Sitting Practice*. Toronto: Thomas Allen Publishers, 2003.

Akenson, Don. *At Face Value: The Life and Times of Eliza McCormack/John White*. Montreal: McGill-Queen's University Press, 1990.

Akenson, Don. *An Irish History of Civilization*. Montreal: McGill-Queen's University Press, 2005.

Alexis, Andre. *Asylum*. Toronto: McClelland & Stewart, 2008.

Atwood, Margaret. *Alias Grace*. Toronto: McClelland & Stewart, 1996.

Atwood, Margaret. *Cat's Eye*. Toronto: McClelland & Stewart, 1988.

Atwood, Margaret. *Oryx and Crake*. Toronto: McClelland & Stewart, 2003.

Atwood, Margaret. *The Penelopiad*. Toronto: McClelland & Stewart, 2005.

Atwood, Margaret. *The Year of the Flood*. Toronto: McClelland & Stewart, 2009.

Barfoot, Joan. *Critical Injuries*. Toronto: Key Porter Books, 2001.

Barfoot, Joan. *Exit Lines*. Toronto: Alfred A. Knopf Canada, 2008.

Barfoot, Joan. *Luck*. Toronto: Alfred A. Knopf Canada, 2005.

Bissoondath, Neil. *The Soul of All Great Designs*. Toronto: Cormorant Books, 2008.

Bock, Dennis. *The Ash Garden*. Toronto: HarperFlamingo Canada, 2001.

Boyden, Joseph. *Three Day Road*. Toronto: Viking Canada, 2005.

Bush, Catherine. *Claire's Head*. Toronto: McClelland & Stewart, 2004, 2006.

Bush, Catherine. *Minus Time*. Toronto: HarperCollins Canada, 1993.

Charney, Ann. *Distantly Related to Freud*. Toronto: Cormorant Books, 2008.

Charney, Ann. *Rousseau's Garden*. Montreal: Véhicule Press, 2001.

Choy, Wayson. *All That Matters*. Toronto: Doubleday Canada, 2004.

Choy, Wayson. *The Jade Peony*. Vancouver: Douglas & McIntyre, 1995.

Clarke, Austin. *More*. Toronto: Thomas Allen Publishers, 2008.

Clarke, Austin. *The Polished Hoe*. Toronto: Thomas Allen Publishers, 2002.

Clarke, George Elliott. *George & Rue*. Toronto: HarperCollins Canada, 2005.

Coady, Lynn. *Mean Boy*. Toronto: Doubleday Canada, 2006.

Cohen, Matt. *Elizabeth and After*. Toronto: Alfred A. Knopf Canada, 1999.

Cole, Trevor. *Norman Bray in the Performance of His Life*. Toronto: McClelland & Stewart, 2004.

Corbeil, Carole. *In the Wings*. Toronto: Stoddart, 1997.

Corbeil, Carole. *Voice-Over*. Toronto: Stoddart, 1992.

Coupland, Douglas. *JPod*. Toronto: Random House Canada, 2006.

Coupland, Douglas. *Microserfs*. Toronto: HarperCollins, 1995.

Durcan, Liam. *Garcia's Heart*. Toronto: McClelland & Stewart, 2007.

Endicott, Marina. *Good to a Fault*. Calgary: Freehand Books, 2008.

Endicott, Marina. *Open Arms*. Vancouver: Douglas & McIntyre, 2001.

Engel, Howard. *Memory Book*. Toronto: Penguin Canada, 2005.

Fawcett, Brian. *Gender Wars*. Toronto: Somerville House, 1994.

Ferguson, Trevor. *Onyx John*. Toronto: McClelland & Stewart, 1985.

Findley, Timothy. *Not Wanted On the Voyage*. Toronto: Viking, 1984.

Foran, Charles. *Kitchen Music*. Dunvegan, Ont.: Cormorant Books, 1994.

Fraser, Keath. *Popular Anatomy*. Erin, Ont.: The Porcupine's Quill, 1995.

Garnett, Gale Zoë. *Visible Amazement*. Toronto: Stoddart, 1999.

Gowdy, Barbara. *Falling Angels*. Toronto: Somerville House, 1989.

Gowdy, Barbara. *Helpless*. Toronto: HarperCollins Canada, 2007.

Gowdy, Barbara. *Mister Sandman*. Toronto: Somerville House, 1995.

Gowdy, Barbara. *The Romantic*. Toronto: HarperFlamingo Canada, 2003.

Gowdy, Barbara. *The White Bone*. Toronto: HarperCollins Canada, 1998.

Greer, Darren. *Still Life with June.* Toronto: Cormorant Books, 2003.

Griggs, Terry. *Thought You Were Dead.* Emeryville, Ont.: Biblioasis, 2009.

Hage, Rawi. *Cockroach.* Toronto: House of Anansi, 2008.

Hage, Rawi. *DeNiro's Game.* Toronto: House of Anansi, 2006.

Harris, John. *Small Rain.* Vancouver: New Star, 1989.

Heath, Terrence. *Casualties.* Regina: Coteau Books, 2005.

Heighton, Steven. *Afterlands.* Toronto: Alfred A. Knopf Canada, 2005.

Heighton, Steven. *The Shadow Boxer.* Toronto: Alfred A. Knopf Canada, 2000.

Helm, Michael. *The Projectionist.* Vancouver: Douglas & McIntyre, 1997.

Highway, Tomson. *Kiss of the Fur Queen.* Toronto: Doubleday Canada, 1998.

Hill, Lawrence. *Any Known Blood.* Toronto: HarperCollins Canada, 1997.

Hill, Lawrence. *The Book of Negroes.* Toronto: HarperCollins Canada, 2007.

Hill, Lawrence. *Some Great Thing.* Winnipeg: Turnstone Press, 1992.

Hood, Hugh. *Near Water.* Toronto: House of Anansi, 2000.

Hospital, Janette Turner. *Orpheus Lost.* Toronto: Alfred A. Knopf Canada, 2007.

Huston, Nancy. *Plainsong.* Toronto: HarperCollins Canada, 1993.

Ignatieff, Michael. *Scar Tissue.* Toronto: Penguin Canada, 1993.

Itani, Frances. *Deafening.* Toronto: HarperCollins Canada, 2003.

Johnston, Wayne. *The Colony of Unrequited Dreams.* Toronto: Alfred A. Knopf Canada, 1998.

Johnston, Wayne. *The Custodian of Paradise.* Toronto: Alfred A. Knopf Canada, 2006.

Johnston, Wayne. *The Navigator of New York.* Toronto: Alfred A. Knopf Canada, 2002.

Kelly, M. T. *A Dream Like Mine.* Toronto: Stoddart, 1987.

Kelly, M. T. *Save Me, Joe Louis.* Toronto: Stoddart, 1998.

King, Thomas. *Green Grass, Running Water.* Toronto: HarperCollins Canada, 1993.

Kulyk Keefer, Janice. *The Ladies' Lending Library.* Toronto: HarperCollins Canada, 2007.

Kulyk Keefer, Janice. *Thieves.* Toronto: HarperFlamingo Canada, 2004.

Lai, Larissa. *Salt Fish Girl.* Toronto: Thomas Allen Publishers, 2002.

Lawson, Mary. *Crow Lake*. Toronto: Alfred A. Knopf Canada, 2002.

MacDonald, Bruce. *Coureurs De Bois*. Toronto: Cormorant Books, 2007.

Maharaj, Rabindranath. *Homer in Flight*. Fredericton: Goose Lane, 1997.

Maillard, Keith. *Gloria*. Toronto: HarperFlamingo Canada, 1999.

Manguel, Alberto. *News From a Foreign Country Came* Toronto: Random House of Canada, 1991.

Martel, Yann. *The Facts Behind the Helsinki Roccamatios and Other Stories*. Toronto: Alfred A. Knopf Canada, 1993.

Martel, Yann. *The Life of Pi*. Toronto: Alfred A. Knopf Canada, 2001.

McAdam, Colin. *Some Great Thing*. Vancouver: Raincoast Books, 2004.

McGillis, Ian. *A Tourist's Guide to Glengarry*. Erin, Ont.: The Porcupine's Quill, 2002.

McLaughlin, Karen. *From This Distance*. Toronto: Cormorant Books, 2009.

McNeil, Jean. *Private View*. London: Weidenfeld & Nicolson, 2002.

Mistry, Rohinton. *A Fine Balance*. Toronto: McClelland & Stewart, 1995.

Mootoo, Shani. *Cereus Blooms at Night*. Vancouver: Press Gang Publishers, 1996.

Moore, Brian. *Black Robe*. Toronto: McClelland & Stewart, 1985.

Moore, Lisa. *Alligator*. Toronto: House of Anansi, 2005.

Morrissey, Donna. *Downhill Chance*. Toronto: Penguin Canada, 2002.

Morrissey, Donna. *Sylvanus Now*. Toronto: Penguin Canada, 2005.

Morrissey, Donna. *What They Wanted*. Toronto: Viking Canada, 2008.

Munro, Alice. *The View from Castle Rock*. Toronto: McClelland & Stewart, 2006.

O'Neill, Heather. *Lullabies for Little Criminals*. Toronto: HarperPerennial, 2006.

Oliva, Peter. *The City of Yes*. Toronto: McClelland & Stewart, 1999.

Oliva, Peter. *Drowning in Darkness*. Dunvegan, Ont.: Cormorant Books, 1993.

Ondaatje, Michael. *In the Skin of a Lion*. Toronto: McClelland & Stewart, 1987.

Patterson, Kevin. *Consumption*. Toronto: Random House Canada, 2006.

Pountney, Christine. *Last Chance Texaco*. London: Faber & Faber, 2000.

Poliquin, Daniel. *A Secret Between Us*. Donald Winkler, tr. Vancouver: Douglas & McIntyre, 2007.

Quarrington, Paul. *Galveston*. Toronto: Random House Canada, 2004.

Rau Badami, Anita. *Can You Hear the Nightbird Call?* Toronto: Alfred A. Knopf Canada, 2006.

Rau Badami, Anita. *The Hero's Walk*. Toronto: Alfred A. Knopf Canada, 2000.

Ricci, Nino. *The Lives of the Saints*. Dunvegan, Ont.: Cormorant Books, 1990.

Ricci, Nino. *Testament*. Toronto: Doubleday Canada, 2002.

Richards, David Adams. *Evening Snow Will Bring Such Peace*. Toronto: McClelland & Stewart, 1990.

Richards, David Adams. *For Those Who Hunt the Wounded Down*. Toronto: McClelland & Stewart, 1993.

Richards, David Adams. *The Friends of Meager Fortune*. Toronto: Doubleday Canada, 2006.

Richards, David Adams. *Nights Below Station Street*. Toronto: McClelland & Stewart, 1998.

Richards, David Adams. *River of the Brokenhearted*. Toronto: Doubleday Canada, 2003.

Richardson, C. S. *The End of the Alphabet*. Toronto: Doubleday Canada, 2007.

Richler, Emma. *Feed My Dear Dogs*. Toronto: Alfred A. Knopf Canada, 2005.

Richler, Mordecai. *Barney's Version*. Toronto: Alfred A. Knopf Canada, 1997.

Richler, Mordecai. *Solomon Gursky Was Here*. Markham, Ont.: Viking Canada, 1989.

Robertson, Ray. *Gently Down the Stream*. Toronto: Cormorant Books, 2005.

Robertson, Ray. *Moody Food*. Toronto: Doubleday Canada, 2002.

Robinson, Eden. *Blood Sports*. Toronto: McClelland & Stewart, 2006.

Robinson, Eden. *Monkey Beach*. Toronto: Alfred A. Knopf Canada, 2000.

Ruth, Elizabeth. *Smoke*. Toronto: Penguin Canada, 2005.

Salutin, Rick. *The Womanizer*. Toronto: Doubleday Canada, 2002.

Schoemperlen, Diane. *In the Language of Love*. Toronto: HarperCollins Canada, 1994.

Scott, Gail. *Heroine*. Toronto: Coach House Press, 1987.

Shields, Carol. *Swann*. Toronto: Stoddart, 1987.

Singh Baldwin, Shauna. *The Tiger Claw*. Toronto: Alfred A. Knopf Canada, 2004.

Škvorecký, Josef. *The Engineer of Human Souls: An Entertainment on the Old Themes of Life, Women, Fate, Dreams, the Working Class, Secret Agents, Love and Death*. Translated from the Czech by Paul Wilson. Toronto: Lester & Orpen Dennys, 1984.

Smith, Brad. *Big Man Coming Down the Road*. Toronto: Penguin Canada, 2007.

Smith, Brad. *One-Eyed Jacks*. Toronto: Doubleday Canada, 2000.

Smith, Russell. *The Princess and the Whiskheads: A Fable*. Illustrations by Wesley W. Bates. Toronto: Doubleday Canada, 2002.

Stenson, Fred. *Lightning*. Vancouver: Douglas & McIntyre, 2003.

Swan, Susan. *The Wives of Bath*. Toronto: Alfred A. Knopf Canada, 1993.

Tamayose, Darcy. *Odori*. Toronto: Cormorant Books, 2007.

Taylor, Kate. *Mme. Proust and the Kosher Kitchen*. Toronto: Doubleday Canada, 2003.

Taylor, Timothy. *Stanley Park*. Toronto: Alfred A. Knopf Canada, 2001.

Tefs, Wayne. *Red Rock*. Regina: Coteau Books, 1998.

Thien, Madeleine. *Certainty*. Toronto: McClelland & Stewart, 2006.

Toews, Miriam. *A Complicated Kindness*. Toronto: Alfred A. Knopf Canada, 2004.

Uppal, Priscila. *To Whom It May Concern*. Toronto: Doubleday Canada, 2008.

Urquhart, Jane. *The Stone Carvers*. Toronto: McClelland & Stewart, 2001.

Vanderhaeghe, Guy. *The Englishman's Boy*. Toronto: McClelland & Stewart, 1996.

Vanderhaeghe, Guy. *The Last Crossing*. Toronto: McClelland & Stewart, 2002.

Vassanji, M. G. *No New Land*. Toronto: McClelland & Stewart, 1991.

Whittall, Zoe. *Bottle Rocket Hearts*. Toronto: Cormorant Books, 2007.

Winter, Michael. *The Architects Are Here*. Toronto: Viking Canada, 2007.

Winter, Michael. *The Big Why*. Toronto: House of Anansi, 2004.

Winter, Michael. *This All Happened: A Fictional Memoir*. Toronto: House of Anansi, 2000.

INDEX